INCENTIVE
MANAGEMENT

BY

JAMES F. LINCOLN

A New Approach to Human Relationships in
Industry and Business

Published by

The Lincoln Electric Company
Cleveland 17, Ohio

1951

PREFACE

This book discusses an age-old problem. It approaches it with obvious facts. Their application to industry, however, is believed to be new. At least, there has been no application of incentive management as herein outlined in any industry known to the writer.

The author has been the executive head of a manufacturing company for the last thirty-eight years. The company of which he is the executive head has grown from bankruptcy to the leader in its field during his term as president. The discussion herein is not theoretical, therefore it is proven fact, based on the actual record of a going concern.

It is very difficult for the author to understand why the program outlined herein has not been followed by all industrialists. It is especially hard to understand why companies which have been vexed by labor-management friction do not go to incentive management. How long must the country wait before it can have these benefits of such natural and obvious cooperation in industry? Such cooperation is taken for granted and is continuous in many other activities of man. It is in industry, however, where it is most needed. It is industry that determines our world position and our standard of living. We cannot safely neglect this progress. Public patience is wearing thin.

I have been very fortunate in writing this book in having

the help of Mrs. Rose Wilder Lane, Miss Marjorie Wilkie, Mr. C. G. Herbruck and Dr. A. F. Davis. Their criticism and suggestions have been most helpful. The data given in the Appendix was compiled by Dr. Theodore N. Beckman of The Ohio State University. The supporting facts are given also.

I am especially fortunate in having had the friendship over the last thirty-one years of Dr. Frank Halliday Ferris. His example and philosophy of life have been priceless to me in the development of this start toward the final accomplishment of INCENTIVE MANAGEMENT.

James F. Lincoln

Cleveland, Ohio
September, 1951.

CONTENTS

PREFACE

CHAPTER   PAGE

    I. THE NEW AGE IN INDUSTRY 1

   II. IT IS INDUSTRY'S RESPONSIBILITY TO ELIMINATE JOBS 19

  III. THERE IS NO LIMIT TO THE POSSIBLE STANDARD OF LIVING 36

  IV. DEVELOPMENT OF PERSONNEL 51

   V. WHAT AND WHY THE DRIVING FORCE OF INCENTIVE. 76

  VI. INCENTIVE 89

 VII. HOW TO INSTALL THE INCENTIVE SYSTEM . . . 120

VIII. PIECEWORK IN INDUSTRY 132

  IX. WHY INCENTIVE SYSTEMS FAIL 146

   X. SECURITY 158

  XI. HOW BIG IS TOO BIG? 174

 XII. THE PLACE OF THE UNION 197

XIII. HOW TO FINANCE THE COMPANY 217

XIV. CONCLUSION 229
     APPENDIX 251

THE ACTUAL IS LIMITED:
THE POSSIBLE IS IMMENSE.

Chapter I

New Age in Industry

The world is going through a revolution. Progress in all branches of industrial development is at a higher pitch now than at any other time in the history of man. New devices of every kind are being developed at a previously unheard-of rate. The standard of living, insofar as it has to do with things, is advancing as never before. Many of our economic ideas which have been considered basic truth up to this time have been rudely upset. We hesitate now to believe anything regarding science as fundamental truth. Our confusion is very great.

While this lack of understanding covers all fields, the place where it is most marked is in our understanding of man himself and his proper position in the industrial economy. The only fact that we are sure of is that past custom is being changed. We are not at all sure yet as to what the net effect of this change is to be.

At first, all people were arranged in neat classes whose authorities and rewards were well known and accepted. The slave then had no rights the master had to respect. The upper classes were supreme. Later under the feudal system the lower classes had some rights, but still few that the feudal lord had to consider.

When the industrial revolution came, two hundred years ago, the relative position of the owner and worker did not change greatly from the feudal system which it supplanted. The change which was made in the economy was mostly mechanical, not human. The worker was still completely subservient to the boss in all their relationships. Position of all people depended on birth or wealth rather than on the real worth of the individual in the world.

COMPETITION DEVELOPS ABILITY

As industrialization progressed, however, a new need arose that was very urgent. Progress in efficiency had to be made continuously to keep up with the competition of other organizations who were in the same field of endeavor. *The individual then had his chance.* He could and did develop abilities that the boss did not have, and that the boss needed in his operation. Respect for ability wherever found then began to develop. The change was slow at first, but its speed accelerated as the need for industrial progress became more insistent. That precipitated the present world revolution wherein we begin to recognize that ability is of supreme importance in our economy and that it *does not depend on birth or wealth.*

Ability is the power to perform that is acquired from the development of an accumulation of traits by the individual himself. It is the result of the desire to develop in an economy that presents for the first time in history opportunity and incentive for development to anyone who has the desire and will pay the price in effort. This is possible here because of the personal freedom inherent in the government as established by our Founding Fathers.

It is the intent of this book to outline the principles and

2

philosophies in industry that produce the atmosphere and incentives which will far more rapidly develop in the individual his latent abilities. These abilties have always been part of the individual's equipment. For lack of incentive, he has not developed them, however, to any great extent, heretofore, except in a few rare cases.

The present world revolution is the preliminary stirring of the desire inherent in all people which has not had the opportunity for outlet except only for the favored few who happened to live in the countries where freedom of opportunity existed and where circumstances happened to produce the necessary incentive.

This overturn of ancient custom that we are now witnessing should not disturb us, even when some developments are no doubt wrong and even evil and dangerous. All progress that man has made has been made by going a more or less circuitous route. Progress is usually made by exploring all possible detours, most of which lead nowhere or even in the opposite direction from that we actually want to travel. These detours should not disturb us as long as we do not lose sight of the real goal in our wanderings.

NEW AGE WILL DEVELOP MEN

Industrial progress up to the present, and even at the present time, is made largely by development of machines. In the new age to which we are coming, progress will be made mainly by development of men. Previously, we have thought of man as a necessary part of an operating machine. In the future, we will see the machine as the creation of the imagination of man and as one expression of his genius. New development of man will produce new and much more wonderful machines as a normal outlet of his

3

development. That changed point of view and its consequent development of man will have a revolutionary effect on the economy.

The development of individual latent ability has received, so far, little attention. We have always considered that man was born to be a certain person. We have been very slow to accept the fact that man can develop into almost any person that his ambition and opportunity make him. He is a product of his determination and opportunity. The present revolution comes from the partial recognition of this concept by man himself. This idea shocks the man of custom. Many are not yet ready to accept the fact, evident as present results are proving it to be.

INCENTIVE IS KEY TO DEVELOPMENT

Incentive management, which is the method outlined herein for the gaining of such development in industry, is a means of giving the opportunity and spur to the individual so that he will develop these abilities of his, now latent.

It is obvious that there are no set rules that can be followed that will succeed in producing this development in all cases. Man is too complicated for that. The attempt is made here, however, to establish principles that have universal application, even when the detail of application will vary widely in all cases. Principles are immutable.

The governing fact in incentive management is this: developed man will be a far abler person than he was before such development took place. Developed man will be a genius compared to the same individual who now under our present lack of incentive remains almost completely undeveloped. Incentive management as shown here is a plan of management as it may be applied in industry.

4

However, the same principles are governing in all incentives in life. They determine the measure of the development of man who then determines the direction and progress of development of the whole economy.

CRISES CREATE LEADERS

The leaders who have shaped the history of the world would never have been leaders had they not developed their latent abilities in the white heat of crisis. That is how leadership is born from its latent state. The point that we usually miss is that millions of incipient leaders, some of whom would have been even greater than those we know, have gone to their graves as unknowns because they did not, or would not, face crises which would develop the latent abilities which would have made them leaders. Their leadership would have been different from what we have had. History would have been changed by such leadership. Perhaps such a conclusion is difficult to believe at first. Consideration of all the facts involved, however, can lead to no other conclusion.

We cannot believe that the leadership of George Washington would have been developed had he not faced the crisis of the American Revolution and the formation of the colonies into a new nation. Washington instead, without this crisis, would have been a very delightful neighbor of the farmers of Virginia, who would have been much sought after as a friend. Washington would have wanted it that way himself. He did not at first want to be the leader of the American Revolution.

We cannot believe that Abraham Lincoln would have been the same leader that he was, had he not had the crisis of slavery and the Civil War to handle when he was President.

We cannot believe that Woodrow Wilson would have been the same leader, had he not been forced to lead the country during the crisis in America in the First World War.

The most striking evidence of development of latent abilities was the change that took place in the disciples during and after the life of Jesus. We are perhaps prone to feel that such change was a miracle rather than individual development. No such conclusion is obvious, however. All the disciples left Jesus at the time of his trial and crucifixion. They were obviously not the inspired leaders who afterwards made Christianity a world moving philosophy. It was only after his crucifixion and resurrection that the disciples developed their great abilities of leadership.

We certainly would not think that Paul was the same man before and after his vision during his journey to Damascus. It is even hard to believe that Jesus was the same man at the time of his trial and crucifixion as he was in Gethsemane, the night before.

Perhaps we consider all these changes as the miraculous working of an all powerful God. It is very doubtful that Jesus and his disciples had the same feeling. In any case, whether the changes were God directed miracles or the development of latent abilities, is of no consequence. The results are the same. Perhaps all development of latent ability is miraculous. Much of it seems to be.

We cannot believe, in the light of these facts, that anyone would be the same person, were he to have other incentives than those he had which forced him to develop in a certain direction because of the needs and desires that were put on him by the various conditions that he met.

Carrying the matter further, we cannot believe that no person ever lived before who could bat a baseball as could

Babe Ruth. We can be sure also that if the Babe had lived in England or Europe or any place other than the United States, he never would have been a great batter. He never would have had the competition and incentive needed to so develop.

There are obviously others who with the same opportunity and incentive would have made as great and even greater baseball players, who never had the opportunity and desire to strive so mightily as did the Babe to develop the ability that made him the player he was.

ALL MEN HAVE LATENT ABILITIES

The same development in many directions is latent in every person. The difficulty has been that few recognize that fact. Fewer still will put themselves under the pressure or by chance are put under the pressure that will develop them greatly. Their latent abilities remain latent, hence useless.

There were obviously millions of people in previous generations who could have done as well or better in any and all fields of endeavor if given the same incentive and opportunity as those who were the actual leaders we now recognize in any field.

This same thing is true of every accomplishment, either mental or physical. The latent ability is there. The spur or the environment or the ambition is lacking if it does not develop. Thus is man usually only a shadow of his possible self.

Man is not always content to remain a small part of his possible self. He craves greatness. He has had a taste of what he can do in the opportunities given by the industrial revolution. He will not now stop. Incentive management is a means of encouraging this possible development of man.

7

It is an obvious, although radical step, compared to previous custom. That is not strange, since any new development must be a change from previous custom. If it were not a change, it would not be development. Let us approach the matter in this light.

It is of course obvious that the development of man, on which the success of incentive management depends, is a progressive process. Any results, no matter how good, that come from the application of incentive management cannot be considered final. There will always be greater growth of man under continued proper incentive. Therefore, what he can and will accomplish will be progressively greater as latent abilities are developed and become usable.

The results so far obtained by incentive management are very great compared to what is usual in industry under so-called collective bargaining. Low costs, low selling prices, high profits, high wages, because of greater efficiency, and general satisfaction of all involved, are the present results.

POSSIBILITIES UNLIMITED

The obvious question is: how far can this progress be carried and what should be the goal that is sought from such progress? No one can know how far man can develop his latent abilities. It is obvious that the Creator in giving to man such abilities expected them to be used. Therefore, the ultimate goal will always be a challenge to any man, no matter how far he goes in his development.

Even under present limited development resulting from present incentives, more than four times previous production is easily obtained. This comes from increased skill, increased imagination and the elimination of overhead and waste, the necessity for which is past because of the new attitude of all.

It is not necessary to check on a player in an amateur game to see if he tries. There is no doubt he will try. Likewise, in industry under incentive management, all try. Many overhead jobs, therefore, such as many foremen, inspectors and clerks are needless, since the desire to produce at top speed and accuracy is inherent in all involved— they do not need to be watched.

WHAT TO DO WITH INCREASED PROFITS?

Such increase of efficiency poses a very real problem to management. The profit that will result from such efficiency obviously will be enormous. The output per dollar of investment will be many times that of the usual union shop which practices output limitation. The labor cost per piece will be relatively small and the overhead will be still less.

The profits at competitive selling price resulting from such efficiency will be far beyond any possible need for proper return and growth of any industry. Hence, new thinking must be done. Where should such profits go? There is a case that can be made for all those involved who accomplished such a result. The worker can say the increased profits belong to him because of his increased productive efficiency. The owners of the tools can say that the extra profit belongs to them. This conclusion is frequent in the present-day thinking. Management can say these profits belong to them since they applied incentive management which resulted in the profits. None of these conclusions is right. A new view must be taken if incentive management is to succeed. Such enormous profits cannot fairly nor properly be taken wholly by either labor, owners or management.

The real and ultimate boss of industry is the consumer.

He pays all wages and salaries, all taxes, all profits and all other costs. He can, whenever he wishes, stop all operation and all profit of any industry by stopping his buying. Hence, he must be the first to be considered in profit distribution. If we are to please him, he must continuously be given lower prices for a better product. Only so can industry expect to continue to sell him increasing quantities.

If, as is now customary, the stockholder takes all or most of these profits resulting from increased efficiency, the worker and customer have a real gripe. Such a plan is doomed to failure. If the worker takes all, the customers have a real cause for complaint. Even if the customer gets all the increased profit in lower prices, both labor and the owner will have a complaint. They have not been given proper recognition. Not only that, but the government would immediately institute proceedings to destroy any such successful industry because it would take all business in its line and become a monopoly. Competition would disappear. Government will not let the consumer have such a good deal.

CUSTOMER, WORKER, OWNER ALL MUST SHARE PROFITS

How, then, should the enormous extra profit resulting from incentive management be split? The problems that are inherent in incentive dictate the answer. If the worker does not get a proper share, he does not desire to develop himself or his skill. Incentive therefore would not succeed. The worker must have a reward that he feels is commensurate with his contribution.

If the customer does not have a part of the saving in lower prices, he will not buy the increased output. The size of the market is a decisive factor in costs of products.

Therefore, the consumer must get a proper share of the saving.

Management and ownership are usually considered as a unit. This is far from a fact, but in the problem here, they can be considered together. They must get a part of the saving in larger salaries and perhaps larger dividends.

There is no hard and fast rule to cover this division, other than the following. The worker, (which includes management), the customer, the owner and all those involved must be satisfied that they are properly recognized or they will not cooperate, and cooperation is essential to any and all successful applications of incentives.

SUCCESS DEPENDS ON FUNDAMENTAL PHILOSOPHY

The details of the incentive management plans followed are of little importance if the fundamental philosophies are adhered to. Whether the division to the worker is made monthly or yearly or at the end of his active life is of little importance, provided he believes in the plan and *wants* to do his best.

It will make little difference whether an annuity is part of the plan or not, if all workers believe in the program as used and *want* to do their best in the needed cooperation.

It will make little difference what the actual split between consumer, worker or owner is, as long as all feel it is fair and honest and worthy of their cooperation.

The fundamental effect that determines success or failure of incentive management is the development of the individual through his desire to rise in his usefulness in industry and through his desire to work together with his co-workers from top to bottom to produce better products more efficently. If all do this, success is assured under normal leadership following the same philosophy.

11

Failure always will come if the program falls short in understanding and/or resulting desire in accomplishment of these real and proper ends.

If the enthusiasm of the amateur athlete could be put into industry, results ten times greater than anything yet accomplished would become automatic. No one can doubt that such progress will eventually be made. This horizon is far beyond any present accomplishment, however.

That is the challenge and the goal that is inherent in incentive. That it will be accomplished eventually is obvious to anyone who can imagine and believe. These much greater results will come. Who will do it is the only question.

There are concomitant results that come from a proper application of incentive management that should be noted, since they are more important than mere increased efficiency of production.

The first is the change in the goals that industry has in its program. Profit under incentive management is no longer an end in itself. It is a by-product.

INCENTIVE MANAGEMENT GUARANTEES FREE ENTERPRISE

The second beneficial result to the economy is the guarantee that incentive management gives to the continuance of freedom of the people. For the first time in American history, free enterprise is being destroyed by high-minded incompetents who have only the best interests of America at heart, but whose knowledge of what makes the economy successfully progress is completely nil. Because of this and their soft-hearted "do-gooder" attitude, in which they are perhaps entirely honest, they are destroying America in the same way that a widowed mother is apt to ruin an only son. Our present policy of government-promised security is producing a race of incompetent softies, who will, because of their lack of vigor, be unable to continue the greatness of our country.

Free enterprise, which developed in the United States largely by luck, is the only reason why America is at the top now. The program of the various deals, "New" and "Fair", has already stopped and reversed the development on which we depend for our future progress and national security. It also has made the man of pioneer spirit a memory and replaced him by a seeker for politically-promised security who will never pioneer and hence will never progress beyond a crank-turner under the present socialistic philosophy.

These concomitant results of incentive management are perhaps equally or more important than production efficiency. They are not, however, the direct end sought by incentive management as shown here.

PROFIT NOT SOLE PURPOSE OF INDUSTRY

Incentive management cannot have successfully a narrowly selfish outlook in any industry which adopts it. The economy has progressed far beyond the point where profit only can be made the reason for industry. That plan is too narrow and will not succeed for long for any of those involved, be they owners, managers, workers or customers.

Successful industry cannot be operated for the sole purpose of profit. Such plans will fail. They will fail for three reasons: first, they direct the planning and thinking of the organization to the wrong objectives; second, they alienate the customer; third, they do not develop the latent ability and cooperation of the group. Any one of these will wreck any company in competition with an industry that has an enlightened objective.

If any industry has for its target the making of profit

only, it will largely overlook the goal of bettering its product. If its thinking is, "How much more can I get?" it cannot also be thinking, "How much more can I give?" If we think, "How can I raise this price to make more profit?" we cannot be thinking, "How can I make this more economically, so as to sell it at a lower price?" If we try to attain the first stated aims, by so doing we eliminate the possibility of seeing and attaining the second and proper objective. "No man can serve two masters" illustrates the dilemma of the industrialist who tries to seek profit as an end, and also service to the consumer with profit as a by-product only.

The second difficulty with this philosophy of profit only is the alienation of public goodwill. This public also includes the industrial workers in all plants. If we are self-seeking, as the philosophy, "This company is organized for profit," indicates, we will not win the buying public to our program. It already thinks prices are too high and higher than needed for a prosperous economy.

The third difficulty is that cooperation of labor and management disappears. No worker is keen in his desire to make more profits for absentee stockholders. We cannot expect that the worker will be greatly interested in such a program. He already thinks the owners get too much. No worker so believing will grow in skill and developed ability.

THE PRIMARY GOAL OF INDUSTRY

The primary goal of any industry to be successful continuously must be *to make a better and better product to be sold to more and more people at a lower and lower price.* Profit therefore will and must be a by-product of service only. That must be the fundamental philosophy in any

14

industry if it is to adopt incentive management.

These facts are perhaps obvious. However, they are not given their true significance by many people who should know better. Every scheme to maintain a high price by patents, agreements or other forms of monopoly has never given the profit to the monopolist that is obtained when competition sets the price and free competition fires the imagination of all manufacturers so that the lowest cost and greatest usefulness of the product is obtained. The Selden patent and comparative automobile production and profit before and after its invalidity is a good example. In the light of its history, it is hard to understand how any industrialist can still approve the price policy of "all the traffic will bear."

"MORE AND MORE FOR LESS AND LESS"

There are many other favorable results that flow from the plan of "more and more for less and less" which we may well consider. The American industrialist has always paid small attention to the foreign market. This is most surprising. The population of the United States is less than six per cent of the total population of the world. Under proper conditions, the foreign market obviously can be developed to sixteen times that of the United States. It is not larger now because the high cost of our production and because the foreigner's small income make it impossible for him to buy our products. This is not because he does not want them. He does, as is shown by the enthusiastic way he embraces our standard of living when he comes to live in this country and has the American opportunity. He would do the same when he is at home if he had the same opportunity.

If we made our products available to him, our market

would be expanded many times. If that were done, the cost of our production here would be much reduced by our higher output. Hence, our own and the foreigner's living standard would both increase. All would gain; none would lose. However, we will not do that. We insist on forcing artificially high prices, both by our tariff policy and by our own stupid selfishness, which leads us in many cases to charge much higher prices abroad than we do at home on the same product.

This policy of gouging the foreigner is so universal that foreign companies who do much buying of American products put their own purchasing departments in America to buy American products controlled by American competition, since the price charged abroad is artificially inflated.

Profit as a goal for our efforts fails in the same way and for the same reason that an attempt to capture happiness as an end in itself would fail.

We all desire happiness. No one will doubt that this aspiration is most sought for. However, anyone who strives for happiness as an end in itself will never be happy. Such a person will probably be miserable. Happiness is a by-product of many other things. Many of these things are of themselves the direct opposite of what we might think of as happiness. Self-restraint, generosity, treating others as we are bidden in the Sermon on the Mount, all lead to happiness, but none of them is itself happiness. Long experience has, however, shown that these seemingly opposite actions are the only road we can take which will finally make a happy person.

NEW PHILOSOPHY—NEW VISION

If we accept this philosophy of more and more for less and less, we have a new vision. Our activity will be geared entirely differently. Let us approach the problem from this point of view and see where it leads.

The first step we will take is to recognize that what we are now producing can be greatly bettered and greatly reduced in cost. There can be no doubt that such a conclusion is true. We need only to look back at what has gone before in industry to be sure of this. Everything that we now do is wrong compared to the better results that can be obtained. Every design can be bettered. Every method can be improved. Every skill can be increased. We are surely aware that these results will come eventually. The only question is, how soon and by whom will the progress be made?

INDUSTRY HAS HIGH RESPONSIBILITY

Industry's responsibility is just as great and perhaps greater than the school teacher's, the doctor's or the minister's. The outlook of each of these must be far broader than merely money as his final goal. We would not countenance the police officer's running his job as a money-making activity. We would put him in jail if he did. Industry's responsibility to the economy is equally great or greater than any of the above examples. So industry eventually must acknowledge.

This revolution in the place of man and of industry in the economy is the result of our natural growth. When we remember that industry as now organized is only a little more than two hundred years old, we can expect great growth and great change resulting from such growth. The remarkable fact is that such change has not proceeded much further and much faster than it has.

This book approaches the problem of management from the fundamental belief that enormous progress can be made compared to what is now happening in industry. This can be done first by the development of man's latent abilities, then by directing these developed abilities to producing better and better products at lower and lower prices for more and more people. The progress to be made is very great compared to anything yet seen, since we are dealing with the development of that marvelous being, man.

CHAPTER II

Industry Must Eliminate Jobs

We are now in an era when the individual greatly desires security. To many it is the first requirement to make any future attractive. This fact is remarkable since it is new to Americans. The Founding Fathers did not value security; if they had, they would not have been Founding Fathers. Security was the thing they renounced when they came here to get what to them was a much more desirable attainment; which was, personal freedom.

WE HAVE SACRIFICED FREEDOM FOR SECURITY

The Founding Fathers would not understand our present desire to sacrifice freedom to make our future more economically secure, or at least seem to make it so. Freedom, pride, self-reliance, personal responsibility, all are now forgotten if we only can get someone to assume the responsibility for a necessary income in a competitive economy. Seemingly, we do not want to meet the competition of our fellows. Meeting life is a responsibility many want someone else to assume for them.

Yet in shedding this responsibility we do not want to admit to ourselves that we are lazy or incompetent. We cannot do that and be content. We cannot admit that we are dubs or too lazy to meet life in competition with our fellows. For that reason, we try to change the rules of the game. We try to make self-support not an individual responsibility, but instead, a responsibility of the national government. If we can succeed in doing that, we do not have to admit to ourselves that we cannot meet the competition of the rest of the world. We can say instead that there is no such game in which we must compete. That allows us to be defeated without loss of personal pride. The present generation has succeeded in doing that, seemingly, to a satisfactory extent.

It is obviously true that many people now believe that it is up to someone beside themselves to take care of them, particularly if they are in trouble. There is little doubt that anyone in public office in America who would advance the idea that the individual is responsible for his own welfare would not remain a public official long. We do not want such public servants.

We now value liberty very little. We have developed a philosophy which shuns individual responsibility. Looking ahead is a lost art for many people. Many an American concludes that if he has a hot dog in his hand, a shot of liquor under his belt and a gallon of gas in his car, he is free from responsibility. If any of these things is missing, he feels that government should take steps to supply it. Perhaps this is a natural development of a prosperous people.

This is a very recent development in our country, however. Our forebears never had that philosophy. Desire to be supported by government or even by one's own family was a weakness that no normal individual then would ever countenance. The pauper then was a man despised. No pauper could hold his head up regardless of the reason for his condition. All that has changed now.

GOVERNMENT OWES US A LIVING

One of the striking illustrations of this present yen for someone else to give support to those who do not support themselves is the attitude that is now usual regarding industry's responsibility to the worker for jobs. Most workers have the feeling that the main purpose of industry is to produce jobs for them. They further feel that if industry does not give jobs of a kind and to the extent that is desired by the worker, government should step in and rectify the fault by any action that the government planners may suggest, including nationalization of industry. If this action should not put men to work, then government should make jobs by spending the taxpayer's money. Present government has largely accepted this responsibility.

It is interesting to note that jobs have always been and always will be available to every person. The same job opportunities that were present when the Pilgrim Fathers came to this country in 1620 have always been present ever since and are now present and in enormously greater volume. There has never been, nor will there ever be, a time when any man could not get a job that would support him much better than the Pilgrim Fathers could and did support themselves when they came to these shores.

EMPLOYMENT INCREASES WITH EFFICIENCY

Unemployment is a misnomer. The only unemployment that ever has existed, or ever can exist, is lack of specific

21

jobs, not lack of any job. As an illustration, if every person came to the conclusion that the only job he would take would be the Presidency of the United States, there would be at least 60,000,000 unemployed. There are always other jobs to be had, if we can and will take them.

The proportion of people who are employed by industry has continually increased as the efficiency of production has increased. This explodes the stubbornly held theory often urged by union labor leaders, that more efficient machines of production decrease employment. The facts prove the exact opposite. As efficiency of production increases, industrial employment increases also.

The development of a higher standard of living must be made by replacing the present skills and abilities by new ones that will make our present production methods out of date. This perhaps would seem impossible now to the unthinking. However, the newer and better methods will be obvious to us when we develop them. In industry that is the incentive and virtue of the free competitive system which has been developed so greatly in America.

A higher standard of living comes to any economy because of the lower costs of the products necessary to make up that standard of living or because of larger income of the individual to buy that standard of living at stationary prices, or both. History shows that both usually occur at about the same time.

No one ever has a satisfactory standard of living, no matter how high it may be. We always want to progress to a still higher standard and always will. That is the drive that has made the human race what it is. That is the reason why there will never be any lack of jobs if we make efficiency of production a progressive thing. Jobs will disappear if efficiency is reduced. Jobs increase when low costs, the result of high efficiency of production, reduce costs and prices. All history in industry proves this fact. The proportion of workers in industry is continually increasing as efficiency of production increases. The only time when jobs disappear in industry is when progress is not made in efficiency so that progressively lower prices can be given to the consumer so he can buy a progressively higher standard of living.

Perhaps this statement is surprising to those who believe that there is only so much work, so much market and so much profit to be made. Perhaps the so-called "hard-headed business man" will completely reject this conclusion. The fact, however, will still remain.

There is no doubt that it takes vision to see this new goal for industry. There are countless people who have held the opposite view and their temporary success by monopoly or cartel is convincing to many. The two courses are diametrically opposed. One or the other must be followed. One course obviously excludes the other.

CHANGE IS NECESSARY FOR CONTINUOUS EMPLOYMENT

New education, new skills and new locations are the changes necessary if anyone is to be continuously employed. Technical and industrial progress not only eliminates old jobs, but also continuously produces more new ones. We must be prepared for such progress and change.

All unemployment is the result of lack of skill, or desire for too high wages, or the fact that the worker is not in the right locality to take the available jobs. There are always jobs to be had if we are able and willing to take them and always will be.

A job in many minds is employment in the city where one is located, at work he has done before, at wages that are high, at hours that he likes. No other job will do. That is the reason for all unemployment that now exists or ever will exist. The reason a totalitarian state always has jobs is that the worker learns the skill and goes to the place required at the order of the state. Such jobs are always available in any economy.

Some jobs disappear as industrial progress is made. For instance, there is little need for the carriage builder now. If he has not taken some other job at new skill, he is on relief. There is little use for the village blacksmith. If he has not taken another job and acquired new skills perhaps in a new location, he also is on relief.

The important point is that only by changing to new jobs at new locations with new skills can anyone get continuous employment. So rapid is the development of industry, that if such foresight is not displayed by most individuals, almost all would be on relief within a generation.

WHO SUPPORTS THOSE WHO CANNOT OR WILL NOT CHANGE?

Since a large part of the people can and do change their skills so that they can do new jobs, the question is, why cannot all do the same? Why should the taxpayer support those who have not the ambition to prepare themselves for these changes? Why should those who pay their way by proper preparation for the future also have to support those who are too thoughtless or lazy to do so? These questions must be answered soon. We shall be running out of supporters for the supported with our present program.

INDUSTRY MUST ELIMINATE JOBS

We can cure the trouble in one of two ways; by placing the responsibility for our personal support on ourselves, or by giving it to government. We must, however, give government the power to do the job if we are to give it the responsibility. Government can only spend money, government cannot make it. Hence, it must have the power to take the needed money no matter how much, in taxes from all who work. As the taxpayer's resentment rises with increased taxes, the state must have the power to quell the disturbance. That form of government is called totalitarianism.

TOTALITARIANISM HAS ONE ADVANTAGE

When all citizens depend on governmental support, it takes most of the earnings of most producers to produce a bare living for all. Because of the inefficiency of government bureaucracy, it is also necessary to make all work to get enough income for government to do even that. Only so can enough money be taken by taxes to make a bare living for all. Russia has shown the way on this phase of security. No one, except those in power, likes such a government. That is too bad. However, it will have no effect on governmental policy. There is one advantage of totalitarianism. No totalitarian government ever runs out of jobs. Job security is certain. Foresight of the enslaved individual is not needed.

INDUSTRY MUST ELIMINATE JOBS

The reason for discussing this matter of jobs and who can make them is to see what industry's function should be. The first fact we must accept is that industry is not

25

for the purpose of creating jobs. As a matter of fact, the sole function of industry is to eliminate jobs. It is only to the extent that it eliminates jobs that industry can justify itself in the economy.

Perhaps this sounds untrue. Let us analyze the matter. The only reason why people buy the product of industry is because it is better and/or cheaper than the same product would be if made by the buyer himself. It is only because of this cheaper price and better product that industry is maintained by customer buying of its product. When industry ceases to give a better value at a lower price than the buyer can produce for himself, obviously it must disappear, since there will be no market for its products. Unless the price is reduced enough by the efficiency of the producer, the customer cannot and will not buy the product at all. At the same time, there are many things that the consumer could not make himself because of lack of skill and time and he can't afford what is offered. He therefore would buy nothing. That means that the standard of living then would go down. Put another way, our standard of living depends on the cost and availability of the things that go to make that standard of living. Only as these costs decrease can our buying increase and living standard rise.

LIVING STANDARDS RISE AS JOBS ARE ELIMINATED

The cost of any product is dependent on the time taken by man and machine to make and distribute it. This means not only the time of making the product by the worker, but also the time taken in producing and maintaining the machinery that is used by the producer. As the time of production is reduced, the cost is reduced. This time of production can only be reduced by eliminating jobs that were previously needed. The service of industry to mankind, therefore, is in direct proportion to the number of jobs that are eliminated by it in making the products that make up our standard of living. The responsibility of industry, therefore, is the elimination of jobs.

Our industrial system of free enterprise has made great strides in eliminating jobs by its efficiency. The number of hours needed to give us our present higher standard of living has been reduced tremendously in the last century. Further reductions are in the offing; as a result the standard of living is continually rising for all people. The wage earner has had his job changed by our industrial progress, but the change has given him not unemployment, but a new job and a higher living standard and continually will.

Perhaps the making of the common pin is a useful illustration. Two hundred years ago pins cost about eight cents each. They now cost much less than eight cents per hundred. During the intervening two hundred years, the wages of labor per hour for making pins has increased more than ten times; yet in spite of this the cost of the finished pin is less than one per cent of what it was then. Obviously, the number of operations to produce a pin has been cut to one one-thousandth of what it was two hundred years ago. Put in another way, 999 jobs out of 1,000 have been eliminated in two hundred years in the producing of pins. We, the buyers, like that. We are buying millions of pins at the present price compared to one that our forebears bought two hundred years ago. Total jobs for making pins are now greater than before because of the lower cost to the user and his resulting greater purchases. That is the justification for the industrial system. Industry's value to mankind obviously is in direct proportion to the number of jobs it eliminates in making its products and the price reduction that comes from this greater efficiency.

This same kind of industrial progress has been made in producing every popular item that makes up our standard of living. That is why our living standard has risen.

EVERYONE WHO BUYS WANTS LOW PRICES

It is an interesting fact that no buyer of any product ever disputes this statement. It is only the starry-eyed theorist and labor leaders who try to think otherwise. It is instructive also to note that even these starry-eyed theorists and labor leaders who promote industrial inefficiency do not believe their own theory. They scream to high heaven when costs of what they buy go up because of the inefficiency which their program promotes.

Up to the present time there is no record of any buyer of any product who thought that the price he paid for his living was too low. No one yet has insisted that the asking price of the things he buys be raised so as to support useless jobs. That was also true when child labor at long hours and starvation wages, which reduced prices, was the custom. This statement is equally true of housewives, business men, ministers, labor leaders and also of the starry-eyed do-gooders. That is one place where all are agreed. All want low wages and job elimination when they buy any product.

In any approach to this problem of jobs, wages and working conditions, the seeming contradictions actually are not really contradictions. Properly understood, everyone's interest lies in the same direction. Everyone actually wants job elimination. This is true of the buyer, the worker and the industrialist. They all want lower prices and

28

its raising of living standards.

The development of a higher standard of living must be by replacing the present skills and abilities by new ones that will make our present production out of date. It may seem impossible now since we are doing our best with our present state of development as we see it. The new methods will be obvious when we develop them.

EFFICIENCY=PROGRESS=JOB ELIMINATION

All progress in our living standards is the result of efficiency of production. These new methods usually mean the changing from hand operation to machine production. This change often eliminates most of the labor and time of production. Few men are needed to tend a machine compared to those needed before when production was hand operations. We all want the change made. The worker wants to be rid of his former drudgery. The manufacturer wants more production from his plant so that he can satisfy the greater demand caused by the lower price of the machine-made product. The buyer likes the accuracy, appearance and low cost. It is well to remember also that the maker and the buyer are eventually the same man.

No man ever has all of the things he wants. What possessions we have are determined by our ability to buy, not by our desire, for there is no end to desire. Every time our wages go up our living standard rises if costs do not. If prices go down and wages remain constant, the same thing happens: our living standard rises. The only limitation on our standard of living is ability to pay for the things we want. Cost obviously determines price and hence availability of all things and the resulting standard of living.

COST REDUCTION MUST BE HANDED TO CONSUMER
TO AVOID SLUMP

There is another fact illustrated above. It is obvious that if a job is eliminated and the cost reduction is not handed on to the consumer, no progress is made. We have made the product cheaper. We have eliminated jobs but we do not, as a consequence, make more demand for the product nor the consequent new jobs.

When we fail to hand on the savings from job elimination or when government takes the saving in taxes so that the producer cannot hand the saving to the consumer, the economy is in for trouble. That result we call a slump, a recession, a crisis or a healthy readjustment, depending on our point of view.

Every so-called slump is the result of cost going beyond the consumer's ability to pay. In the past, some slumps have come from the mistaken economic thinking of those who produced and distributed the products. Slumps also come from improper economic thinking of the consumer. During a boom, the consumer sets his standard of living at the maximum point that his income then warrants. The industrialist sets his selling price at what the market will support. Government increases its tax take. The worker, particularly under present short-sighted leadership, raises wages by his unlimited power to a point that will price him out of the market. This wage tendency is particularly effective when output limitation adds to the price the customer must pay for the product.

There is no trouble as long as buying continues. Under such a program some one will get pinched eventually. The person who feels the pinch first during the progress of such a boom is the consumer. He awakens some morning to find that he spent more on his automobile or his headache than his income can stand, so he decides to cut down on his purchases. In fact, he decides to live on what he has on hand for as long as he can. This feeling takes possession of many people about the same time. Economic pressures hit all and at about the same time during any boom.

The purchaser's reaction must result in low purchases. The buyer has made up his mind to save by buying less. He therefore needs nothing for some time. This means low demand, low demand means fewer jobs, fewer jobs means less purchasing power and more fright. All of these tendencies feed on themselves. The slump becomes progressively more severe.

GOVERNMENT SPENDING NO CURE FOR SLUMP

One way to remedy a slump is to borrow from the future and live at the old rate on this borrowed money. That is something that many people cannot do because no one will lend them the money on their promise to pay. Most of those who can borrow will not do it since it means bankruptcy and they look that far ahead. This difficulty can be so easily overcome, we think, if we have government do the borrowing for us.

Few seem to think that government spending is money that they themselves furnish. They think that it is produced by government. Hence, government spending, although unbelievably extravagant and dumbly done, does not affect our thinking in the same way that our wives' improper spending would.

The fact remains that both those who cannot themselves borrow and those who can are rather well satisfied when government borrows in their names and continues uneconomic spending that they would not or could not do

31

themselves. Such debt spending answers the question of slump elimination; at least for the present time. That is as far as this generation seemingly is interested. The problem of the next generation suffering for our sins leaves us cold. "Why worry about them? They are not even born yet."

LOWER COSTS OVERCOME SLUMP

Of course, the honest and proper way to overcome a slump receives scant attention from such people. The proper solution for our trouble is to stop the habits that caused our sickness. That means lower prices for our products. To obtain lower prices, the need is lower fundamental cost, obtained by higher efficiency or lower wages per hour or less taxes or less distribution costs or all four means. If these things are immediately done to the extent that they can be, the slump is over.

No one ever passed up a bargain if the bargain was real enough. A sale at really low prices always has purchasers standing three deep before the counter. When these new low prices, the result of lower profits, greater efficiency, lower taxes, lower wages and lower distribution cost, are available to the consumer, there will be no slump.

So far, such an obvious correction for any slump cannot be followed because of our short-sightedness. We will not accept the needs of the situation. We will not take the added personal responsibility. We try to coast to the goal rather than work to it. We will not produce at a lower cost by any and all means that may be available. This is the obvious and sure cure, however. We must accept it.

32

INDUSTRY MUST ELIMINATE JOBS

COMPETITION IS SPUR TO PROGRESS

Competition is the foundation of man's development. It has made the human race what it is. It is the spur that makes progress. Every nation that has eliminated it as the controlling force in its economy has disappeared, or will. We will do the same if we eliminate it by trying to give security, and for the same reason. Competition means that there will be losers as well as winners in the game. Competition will mean the disappearance of the lazy and incompetent, be they workers, industrialists or distributors. Competition promotes progress. Competition determines who will be the leader. It is the only known way that leadership and progress can be developed if history means anything. It is a hard taskmaster. It is completely necessary for anyone, be he worker, user, distributor or boss, if he is to grow.

If some way could be found so that competition could be eliminated from life, the result would be disastrous. Any nation and any people disappear if life becomes too easy. There is no danger from a hard life as all history shows. Danger is from a life that is made soft by lack of competition.

COMPETITION FOR JOBS IS NECESSARY

The threat of losing his job makes a worker keen to protect himself so that his job is secure; however, this security is obtained by developing his own perfection. This perfection, however, endangers the job of the less perfect worker, and so it must be if our economy is to grow. We may not like the threat, but we must meet it or progress stops and with this lack of progress, the nation loses its place in the world. Then men go back to savagery and extinction. We either go forward or back. We can't stand still.

We must meet this challenge. Only so can we be men in a man's world. This competition is universal. It is between individuals in their strife for a mate, for money and position, for an education or for a place on the football team.

The competition between industries for the market is another one of these struggles. Of course, the struggle between workers for the job is only a miniature parallel to the competition between the industrial organizations themselves.

All these struggles are necessary if we are to grow and be content. Human beings, since they developed through competition, must of necessity continue with this competition or they will disappear.

If we try to sidestep this program of competition, we will fail, since it is the stuff of which man is made. When we try to cushion the result of failure, as our social security program attempts to do, we are not helping, we are only courting disaster. We would recognize that in an athletic event. We want competition when we buy any product. We would resent any other arrangement in selecting a successful author, teacher, doctor or friend. We must see that competition is equally necessary in all walks of life.

EVERYBODY CANNOT BE A WINNER

Caring for the losers in industrial employment is a problem that we must face. We have not done that yet with any degree of success since we consider that in the industrial field, unlike any other, all must be winners; at least no one can be the loser. A man's job is his personal right under present union labor rules. This philosophy is suicidal nonsense as all history shows. If we do not face up to the reward of winning and the penalty of losing, we will upset the whole system on which progress of the human race is based.

The fundamental fact is that when the reward and penalty are allowed to have their natural effect, there are many more winners and many less losers. The natural ambition inherent in man makes him develop his latent abilities so that we have more experts and fewer incompetents. In fact, the loser in this game is almost sure to develop to new skill from his failure and develop abilities of a new and different kind. In any case, the failures are fewer and the geniuses are far more numerous when competition has its natural way. It is a completely natural outcome of natural competition.

It would be well to allow this competition to work out its natural laws instead of penalizing the winner by taking his winnings away from him to give a prize to the carefree, as we are now doing. It is too easy to eliminate the winner entirely if we punish him for winning. When we do eliminate him, we will have a nation of soft incompetents who cannot survive.

His own security is an attainable reward for which any normal man can and must be responsible. If we try to make a gift or guarantee of the state, the normal incentive that all must have to grow will disappear. When that happens, the nation disappears with it, as all history so fully shows.

CHAPTER III

No Limit To Standard of Living

We are continuously hearing about standards of living and those whose standard of living is not as high as it should be. We hear much about slums and the disease and crime that are bred there. We hear about the wages that are so low that the earners of such wages are ill-fed, ill-housed and ill-clothed. There have been countless politicians, chief of whom was Roosevelt and his successor, Truman, who have ridden this theme to great political success. The future politicians are fitting up the various changes in the theme for their own future use. Any politician who did not ring these various changes on this theme will not now remain a politician long, as past experience shows.

STANDARD OF LIVING IS RELATIVE

Therefore, we may well ask the question: what is a proper standard of living? As is true with many popularly held ideas, it is a current myth. The living standard of a king of a few generations ago is poverty and unthinkable destitution for even a person on relief now. A standard of living is actually a comparison that has to do with keeping up with the Joneses and not with any fundamental need.

The best proof of this statement is that no standard of living in this country at any time would have been tolerated by the following generations. A living standard does not deal with fact. It deals only with relationship to what has gone before or what exists elsewhere.

The standard of living of King Solomon would mean unthinkable hardship to the American of today. The standard of living of Louis XIV, "The Grand Monarch," would be unendurable hardship to the present Frenchman. No present-day civilized human being will stand the lack of central heating, transportation, medical care, communication and hard roads which were usual even seventy-five years ago in this country. Any such present-day citizen would probably die within a year if he were forced to live as even the most pampered did centuries ago.

A standard of living is actually what a generation is accustomed to. What we consider today an excellent standard of living will be thought of by our children as poverty that must not be allowed to exist.

The social worker who continually berates the supplier of his clients' present standard of living will have a progressively better story to give to the newspapers as our ideas change with the advance of science and industry. The "minimum standard of living" will always be beyond anything that can be given since the size of that minimum will be always progressively higher. An automobile, telephone, gas or electric range and modern medicine are now considered minimum. A few generations ago, none was even known. A generation hence, they will represent unthinkable poverty.

There is no doubt that everything now necessary as a standard of living will be replaced by a different and more useful product. It is also sure that the number of products that make up the standard of living will be enormously increased. There is no possible end to such progress except the imagination and ability of the industrial team.

PRESENT STANDARDS WILL CHANGE

Science and industry can and will change our desires as to our living standard almost overnight. It is obvious therefore that such changes do not come from bodily or spiritual need of the citizen. It comes only from custom. What is a proper standard of living in America is not a proper one for the Kaffir of Africa. This is true not because of fundamental differences of need, but solely because of custom. If we need any proof, compare the needs of any American in America with those of his cousin in Africa, Asia or Europe. They were blood brothers a few generations ago.

The conclusion to be drawn from these facts is this: every person in the world has the same fundamental desire as to a standard of living. That desire is to have his standard higher than others. He here displays the fundamental drive that has made man what he is. He wants to rise above his fellows. That is man's chief desire and incentive.

From this fact, we know that there is no limit to the need for industrial and scientific progress. We could sell seven hundred million automobiles to the rest of the world if we would make the conditions the same there as they are here so that the rest of the world would want an automobile in the same way and for the same reason that we want it here.

The automobile is not necessary in itself. A few years ago we were content without it. It has been made necessary by custom only. It will be replaced by custom in the not too distant future by something we would scoff at now as we did the automobile a generation ago, but which we will insist is necessary then. What that will be depends on science and management, not on actual human need.

It is obvious there is no end to this program. It will not make the people happier, more healthy or more useful. As a matter of fact, it will frequently do just the opposite as ease takes the place of effort. It is, however, the necessary concomitant to man's progress. He struggles for this progress as an end in itself. He is so made that he must so struggle. He cannot help trying to go forward in this living standard so that he can feel his superiority over his contemporaries.

EFFICIENCY DETERMINES STANDARD

The standard of living is determined by the efficiency of production of industry. As less man hours are needed to produce products that make up the standard of living, more products can be made by the same number of man hours.

This may mean more and cheaper products which are now common or new products developed by the labor-management team that is released by the greater developed efficiency in making the present products.

This fact, so obvious when viewed from without, has produced a major problem in many labor-management relationships. Greater production efficiency eliminates certain jobs, as has been discussed before. This has in many cases thrown certain workers out of work. Often these idled workers were not immediately re-employed. Their reaction was fear and distrust of industrial progress for that reason. They would not, or did not see that eventually all benefit by such progress. They would not or did not see that only so could they have the desired higher standard of living they craved.

INEFFICIENCY LOWERS EUROPEAN STANDARD

In the mind of the usual worker, the greatest threat to his future is the danger of working himself out of a job. That is the primary problem in his thinking and in the thinking of most union leadership. Most union planning is based on that premise. Not only that, both workers and union leaders can cite any number of instances which in their minds prove their conclusion completely. The philosophy of industry in Europe is based entirely on this theory that there is only so much work to do and only so much product to be made. Because of this assumption, almost all European industry forms itself into cartels to allocate this limited business among the members of the cartel. In its opinion, only in that way can any industry continue to exist.

It is obvious that allocating the available business by cartels has two suicidal results. The first is that the price agreed on will be that needed to make a profit for the least efficient producer. This means that the price will be much higher than if it were set by competition. Competition would set the price at a profit point needed by the most efficient producer instead of the least efficient. The result of this cartel system pricing means that prices are continually increasing, thus making the market less and less.

This means still higher prices are necessary for a profit as the market shrinks.

European economy shows the results of this cartel system. Wages per hour in Europe are less than a quarter of those paid in the United States, yet the price of some products, exactly the same as those made under incentive management, cost more than twice the cost of production here. The fundamental truth that a large part of nothing is still nothing does not make much impression on the leadership in Europe. It still believes in output limitation as the answer to its troubles.

The labor leader there feels if he can divide up the work he will succeed in giving continuous employment to all his men. The governmental bureaucrat believes if he can restrict imports by tariff or edict he will save the sick industries in his country. The industrialist still feels that if he can only charge a high enough price for his product he can still make a profit. The only difficulty is that these policies have largely eliminated the use of the product because it is priced out of the market.

LACK OF COMPETITION STIFLES ABILITY

The second result of such price fixing and the elimination of competition means that the able do not rise to the top of industry. There is no use for ability in a cartel, hence, great industrial leaders are not produced. The hot pace of competition never comes.

We have seen from the previous discussion that ability is forged in the heat of competition. Only so will the leader develop his latent abilities. It is obvious, therefore, that if such competition does not exist, individual development will not occur. Because of this fact, industrial leadership is not developed in cartel countries.

41

No more destructive philosophy than that of cartels has ever been developed in industry. This is the handicap that is vexing Europe now. It is because of this that America, which has developed its industry in the forge of free competition, must assist the people there.

It is not surprising that labor believes that limitation of production is proper when industrialists under the cartel system support such a philosophy. As a matter of fact, having the cartel philosophy of management, the European manufacturer leaves himself open to entirely justified criticism when he does not allocate to each worker in his employ a given limited amount of work (since his cartel tells him how much he is to get), so that this limited amount of work can be spread to give continuous employment to those employed in such factories. Only so can the manager play fair with his men. He knows how much product he will sell, therefore he should tell his workers the facts and allow them to limit their production accordingly.

THE MARKET CAN BE MADE INFINITE
IF PRICE IS LOW ENOUGH

If the idea that market division and agreed prices is sound, then the whole incentive philosophy of lower prices and better product in larger markets is wrong. What are the facts as to market size and price influence on it? There is no instance wherein the market for any useful product cannot be made infinite if the price is low enough. The converse of this is equally true. There is no market for a product, no matter how useful, if the price is high enough. In general, raising the price of a product merely drives the purchaser to a competitive product that may not be as good but which will do in his estimation because

42

of the lower price. However, if no such cheaper product is available, the purchaser merely goes without.

There are countless illustrations of this reaction. Everyone prefers tailor-made clothes. Few buy them because of the price. Everyone wants a new car. Fewer buy them than second hand cars, again because of price. Everyone would rather ride in a drawing room than in a berth in the usual Pullman car. Few ride in one, however. Everyone would rather ride in a special car than in a car seat. Few do, because of the cost. Every electrical machine could be made more efficient, lighter and with greater freedom from failure if silver instead of copper were used for the windings. Copper is always used because it is cheaper. Gold or platinum is a better coating material for the protection of steel than zinc. It is never used commercially because of cost. Stainless steel is better than galvanized iron for resisting rust. It is seldom used because of price. Distilled water is better than the normal unpure water that every city uses in its water system; distillation would remove the danger of much disease and the bad effects of the dissolved solids that are usually called "hardness." No city has ever even considered it, because of cost.

There are countless cases that could be added to this list. Every housewife, every man and every buyer are continually substituting a cheaper product for a better one in their purchases because of price. This judgment is one that the engineer, the purchasing agent and the housewife continually exercise. All this is obvious.

MANUFACTURERS DISREGARD SIGNIFICANCE OF PRICE

In light of these facts, it is odd that the effect of price on purchasing, so well understood when one is a buyer, is largely disregarded when one is a manufacturer and makes a product to sell. It is almost a universal reaction that in the case of one's own product, high price is of no importance. The industrialist's reaction usually is that high price can be asked and the market will not be affected in the case of his product. The same industrialist will place his own buying wholly on a quality-price basis, however. He does not "wish-think" when he spends his own money.

I have been told many times that the user of welding will not reduce his buying of welding rod if the price is increased; the theory is that the buyer pays only a small proportion of his cost of production for electrodes and machines, therefore he will not think of price when buying welding. The same person will agree that all the previous facts on market-price relationship listed above are true. He always comes back with the statement, however, "welding is different." He will admit that there is much more welding done in the United States than in all the rest of the world combined, but he will always insist that the reason is some other than the fact that in America the cost of welding machines and electrodes is the lowest in the world.

There is even much criticism of the action of the United States government in outlawing price agreements. Any act of government of an administrative nature must be clumsy and very inefficient. There is no doubt, however, that in this field of keeping industry competitive it has gone some distance in justifying its place in industry.

The effect of competition on price is very far-reaching. Competition makes the industrialist develop the unusual in his product and in himself. Competition develops needs and abilities that make the impossible a practical and usable development. Competition is the incentive that has made the human race what it is. Competition is the incentive that will make all future development feasible.

OUR NATIONAL PREDOMINANCE RESTS ON OUR EFFICIENCY

The eventual outcome of the policy of cost and price reduction is of far-reaching importance. If costs and prices are reduced, as has been done by the application of incentive, far-reaching results occur. Manhours for the production of the same products have been reduced in the last fifteen years by more than eighty-five percent in one well-known case. That means that each person produces more than six times as many pieces as he did fifteen years ago. Continuous growth, more jobs and greater prosperity for all concerned have been the result.

It is well to remember that we are in competition with the rest of the world. America's tremendous ability in industry was the reason for our position, compared to other countries. That ability can only be developed by a free people under incentive. We do not have our power because of great numbers of people or great natural resources. Several nations have much more of both. We are great because of our industrial ability. When that is surpassed, we disappear as the dominant nation. The danger of being surpassed is particularly cogent now. We have by our governmental policy, largely eliminated incentive for the efficient producer. We punish him for his excellence by union rules and at a progressively steeper tax rate as he excels.

Russia has a system of incentive that is different. She rewards the efficient with better housing, better food, better facilities of all kinds. Russia punishes the laggard by putting him in a prison camp in which he has less food and more interference with his personal freedom and perhaps death. There is no doubt as to the reality and direction of Russian incentive.

RUSSIAN INCENTIVE REMOVES FREEDOM

The weakness of the Russian incentive system is that it takes away freedom from the individual. He is merely a puppet of the state. This removes the possibility of development of his latent abilities. He is rewarded for hard work, but he cannot rise to important leadership. The only ones who can lead are the bureaucrats. Even they cannot develop the abilities that make great industrialists since they come in contact with industry, not in its productive and inventive phases, but only as supreme bosses of all industry, which is a very different thing. It is not possible to develop new forms or methods when the contact with industry is not more intimate. Progress in the individual comes from authority and responsibility, neither of which the bureaucrat in Russia can allow to the worker.

OUR TAX PROGRAM KILLS INCENTIVE

Our government has adopted a completely different philosophy from that of Russia. We give a measure of freedom to the individual. He can therefore develop his latent ability if he wants to. However, we take away the incentive to develop his skill or desire to progress by our plan of taxation. If he produces at a high rate because of his skill and earns more wages, he is taxed at a progressively punitive rate, far above the less skilled. If he becomes a loafer and refuses to work at all, he is put on relief at the expense of the already tax-penalized producer and rewarded with a livelihood without effort on his part.

Aside from the gross injustice of this program, it is plain suicide for America in competition with Russia, which has progressed in the development of industry at a very much higher rate than any of the Western powers. Russia will obviously dominate the West completely, because of incentive there and lack of incentive here, if the present program continues. Any American who can view this tendency with equanimity is an unusual character.

HIGHER WAGES CAN MEAN LOWER COSTS

There is another problem that bears on the standard of living. That is, wages. There is a very misleading conclusion that is almost universal in industrial thinking regarding the result of wages on cost. There are few industrialists who do not think that higher wages per hour mean higher costs of the finished product. The whole theory of tariffs and resistance to wage increases is based on this error. Actually, wages that are higher per hour may or may not increase the cost of the product made. Higher wages will not mean higher costs if the problem is properly handled by the industrialist. In fact, often higher wages mean lower costs and lower wages mean higher costs.

It is not necessary to prove this, since our own experience with doctors, lawyers and slavery prove the facts conclusively. The cheap doctor usually means higher resulting cost. Slavery meant higher costs also.

If we are to approach the matter accurately, we will not think about wages per hour. They have no bearing on cost. Our thought should be directed to labor plus overhead cost *per piece,* which is an entirely different thing. It is obvious that if wages are increased in direct proportion to production, the labor cost per piece will remain constant.

There is another item of cost, however, that will be

reduced as the efficiency of production of the producer goes up. That item is overhead. In the usual factory, overhead is greater than direct labor costs. Overhead is a constant cost per hour. If, therefore, we can increase the production rate by increased skill of the worker, even when he is paid in proportion, we reduce our total cost by this overhead reduction.

INDUSTRIAL LEADERSHIP MUST PROVIDE HIGH STANDARD

This whole problem of low cost and high wages gives the industrialist his job. It is his genius on which the economy rests its chance not only for the safety of America in its competition with the rest of the world; but also for the continued progress in our standard of living and all other progress that we crave and will always crave.

This higher standard of living comes to labor by higher wages and lower cost of his purchases. This higher standard of living comes to the public as lower cost of its purchases. This higher standard of living comes to the stockholder in larger dividends and lower cost of the things that he buys. The job of the industrialist and labor is to make all of these things possible.

Perhaps this seems a hard and impossible task for industry. It is not. All the proof necessary is to look at our standard of living now and a hundred years ago. That is what our preceding industrial leadership did. We can make even greater progress. We have more knowledge and greater skill. We also know more about that wonderful human mechanism—man.

We have followed the foolish idea that as wages go up, prices must go up also. We gripe about the low wages of foreign countries and the competition that they give us. We feel that such low hourly labor costs mean low product costs. High wages are necessary for low production cost. Only so can the worker have the standard of living and the pride in his ability to make him an outstanding producer.

For example, the true cost of cotton now is much less than it was one hundred years ago when the wages of the slaves who grew it were nothing. The cost of a bushel of wheat is less now than it was when raised by serfs whose wages were infinitesimal in comparison with those of the farm laborer now.

INDUSTRIALIST MUST BE AN EXPERT

It is the industrialist's job to pay these higher and higher wages and still give more and more to the customer for less and less. His success in doing that determines how good an industrialist he is. That is the reason why only an expert can be a successful industrialist. That is why a bureaucrat cannot succeed as an industrialist.

It will be said by many that this standard for the industrialist is too high; that it is unattainable and too few can measure up to it. That is its virtue. Development of the individual's latent abilities can only be accomplished when a high standard is set. Only by reaching out for something that is beyond our present ability can greater ability be developed. We do not make geniuses or record breakers by ordinary striving. Ability of the expert industrialist can only be developed by the intense heat of competition and the setting of a goal that is always unattainable with his present ability. We recognize this, but we perhaps hesitate to put ourselves to this supreme test.

Such leaders, so developed, will be crucified by government which will take the side of the commonplace person who will be jealous of the expert industrialist's success. He will be criticized by the labor leader for his dominance in his leadership of labor. He will be hated by all who say, "It can't be done." He will only be extolled by those who can understand. He will get his reward from the feeling of a job well done. He will know that his leadership was the reason for the progress. He will also show the way to save this country from the crisis now threatening in the labor-management war. He will be content.

CHAPTER IV

Development of Personnel

We all recognize great differences between the abilities of people. That is why every industrial organization has an employment department to pick and choose. We do not as fully recognize the fact that after people are hired, the development that can be accomplished in them will often make far more difference than what is found in them when they were hired.

There is no doubt in the minds of anyone that careful selection of personnel is essential if we are to have a successful organization. We have far less knowledge, however, regarding the development that can occur in this same personnel on the job under proper leadership. This development may be toward greater ability and worth. It can also be toward less ability and greater incompetence. Development surely will take place. What its direction will be is dependent on the leadership of the company. Its importance to industry cannot be overemphasized.

It is usual for those who hire the new recruits to base their decisions largely on the previous experience and record of the applicant. For instance, very seldom is a

51

man hired for a technical job unless he has had technical university training. Also, no man would be chosen as a toolmaker unless he had proper previous training in tool-making. All that is customary.

There is one further point regarding this matter, however, that is often overlooked. The development that can take place in the new recruit, no matter what his job may be, can and should be far greater after he is hired than it was before. That is what incentive management can do. It is this development that is the greatest opportunity of the industrialist. It is that development that is decisive in determining the future of the man and the company.

ABILITY MUST BE DEVELOPED

What a man's ability is at any time depends on two things: first, with what abilities he was born and, second, how much he has developed those abilities. It is obvious that he cannot have abilities if he is not born with them. It is also just as evident that he will never be able to be conscious of abilities with which he was born if he does not develop them from their latent state in which they were at the time of birth. Most latent abilities of most people remain latent. They are then no more useful to anyone than if they never had existed.

Perhaps these examples will illustrate the point. Julius Caesar no doubt could have been a good automobile driver. He never had the chance to drive, however, hence his latent ability along this line remained latent. Neither he nor any of his contemporaries ever knew that he could drive an automobile. Ben Hur would no doubt have been a great airplane pilot had he developed the latent abilities he so fully showed in his chariot races. However, he never piloted a plane. He therefore never developed this latent ability. He went to his grave never knowing he had the possibility of any such skill. Babe Ruth would never have been a great baseball player had he always lived in England. They don't play baseball there and he could never have developed his latent batting ability. Henry Ford would never have been a great manufacturer had he remained on the farm. He could not have developed his great mechanical production genius there.

Perhaps learning to swim will further illustrate the point. Any child can swim if thrown into the water if his attempt is to swim. Many children will drown, however, if thrown into water deep enough if they have never swum before. The difference between those who swim and those who would drown is not difference of latent ability to swim. It is the lack of attempt on the part of those who fail. The failures do not try to swim, they are thinking of something else. They are frightened by the new problem and do not try to solve it. They are too busy yelling for help or crying because that help, which has always before been available, is not at hand. Because they do not try to swim, they sink. Those who try to swim, do swim. They develop from a latent a real ability.

The one most important point to be remembered is that no one would ever have become a swimmer if he were not in water of sufficient depth to make swimming possible and perhaps necessary. If the problem had never been put to the individual he would never have solved it. He was a latent swimmer always. He became an actual swimmer only because of conditions that forced him to swim. Latent abilities are like clay—it can be mud on the shoes, brick in a building or a statue that will inspire all who see it. The clay is the same. The result is dependent on how it is used.

All men would be geniuses if they should develop to the extent they can. All men would be incompetents if they developed their latent abilities not at all.

MUST HAVE DRIVE TO DEVELOP ABILITY

In the same way, we all have great latent abilities in all lines. Those abilities remain latent forever unless there is a sufficient drive founded on intense desire to develop them. Undeveloped, they are no more useful than if they had never existed. Thousands of geniuses have gone to their graves with their genius still latent and unknown. They were incompetents instead of geniuses because ambition and opportunity never was brought to bear on their latent abilities to make them develop to abilities that were real and usable.

Some latent abilities usually develop in almost all people. These are very great developments such as ability to walk, run and talk. We are forced by the circumstances of life to develop these abilities to be able to live in the world. Hence, these very great abilities develop almost universally. Since they are found in all people, we think little of them, great as these skills are. It is because of their universality that we do not think of them as great developments of latent ability. If we will consider the fact, however, we will see that these developments are actually almost awe-inspiring. If parallel abilities were developed in other more uncommon phases of our being, we would call the developer a genius.

The abilities that are usually thought of as evidences of genius are those whose development are not in the usual course of everyday life. If they were, we would not be surprised when we met them. Walking is far more difficult than skiing, yet we admire skill in skiing that we should never notice in walking. Talking requires far more muscular skill than playing a piano, yet we respect talking as a skill not at all. The great piano player is a genius. A normal conversation requires more mental dexterity than making a prepared speech, yet we admire the latter and generally deprecate the former.

We develop these common abilities of walking and talking because every person expects us to do so. Every child feels an intense desire to ask intelligently for what he wants and to be able to go and get it for himself. We therefore develop these very great latent abilities into usable abilities as a matter of course. Those abilities that are not expected from us do not develop unless a person puts into their development an unusual desire stronger than the influence of ordinary routine living.

INDUSTRIALIST CAN STIMULATE DESIRE TO DEVELOP

Herein is the greatest opportunity and challenge to the industrialist. Here is also the measure of his ability. The personnel of any organization has inherent in it the making of a company of unique and outstanding ability if only their environment will stimulate in its members a strong desire to develop their latent abilities.

Man has endless possibilities. The machine has very definite and known limits to its abilities. Most industrial managers, however, have paid more attention to the development of the machine than they ever gave to the development of man. The oncoming industrialist must change this. He must develop man first and the developed man will produce the unique machine. That is the fundamental difference between incentive management and the managements of the past.

HOW CAN INDUSTRIALIST DEVELOP PERSONNEL?

How can the industrial leader develop these latent abilities of his personnel? There are many answers to this question since there are many different persons involved. No two persons are alike in latent abilities nor in ambition to develop them.

The first step for the industrialist to take in his program of development is to recognize the fact of the limitless possibilities of man. He must recognize that if properly inspired and led so that the necessary effort is put forth, there is great genius in everyone. This genius will remain latent and useless if leadership does not give the inspiration and incentive to develop it. The ability that has been already developed is the only ability that is seen by the usual industrialist. That is the only ability that the usual leader expects. That is a very small fraction of what is there. To recognize that the ability that is not obvious is also there is the first step for the leader to take in the development of his personnel.

INTENSE DESIRE NECESSARY

The next step is to recognize that development comes only from intense desire to develop within the person himself. Development of abilities does not occur automatically. It usually is a response to an instigation from without, which arouses the person's desire to do and be and have more.

The man who can and will put on himself the pressure to develop the unusual latent ability is seldom seen. It is a fact that such development, except in a crisis, seldom occurs. A person can seldom put on himself the pressure, desire and crisis to the degree that will develop his greatest growth. Such pressure usually must come from the outside. If we only react to the desires that come normally from within ourselves, we will meet conditions as they are now. In such cases we either side-step the crisis, since we feel we cannot meet it, or we do whatever we can to prevent it. In either case, we do not have the necessary pressure within ourselves to develop our latent powers and change the conditions around us.

HOW TO APPLY INCENTIVE

The leader therefore, must produce the opportunity and apply the incentive to his people so that they call on themselves to the necessary limit to develop that particular quality or ability at that time of crisis.

It is easy to put down those obvious facts. It is not so easy to tell how to apply such incentive in any particular case. Obviously, there is no rule that will accurately answer the question in all cases. However, there are some suggestions that may be helpful to the leader in his job.

AN OPPORTUNITY TO DEVELOP IS NECESSARY

First: occasionally give the person whom you wish to develop a job that is over his head. Show him that you expect him to do it. Do that in such a way that he sees that you believe he can, so that he himself feels that he should be able to do it. This point of view on your part, and also his, must be honest and real, as must be all the actions of any successful leader. Perhaps you can also give him helpful suggestions that he will feel are his own. Light a fire under him by showing that he must progress if he is to take his place as a man among men. Make him see that others before have done the unusual and that everyone can and should.

Make him see that everything is possible. All our failures stem from our habitual approach to any unanswered problem. There is nothing impossible. There is nothing that will not be done eventually. Anyone can do anything if he only thinks so and drives himself to the limit that is necessary to do it. Invention is the doing of the new thing in the obvious way. After an invention has been made, we then see that it was the obvious way; there was nothing unusual in it. It was only our inhibited mind that kept us from seeing this self-evident answer from the very first.

Invention and development of latent abilities have much in common. After we develop any latent ability, we see how natural such development was. It was only because we did not believe in ourselves that such a step was delayed as long as it was. Development is natural and very satisfying.

If this pressure, incentive and crisis are real, any man will often rise to it. By so doing he will develop. He will be a more valued member of a greater team. In passing, you yourself as the leader in inspiring him in this development will develop in yourself new abilities that you did not know you had before. You also are on trial and facing a crisis if you recognize your responsibilities as the leader.

RESPONSIBILITY AND PRESSURE NECESSARY

Second: remember that the men you are leading must have the feeling of responsibility to the team of which they are members. That must be a reality, not an act. Each one must be responsible. He must feel the same responsibility that is felt by the goal kicker after a touchdown.

You, as the leader, must have the feeling of responsibility for your team's success. You are responsible. You are the captain. It is you who must develop the team spirit in your team.

Third: keep the pressure on. After the first step in development has been accomplished, have the next follow quickly. Do not let the man relax to the point that he feels he has arrived. No man ever does or ever can arrive. Keep the same philosophy in your own mind about yourself. There is no end to possible progress in any worthwhile endeavor. This is not slave driving; it gives instead a feeling of accomplishment, which is our greatest satisfaction.

DON'T WAIT FOR FUNERALS

Fourth: advance a man only on his ability and contribution to the success of the company. This is, of course, closely related to the previous incentive. This program of advancement is claimed by most managements as an adopted standard practice. It is not, actually, except in very rare instances. If every man felt that if he had what it takes he could actually go from a new employee to president in one jump, there would be an entirely different attitude than that now present in most industrial organizations.

In most organizations, funerals are necessary for the progress of any individual. Since the average span of life is increasing rapidly, funerals do not occur nearly as often as they should for the best progress of most companies. Also, they frequently do not take the proper people. If the man of ability would be put over the head of the older man who has slipped, funerals would be of far less important to most manufacturing plants. The upcoming man then could go ahead as he should and must.

It is a very difficult decision for the leader to make to advance the able over the head of the old, even when such action is obvious and needed. If the leader cannot bring himself to do it, he should look around for the man to take his own place, for his usefulness has passed. No man's progress should be stopped by failure to recognize his ability and to advance him to his proper place.

Incentive that will give every man recognition as soon as he has the ability, and to the extent of that ability, is an obvious necessity.

BE A LEADER, NOT A BOSS

Fifth: when any man makes the team, accept him as a teammate. You are not a boss, you are a leader. He will be better in some ways than you or anyone else if he develops as he should. You and he are two members of a team, each of whom plays a different position, dependent on developed ability. You are fellow players and each has specialized skills that make him most valuable in his position. There is no relative position one above another except as is shown by the actual contribution that each makes to the team's success. You are the captain. You are the leader. You are not dominant, except as you deserve to be from your contribution to the team's success.

This program is strong medicine to the usual executive. Present day industrial organizations are not built that way. It is, however, an obvious development. No one can see the endless checks that are put on an organization by routine executives without knowing that there is a far better way.

Perhaps we feel that such limited authority is not sufficient to do the job of being a responsible executive. It is true that the fear depended on to boss in the customary way is thrown aside. There is a far stronger hold that can be had, however. This is the hold the good captain of a football team has on his players. He has far better cooperation than any boss of the usual kind who depends on authority only. He also opens new avenues of progress hitherto unknown.

Gray puts it beautifully in his "Elegy"—

"Full many a gem of purest ray serene
The dark unfathomed caves of ocean bear
Full many a flower is born to blush unseen
And waste its sweetness on the desert air."

Making useful these gems and sweetness is the opportunity for incentive management.

Perhaps all this sounds like the vaporings of a theorist. That is not true. It is the pattern followed by a manufacturing organization that has made a uniquely successful record over many years in one of the most competitive fields in industry.

PICK MEN WITH ABILITY AND DRIVE

In selecting personnel it is, of course, best to pick those who have great ability. The person who has ambition with great nervous energy will go much further than a man of even greater latent ability but less drive. The reason for this is not far to seek. The development of the latent abilities of any individual depends on the pressure that he places on himself. Nervous energy is necessary in putting on such pressures as are needed in such development. The man of small ambition is the man who

61

will not and perhaps cannot put pressure on himself. He is prone to let well enough alone. He feels it is far easier to say, "It can't be done," than to go ahead and do it as his ambitious brother will.

CHALLENGE CUSTOM

Do not put men in grooves and expect that they will develop. The greatest difficulty in the usual industry is fitting all people in grooves and allowing them authority only in those grooves. Routine duties can be learned in a short space of time and can be done by the usual person with no application of either imagination or energy. No man can develop in that way. Development comes from opportunity, plus ambition. He may be a good routine clerk, but he will never develop genius in a groove. He may never make a mistake, but he will also seldom make progress.

It is well to remember that if we as leaders follow custom we will not develop the individual. Custom does not do the unusual. Custom follows precedent. That will never develop the latent abilities of anyone since it will never challenge him. The usual individual in the usual industrial environment has no challenge presented to him. Obviously, the result will be the usual.

SENIORITY NO MEASURE FOR ADVANCEMENT

It is obvious from the above that giving men new responsibilities is a very real part of the program of the leader who will develop the latent resources of his men. This means that there will always be the striving of those below in position to out-perform those who are above them. Seniority as a measure to determine who is to be advanced to positions of leadership is wrong. Ability does not necessarily increase with years. Experience shows that seniority is death to progress in industry. It is even more disastrous in management. There is more failure in industry because of this custom than from any other single source. Do not keep the static mind in any place of leadership. Replace it at once.

There is a great advantage in making frequent tryouts of the junior men in any organization to more responsible positions. When such a man succeeds, the whole organization will take on new life. The change will not only develop the men advanced, it will inspire all. It is the strongest and best medicine that any organization can have. Do not fail to use it.

AN ORGANIZATION IS COMPOSED OF INDIVIDUALS— NOT CHARTS

There is a general tendency for those dealing with organization to produce a chart that shows who has authority in all functions and under all conditions. This tendency is often so complete that it leads to the detailing of all duties to the last act and order. Such an organization will never be either efficient or progressive. In fact, such channeling will stifle progress probably as completely as the shop politics that it engenders. An industrial organization must operate as individuals to succeed. Men are not easily made parts of a machine. When they are forced into a groove they do not develop. They resent their consequent frustrations. These organization charts are a throw-back from the military who carry the organizational chart to its logical conclusion. Authority there is supreme, hence, progress is practically non-existent.

If progress is to be made by any organization, it must

be able to use all its resources from top to bottom. If the plan is one that forces all progress to be made by those in top authority, there will be little made. No top management can be nearly as able as the combined ability of all in the organization.

An organization chart concept comes from the belief that one person can know more about a subject than all others combined. If such men could be found, the chart plan would work. Since there are no such persons, the plan must fail in competition with a cooperative setup which uses the knowledge of all the people in it.

WORKERS NOW LACK DESIRE TO DEVELOP

The reason why the industrial revolution did not happen a thousand years ago was not because the latent abilities did not exist. It was solely because there was no incentive present then to bring out the existing latent abilities and develop them, since the reason for such development did not exist. Obviously, millions of Edisons, Ketterings and Fords went to their graves with their abilities still latent when they would have changed the economic world history had they been given the chance and the challenge. The important point to be remembered is that we are now allowing millions of latent geniuses to go to their graves with their abilities undeveloped and unknown because the incentive and desire are not sufficiently urgent in our present industrial system.

This is the worst criticism that can be made of our present economy. Whether it be the deadening effect of chart organizations as now constituted in many industries or the classification of labor as is done by the labor union, the result is frustration and the consequent lack of desire for development.

Let me illustrate the lack of desire in this way. Suppose an all-American halfback is on a job during the summer preceding his last year of football. Suppose he is in the maintenance department and the shop is unionized and he is paid $1.50 per hour, with time and a half for overtime and double time for Sunday. Suppose he is just 100 yards from a breakdown of some machinery in the plant for which he is responsible. The question is: what will be his time in covering the 100 yards to the breakdown carrying his repair tools, to get the breakdown back in operation, compared with his time in covering the same distance carrying a football at the kick-off in his next championship football game? It is well to remember in this connection that the repair of the breakdown is far more important to the economy than is the winning of any football game.

As a sidelight, we will suppose this halfback is that "rare bird," a star athlete and also an amateur getting nothing per hour for playing with no overtime pay for practice or training to condition himself. He does not feel that he is being "sweated" in his extreme effort in the game. He will resent totally any pressure put on him in his job, however.

He is very glad to do all these necessary things in a game without any thought of pay. All this in spite of the fact that in the game his chances of being hurt are at a maximum and there is no social security to take care of him if he has his teeth kicked out or his leg broken.

HARD WORK IS HEALTHY

There is frequently the comment made by the thoughtless that high production, such as is usual with incentive management, must mean that the workers involved will wear themselves out in a short time. Union leadership continually harps on "sweating" the worker by the "speed-up" that they claim results from incentive. What is the relative length of life of a worker and a loafer? If work shortens life, then loafing must lengthen it. The facts show the direct opposite. How long does a worker live after retirement? How good is his health if he stops work and loafs? Ask any man who has had experience.

There is much other experience on this matter. The hardest worker in the world is the mother when she is raising a family. No work done by man is so continuous and demanding. The facts show, however, that women live as an average ten per cent longer than men. Nervous breakdowns and suicide do not come to the producing, progressing worker; they come to the loafer. A healthy man is a man proud of his abilities. It is the dissatisfied man who is unhealthy. Athletes work to the very limit of their endurance. They live as an average longer than the non-athlete. They also are much more content than the loafer who has not the ambition to put forth the effort to go to college, much less the desire to go into athletics.

Hard work in which we can express our personalities and develop our latent abilities is the one thing that will make us contented, healthy and long-lived. Loafing or work that does not extend us and from which we cannot have pride is the source of danger to our health and lives. Here again incentive management proves its case, since it fortifies the very foundation of man's physical and spiritual being.

It is a revealing sidelight on industry incentive and hard and demanding work to remember that the recognized geniuses are not the sons of geniuses. They also

66

are not the sons of wealthy and successful men, yet it is obvious that such sons have the best opportunity of becoming geniuses since they have the example, the training and the expectation of genius in their family. The reason they are not geniuses is because they do not have the pressure that will develop their latent abilities which are the source from which genius is made. They do not have to work hard. They do not have to sweat.

If they had the same pressure that made their fathers geniuses, they would frequently be geniuses also. No successful father can ever put on his son the pressures and deprivations that made himself outstanding. It is perhaps well that this is so, otherwise a few families would dominate the world.

PRESSURES ARE THE SOURCE OF PROGRESS

The conclusion that can be drawn from this is that pressures, such as suggested above, are the greatest source of progress and satisfaction of man. Such incentives are the hope of the future. Do not fend them off Fold them to your bosom.

All world leaders came from the most unlikely parentage if we are to believe the blue blood theory. From Genghis Khan to Napoleon, from Confucius through Leonardo da Vinci to Edison and Kettering, blue blood did not produce genius in any field. Genius comes from most unlikely sources when heredity is considered.

ABILITY IS DESTROYED IF NOT DEVELOPED

Perhaps we can think of undeveloped latent abilities as money that a miser buries in the ground, as did the man with the one talent in the parable of the talents as told by Jesus. There is no doubt that the virtue of thrift

67

was present in this one talent man. The one talent man did not lose the money as he might have done had he used it for another purpose. The difficulty was that this talent did not become useful, therefore there was no gain by having the talent either to the man possessing it or to anyone else.

There is much to be learned from this parable which has to do with incentive management. If we do not develop, we ultimately destroy the ability that we possess.

It is well also to remember that after the five talent man had increased his store to ten talents, he could then increase these ten to twenty in exactly the same way that he increased the five to ten. That was the opportunity that the one talent man had. That was the reason he was punished by having the one talent taken from him. That is what man usually does with his latent abilities when he allows them to remain latent. The parallel to this we see constantly in life. The man who does not develop his talents will progressively decline in stature. The developer of talents will constantly grow into a greater man.

DEVELOPMENT OF ABILITY IS CRUCIAL TO INDUSTRY

Higher efficiency of operation in most plants often means under present managements that the worker becomes less and less an entity and more a part of a machine. He loses his identity progressively as the efficiency of the operation increases. His chance of being an entity, which is his fundamental aspiration, decreases often as production efficiency increases.

His only chance to be **recognized** is to make himself a nuisance. His progress toward efficiency often merely buries him deeper in a rut. That is one of the reasons why there is dissatisfaction in the usual industrial worker. That is the reaction with which we must deal if we are to make progress in developing the worker.

The problem then of the industrialist is to find how this incentive so present in athletics can be put into the operation of industry. When that is done, efficiencies many times those obtained now will be almost automatic. We will not be striving for a ten or twenty percent increase of efficiency. We will get from three hundred to two thousand percent, depending on how great was the lack of efficiency before.

The direction that progress will take depends completely on who develops what latent ability. It is here that the shape of the future is fixed. If an outstanding genius is developed by the fierce competition of circumstances, the direction he takes will determine the future of the world. Had Edison directed his genius to atomic power instead of the electric light, we would now probably be making weekend trips to Mars and Venus instead of to the movies or the seashore. If Kettering had directed his genius to controlling weather rather than perfecting the automobile, we should be reclaiming the deserts of the world to human use. If Ford had been born in Germany and his latent abilities had developed under its philosophy, Germany would now dominate the industrial world. It would be the greatest producer of machines rather than frustrated warriors.

DEVELOPMENT OF MEN CHANGES OUR LIVES

The one thing that we all can be sure of is this. Development of man and man's development of the resources of nature is unlimited. We take these developments for granted when we see them, little thinking that they are changing our lives by their impact and realizing still less that the direction in which we go, because of these impacts, is determined by who develops what latent abilities. We recognize still less that the same leader developed by a different crisis would have made the world a very different place.

If other latent abilities should develop in these same geniuses, the direction of their leadership would have carried us to ends not ever imagined now. If none of these geniuses develop, we are doomed to stagnate in the places in which we are. Thus is history made.

The one fact that we continuously overlook is this: if development does not take place, we will never recognize the lack. We do not crave progress, much as we object to its loss after we become accustomed to it.

Napoleon did not resent the fact that he could not call Paris on the phone from Moscow, much as he needed to do so. He did not know it could be done. The present world would be upset if we could not make such calls now. Napoleon did not resent the fact that he could only go fifty miles per day on his trip from Moscow to Paris in 1812 when speed meant everything to him. Anyone could make the trip in a few hours now. We would expect chaos if such speed were not now available.

In the same way, a generation or two from now the trip to Mars and calling the Martians on a phone may be as necessary and obvious to those who will be alive as are our calls and trips to the corner drugstore now. We do not miss our present lack of telephones and travel to Mars now any more than Napoleon did his far greater lacks. Our grandchildren will wonder as we do now regarding Napoleon, how we could get along without their modern conveniences. That wonder will be continuous in all succeeding generations. Each generation will not miss its own lack of conveniences, however.

The progress will in all cases be determined by those who will at the time be called geniuses or nuts, depending on how intelligent we are. The geniuses will be common people who have been exposed to, and developed from, the explosive driving force that can develop us. They will develop their latent abilities to an extent and in the direction that their desire and leadership produce in them.

INDIVIDUAL RESPONSIBILITY IS OUR STRENGTH

We see here the reason why socialism, communism, the welfare state or any kind of government that gives security to the individual must fail. It also shows why the economy that does not pose problems to the individual that he cannot easily solve will be taken over by the economy that does. Individual responsibility is essential to strength. The individual who throws his responsibility for himself on the state will become soft, static and unprogressive.

Socialism or any other form of welfare state must fail, since it cannot develop citizens who will make a successful economy. This is not obvious at first to those who want to believe that responsibility can be shifted to someone else or by the coward who does not want to deal with reality in life. He can always make a good case for his idea that the state should make him secure because he is a citizen.

It is obvious that such possible progress under incentive management would pose new problems to the economy. There is little doubt, however, that economic progress so far has resulted in a more attractive human race,

71

as well as a more attractive living. The new problems
posed by this progress will be solved by men who are
developed as incentive management will develop them.
Man will gain in stature as a consequence.

The growth that is latent in man as shown by the above
discussion poses a very grave problem to a people who are
drifting to the welfare state as is true now in America.

WELFARE STATE IS STATIC BECAUSE IT DEADENS INDIVIDUAL DEVELOPMENT

The idea of the welfare state and its over-all planning,
even with its necessary domination over the individual, is
very attractive to many Americans now. The idea that a
dominant state could and would do what the individual
is too lazy or incompetent to do himself, or do it better,
has many adherents. Socialism is very attractive to many
undeveloped people. This is not only true of those who
weakly wish-think, it is also true of many who can meet
the challenge of the world successfully if they will.

The fact that these wish-thinkers overlook is that development of the individual can only take place in the
fiercely competitive game of life. State control of the
individual has never succeeded in giving the necessary
incentive and reason for anyone to develop. There is no
way so far known that will fill this void under government domination over the individual.

STATIC UNDEVELOPING CONDITION FATAL IN WAR

The crisis resulting from war is a proof of this statement. History shows that the prepared nation always goes
down to defeat before the unprepared. This fact can be illustrated by all history from David and Goliath to Germany and its enemies in the two world wars. The reason

72

for this failure of the prepared is that preparation is a planned condition, which does not include the progress that can be made. It is static. Such preparation will of course be surpassed by the imagination of progressively developing people. Finished preparation is what a bureaucracy would produce. Progress is what developed latent ability will produce. Planned preparation will of course be surpassed, and quickly, by the crisis of war in the unprepared nation.

The unprepared nation starts from the point where the prepared nation stopped. It starts at the point where the prepared nation went into its coma, having finished its preparation and believing it was invincible. Starting from that point, the unprepared nation calls for help from the scientific and industrial leaders throughout the nation. They are not fitted into a pattern that has been set by a bureaucracy, hence they can develop new ideas, since no such bureaucracy exists. Progress therefore can be made. Progress is made. New war tools and methods are developed by the developed latent ability resulting from the crisis. That is the reason for the universal victory of the unprepared over the prepared when the unprepared are attacked.

This war making progress comes from many sources, but mostly from those who know nothing of war preparation. They therefore proceed without the deadening effects of previous habit to new ideas. They can go forward, and do. The prepared nation is static and advances little or not at all. People who are developing have not come to power in a war bureaucracy. Progress therefore is very limited or impossible.

As an illustration of these facts, when London was bombed at the start of the last war, it had little protection,

73

as none had been made. The Germans were told by Hitler that England would surrender in a few weeks because of this bombing and that Germany could not be bombed. Their preparation had worked all that out. They would have been right if there had been no progress in war making beyond what Germany knew when they finished their preparation. Necessity and lack of preparation made new ideas a must in England. Since no bureaucracy was organized at that time, England's crisis developed an air defense that was far ahead of anything yet known and that largely stopped Germany's bombing.

That was the first step in the development of the English in their ideas of war making. Then came the next progressive step. England and America, because of no organized bureaucracy which felt it knew all the answers, developed an advanced bombing program that defeated the Germans, who were sure they could defeat the world. They could have done so had the war ability of England and America remained static, as did Germany's. This was not such preparation as Germany had made, it was new development of war machines by men who developed their latent abilities under the fierce stress of war, unstopped by bureaucracy.

This illustration indicates the progress that has been made by man under war incentive. When he is so inspired, he develops.

ULTIMATE POSSIBILITIES FAR OFF

Here is the problem posed to all industrial leaders and a philosophy that can solve it. No one has done more than recognize the opportunity and make a few halting steps toward the goal of final accomplishment. No one yet knows the ultimate abilities of man. What little has been seen has amply proved the statement of the prophet that man is only a "little lower than the angels." We have a good way to go yet to have man achieve that goal. However, we must not stop trying.

Government planning has many adherents. There are many reasons that seem to recommend it highly to our present economy. The bureaucrat can make a very attractive argument for his plans of governmental domination of the individual. The duplications, inefficiencies and wastes that go with free enterprise cannot easily be laughed off. These difficulties could be eliminated, so the bureaucrat claims, by the supreme state. The only reason why governmental planning won't work is that progress comes only from developed man.

The greatest waste that can be imagined, far greater than any material waste, is the waste of man. Undeveloped man will always be a far greater loss to the economy than any material loss, no matter how serious that loss may be.

The waste involved in ancient transportation on camel back waited for the ability of the developed pioneer in railroads, trucks and hard roads to eliminate it. The waste involved in delivering information by a messenger only needed the genius of a Bell to eliminate it. Had these men not developed, these enormous wastes would have continued always.

Mistakes are the inspiration that makes man progress. Mistakes are the beacon light that shows us the proper direction in which to go.

Free enterprise has always succeeded in making progress. It has introduced the new and progressive. Little progress has been made otherwise. Progress probably can be made in no other way, since progress depends on men, and men develop only under the incentives that freedom of opportunity gives.

Chapter V

Driving Force of Incentive

There have been many attempts to put some kind of an incentive into industrial operation. None have succeeded to the point that is obviously possible. Few have even paid their way over long periods. Many have been worse than useless. Some have caused the company installing them to fail. No one, however, can doubt, in the light of other incentives that succeed that there is an incentive system that will function well in any industry.

There are countless cases of incentives that are continually successful in any number of activities outside of industry. Incentive never fails in raising children, a garden, or breaking a record in an athletic event. The problem industry has is to apply an incentive which has functioned successfully in other activities and make it succeed in industry. It is in industry that it can be of greatest benefit, since all depend so completely on the products of industry.

SUCCESSFUL INCENTIVE RARE IN INDUSTRY

Successful incentive has seldom been applied in industry. The best so far is a hesitant start compared to what

76

is possible. There have been some cases, however, in which some real progress has been made by the use of an incentive system. In these cases the results relative to the production in competing industry not under incentive have been almost unbelievably great. No one knows what would happen if a plan were devised that would develop a desire to excel and co-operate, such as we see in athletics.

Perhaps the benighted thinking of government bureaucracy and the ultra-conservative industrialist will hold incentive management in check for many years to come. That is not unusual. Flying was obvious from the time man first saw a bird. It took many thousands of years to make it a reality for man, however. The same lack of imagination can hold back incentive. A still more apt illustration of man's resistance to progress is that of the pronouncement by Jesus in His Sermon on the Mount. This philosophy would have eliminated our present and past world chaos, had we had the vision to follow it. It is no assurance, therefore, that truth will be followed in any particular activity just because there is truth announced. Truth must be believed and acted upon to make it useful to man.

Incentive management is a plan that will cause all those in an industrial organization to work together with enthusiasm to produce at progressively lower cost. In this way the consumer, which is all of us, would benefit progressively.

If we are to have such cooperation, there must be two reactions from those involved. First, enthusiastic desire on the part of all in the organization to do their best. Second, development of the latent abilities of all people in the organization resulting from this desire. Because of both of these factors, the efficiency of all in the group will increase tremendously. The result of this greater skill directed by the greater desire is enormous decrease in costs of production.

INCENTIVE MANAGEMENT VITAL TO MECHANIZED INDUSTRY

Incentive management is becoming of progressively greater importance as our mechanization of productive operations advances. When a man dug a trench with a spade, any boss could tell if he was working and how hard. No boss can tell accurately now whether a man operating a ditch digging machine is doing his best, trying to limit output, or is actually wrecking the machine.

As mechanization of industry progresses, the desire of the worker to make the machines work and their skill in using and caring for these machines is of progressively greater importance. Lack of skill and proper desire to use such skill is many times more harmful to efficiency now than before present mechanization of manufacturing operations.

AMATEUR ATHLETICS PROVIDE PERFECT INCENTIVE

There is no better illustration of a perfect incentive than the desire to win in any amateur athletic team. This illustration is obvious to all, since all have had experience in athletics in some form. In such a team, the members first of all will strive to the limit to win the game. There is no doubt of that in anyone's mind who has seen amateur games. That is not all. There is also the rapid development of latent abilities of the players under this stress of competition in playing the game.

It is safe to say that no closely contested game was

ever won except by the team on which one or more of the members did something beyond what he was ever capable of doing before he started that particular game. He developed his latent abilities under the incentive of the game to new, and to him, unknown heights.

No doubt there may be more than one player who has that experience in each game. Most players develop something in each game. The team which develops most, usually wins. We have all seen a team in some game arise to heights of which it was never capable before. That is when many of the players develop under the incentive of the game. They played far beyond what they could have done before. They grew up almost in an instant. That is how latent abilities usually develop. We have also seen a team play a very disappointing game. That is when development does not take place.

No man ever made a great football team who did not have the experience of developing, almost by a miracle, some latent abilities. If he did not, he never made a great team.

INCENTIVE IN ATHLETICS CAN GUIDE INDUSTRIALIST

The football illustration is good because it is so common, and the incentive is so obvious. The problem of the industrialist is to use the possible incentives that are present in the football game to give the same development to those he leads in industry. There has been little accomplished in this regard so far in industry.

It is obviously true that winning a football game is of small importance to the world compared to more efficient production of the necessities of life. In spite of this obvious fact, we have great incentive in amateur athletics and little or none in industry.

In approaching the problem of incentive in industry, it is well to keep in mind the illustration of the football game as a guide. Here there is ample experience for the guidance of the inquiring industrialist in his search for an incentive plan in industry. From this illustration these points are plain:

DESIRE FOR COOPERATION

The first step in developing an incentive is to get the *desire* for cooperation of those involved. This is very easy in the athletic game, but most difficult usually in industry. A football game is not nearly as involved as is industry with its men, machinery, customers, governmental interference and taxation. This complication of industry may make the problem more complex to the industrialist so that he may miss the fact that successful incentive in industry and in a football game both come from the same source and should be obtained in exactly the same way.

ABILITY DEVELOPED IN CRISIS

The second indication for incentive in industry coming from athletics is the development of the individual's latent abilities by the stress and desire inherent in the game. A single new idea has made many industrial organizations outstanding. In fact, most of them depend on some single idea as the foundation of their success. The greatness of the Ford Motor Company resulted from the development of the idea of the assembly line method of production. The airplane was made possible by the idea of warping the edge of the wing.

A specialized skill that is outstanding will often make a company, as well as a football team, dominant. When it is remembered that there are in many men in any organization latent abilities that if developed would make the company outstanding in its field, the opportunity is obvious. The need here is belief and leadership to make the belief a reality.

Each member of an organization should feel under incentive management the continuing desire not only to cooperate with all others, but also the desire to make himself of greater use to the activity. He must want fiercely to rise to new heights in his ability and usefulness. That desire is what the leader must inspire in all in the organization.

The question is: how can this be done in industry? There are numerous ways to accomplish this. Which one should be used in any case is for the executive to decide. In detail, however, they all follow the same fundamental philosophy. The following plan has succeeded in some cases. It will in others. These are not rules to blindly follow, however.

RECOGNITION MUST BE SCALED TO CONTRIBUTION

The worker must feel that he is recognized in accordance with his contribution to success. If he does not have that feeling of self-respect and the respect of others because of his skill, he will think he is being "played for a sucker" if he increases his output so the owners can have more profit.

It is not necessary that this reward be solely in money. As a matter of fact, the amateur athlete gets no money, yet he tries harder than the professional who is paid. This athlete, however, does get the respect and position resulting from his achievement. That is his reward. He wants no other.

When the rewarding is done *to the satisfaction of each*

81

of the workers, then the first step is taken in successfully applying incentive management.

This program of rewarding the worker in accordance with his contribution is perhaps an obvious statement. There is no doubt that most industrialists feel they do that now by job evaluation or piecework or some other way. The fact is that the worker does not feel so. After all, whether management feels that what it is doing is right is of no importance in promoting incentive if the worker does not feel so. The worker must *want* to do his best. Only so can any incentive succeed.

DESIRE TO DO BEST FOLLOWS JUST RECOGNITION

At the present time there are very few companies who reward unusual effort automatically. The worker may over a long period of time be recognized, perhaps by more money or a better position, if someone does not forget. He knows, however, that great effort and reward are not automatic in their relationship nor even closely connected. In fact, if he speeds up his job on piecework, he is very apt to get his price cut in many instances. If he is to do his best, he must feel that he wants to make added effort because it will surely result in the kind of reward he wants.

It is evident, therefore, that the first problem the industrialist has is to make the job one in which the worker will be proud of his skill and desire to increase such skill. Past history has made this difficult. The union leader has a very much easier time getting the man to be proud of his ability to restrict his output than the industrialist has in making the same worker proud of his ability to produce at higher speed. Skillful work by the wage earner has a bad name. That outlook must be changed.

Manual labor in athletics, requiring outstanding skill and endurance can be made, without money reward, the source of great pride and incentive. By using the same basic inspirations, it also can be made the source of great pride in industrial production because of industry's greater importance. That is the industrialist's job in incentive management.

There is one aid in making the application of incentive easier and that is the selection of the proper personnel for the organization. This problem is obvious in athletics. It must be part of the program in industry.

It is not meant that all people cannot be organized into a group that will enthusiastically go along with incentive management. Eventually all people will. In the beginning in applying incentive it is easier to work with those who can and will understand the new philosophy. The others will then follow the established lead.

The psychologists tell us that no man develops as much as fifty percent of the latent abilities with which he was born. That statement is proved by long experience. If we compare any great man before and after he achieves greatness, that statement is completely illustrated. If we look back on our own lives, the fact is obvious. We are what we develop ourselves into, not merely what we were born. All travel this road of development to some extent. The result that we call "man" is determined by how far and in what direction he travels in his development.

THE LEADER MUST LEAD

In this development under incentive management, the effect of leadership is very great as is true in inducing people to go in any new direction in any activity. Obviously, if the industrialist is going to get his organization to go far along the road of development, he will have to travel it himself. He cannot camp out at the start and expect the rest to go where he does not go himself. Here is a test of leadership. Here is the place where many incentive attempts falter. Here is the place where much sober thinking must be done by management before a proper start can be made. Make sure you want to play and hold your place on this new team that is going to show new speed under the new incentive system. Don't expect that you can successfully boss from the sidelines. In fact, you will not boss at all; you must lead.

No man ever developed any latent abilities without an overwhelming desire to do so. It is obvious, therefore, that the first thing for the leader to do is to give to the workers some reason that excites this great desire. Give him a job that will need new abilities. Give this job such an inspiration that when it is accomplished there will accrue to the man who did it the pride and self-respect due him. Make sure this credit makes him outstanding in the eyes of those whom he respects most. That is the greatest of all incentives.

In doing this, make all in the organization conscious of the importance of their work. Make sure those outside who should be interested know of their accomplishment if it merits notice. Make sure also that the facts are real, not the kind of "bunk" frequently spread on the pages of the daily papers regarding these matters. The skill of many people is unique. If we are to give a real incentive, that unique skill must be made understandable to the outside and made the means of making the man unique because of his attainment in the minds of those he respects and likes.

Make the advancement of each in the organization dependent on his development of his latent abilities. **Make the best man the winner. Make him the boss as soon as he is a better man than the present boss.**

Always keep in front of the organization plans that should be matured in one, five, ten and twenty-five years in the future. Progress is fundamental and the thinking of the group under incentive management must be progressive. These plans will perhaps continuously change. That is no handicap. If they do not change, the plans are not properly developing. Interest in the plans will be continuous if the attitude is a proper one.

USE THE DRIVING FORCE OF COMPETITION

Man is always in competition with his contemporaries. He is always trying to excel them in the things he does. He respects himself in proportion to how well he succeeds in outdistancing them. His response to this incentive is often not recognized by man himself, however.

One of the most striking examples of this competition is mob psychology. Man in a mob, because of mob competition, will often pass temporarily out of character. He is temporarily a different man. He is striving to outdo all others in the job at hand. He is so anxious to outdo the others that he thinks little of his normal reactions.

The mob that lynches a negro will carry away with it the normal objectors who would be usually shocked by the very thought of such cruelty. He will not lose face at the time, however, with the rest of the mob since he, from man's natural urge, wishes to outdo them. That is mob psychology. He will therefore devise new and more terrible means of torture to show that he can excel here as well as in other ways. This will not be because of inherent cruelty. He may be a very thoughtful and kind man. It is the natural desire to outdo others that drives him to such extremes in such a crisis.

The same mob psychology causes him to pass out of character at a revival. He will again strive to outdo others in religious fervor. This will not in either case have anything to do with cruelty or religion. It is plain competition. The industrialist must use that driving force of competition. It is a natural and very satisfying reaction to the man involved.

All people want to be part of a group. All want to belong, yet when they are in a group they want to be designated as outstanding in some way. There is always the central desire to outdo in some way those with whom we associate.

This desire often takes weird forms. If we cannot outdo anyone in some normal way, we will often change to another group that will give us a chance to be outstanding. If that fails, then we go to a rather strange device. We set up our group on some new standard of excellence with the idea that we as a group outdo other groups on this newly devised basis. We perhaps know that we cannot meet them in other open competition since they would outdo us. We therefore perhaps set up the idea that our ancestry is better than theirs. That often answers our problem. We have the feeling of superiority without the necessity of competition at which we know we would fail. The allegory, "The Late George Apley," shows the psychology of this type, of which there are many examples, all of which illustrate the insistent craving to be outstanding, no matter how thin the claim of superiority may be.

We see the same attempt to show superiority daily in dense traffic. The young blades, often in their fathers' cars, will drive recklessly and rudely, merely to get ahead of others. They will do this often by breaking traffic laws, merely to force others to notice them. Such a show exhibits neither real skill or actual indication of dominance. They draw attention to themselves, however, by their selfishness. This is sufficient for them, since there is no ability that they possess that will attract any attention otherwise. They feel that they must be outstanding in some way, no matter how poor the exhibition is.

It is of course rather silly to think we can compete with our fellows in this way. It illustrates, however, the fundamental urge in every one of us for some feeling of superiority which will cause us to feel outstanding. We cannot live with ourselves otherwise.

COMPETITION AND PRIDE ARE FUNDAMENTAL URGES

There has been much said about slave driving and sweating in industry when attempts are made toward greater efficiency of production. Union leadership dwells upon this theme. It makes it one of the reasons for output limitation now so usual in manufacturing. Incentive is a complete answer to this objection. Any man would kick any union leader in the teeth if the leader tried to keep him out of such a game as incentive management develops. He would under incentive management work harder than he ever worked on a production job in his life, yet he would not be fatigued at the end of the day since he is developing and showing abilities that make him proud of himself. He knows also that others envy him his ability, which is the source of great satisfaction.

The next step is to make the worker proud of his company. This should be easy. Man likes to feel his importance even if he has to give the major part of the credit to someone else, as he does when he boasts of the importance of his company over which he, normally, has little control and relatively small effect. Pride in one's company is a great driving force if the man feels that his company is one in which he can rightfully have pride.

These fundamental urges are the ones used in applying incentive management. How they are applied is a matter of judgment. There are many ways in which they can be applied. Here great variation is possible. There can be no success, however, unless these basic desires of man are understood and properly applied in some way in any successful incentive plan.

Chapter VI

Incentive

This book deals with incentive management. Incentive management depends on incentives. Incentives come from our inherent selfishness. Selfishness has many aspects.

Selfishness is the driving force that makes the human race what it is, for good or evil. Hence, it is the force that we must depend on and properly guide if the human race is to develop and progress. Selfishness has a bad name. Perhaps the bad name that crassly stupid selfishness deserves, distorts our understanding of what intelligent selfishness is and can be.

There is little doubt that stupidity in its many ramifications has done more to wreck the world than any other excess of man. That includes stupidly selfish aims in industry. There is no doubt, however, that intelligent selfishness has been the driving and guiding force that has produced every advance that man has made. It also must remain the driving force on which we must depend if the world is to continue to progress in any desired direction.

INTELLIGENT SELFISHNESS, THE DRIVING
FORCE OF INCENTIVE

Intelligent selfishness is the incentive that causes the mother to sacrifice herself for the good of her child. Intelligent selfishness is the incentive that makes us loyal citizens who willingly sacrifice our lives in war that our country may survive. It is our intelligent selfishness that is the driving force that results in every advance that man has made in science, in government, in education or in any other field. Selfishness and ambition are interdependent. They must be guided by our intelligence, however, to be eventually satisfying.

The obvious difference between intelligent selfishness and the usual deplored, stupid selfishness is its results. We know from long experience that many acts that we may desire to do because of immediate pleasure will have as their final outcome disappointment and sorrow. Drinking and license are illustrations. Such acts are prompted by stupid selfishness.

All acts of human beings are prompted by selfish motives. Those that are eventually satisfactory are intelligent. Those that are only self-seeking and destructive generally in their eventual outcome are stupid. Both, however, are selfish. Gluttony is a satisfactory action when first indulged. It is not satisfactory to even the glutton over his life. Laziness is satisfying at the time. It is far from satisfactory over a lifetime. Those are illustrations of motives that are stupidly selfish compared to self-control that is intelligently selfish.

"Love thy neighbor as thyself" in the final analysis means love thyself. "Do unto others as you would that they should do to you" in the final analysis means that what you do to others you in effect do to yourself. If you kill

90

all people on the earth, you will by that act also kill yourself, since life alone on the earth is impossible.

When we help others, we by that act help ourselves. No member of any group, be that group an athletic team, a manufacturing plant or any other activity that we are connected with, can progress for himself except by progressing for all others involved. When we cooperate, therefore, we are obviously doing the selfish thing, for we eventually benefit from proper cooperation.

In the final analysis, all people on earth are on **one** team. What helps others will also help **us.** If we could make all men good, honest, happy, healthy, intelligent and prosperous, there would be no difficulties to face in being all these things ourselves.

To the extent that we make others poor, vicious, dishonest, sick, we increase our chances of being the same ourselves.

It is intelligent selfishness that is the driving force in the incentives that are outlined herein. It is intelligent selfishness that is developed by the industrial philosophies suggested. Intelligent selfishness therefore, is in the final analysis attractive; not a fearsome thing, as is often supposed.

INTELLIGENT-VS-STUPID SELFISHNESS

It is intelligent selfishness that causes a man to struggle toward perfection so that he becomes more prosperous. It is stupid selfishness that prompts him to steal. It is intelligent selfishness that incites a man to become outstanding in his development of his latent abilities. It is stupid selfishness that prompts man to try to gain such position by tearing down those who have already gained such position by their abilities. It is intelligent selfishness that makes a man struggle by research to develop new progress in medicine. It is stupid selfishness that prompts a man to advertise quack medical cures that cannot be accomplished. In industry, it is intelligent selfishness that incites an organization to give more and more of a better and better product for a lesser and lesser price with profit as a by-product. It is stupid selfishness that prompts an industrial company to charge all the traffic will bear.

Custom has surrounded the word "selfishness" with wrong connotations. Unless its real meaning is made clear, the reader may reject fundamental philosophies because of a pre-formed conclusion which is not based on the facts involved..

This discussion of selfishness is needed since that is the driving force which the industrialist must work with in his program of incentive management.

MAN IS NOT A MACHINE

Many an industrialist has not let the inherent aspirations of man work with him to benefit him and everyone else. He has considered the worker largely as a part of a machine.

This attitude comes from very ancient times. It is a survival of the slave psychology which always hurt the master as much or even more than the slave. It is the false belief that God creates *classes* of men, some classes inferior, some superior. In this thinking, the worker is not an individual but a member of the lower class. It will make little difference in the final analysis whether such an employer patronizes workers as a class or despises them as a class, the result will be wrong. The worker is a man like his boss. In fact, in a few years or a few generations, the positions of the two will often be reversed.

92

Most of the trouble that has vexed industrial leadership stems from this lack of appreciation of what man actually is. The industrialist has not only passed up the enormous resources of the worker, but also he has courted the worker's hatred because of his lack of understanding of the fact that the worker is a man like himself, not a machine or part of a machine.

The industrialist by his lack of vision lost out on two counts, both of which have made the future tremendously more difficult. He lost because the opposition engendered in the worker by his lack of understanding has been so powerful that he cannot now get the worker's cooperation. He lost also by not developing the wondrous ability inherent in his workers which his lack of vision failed to recognize and hence to develop and use.

The progress of mankind depends on human beings. Human beings act on their incentives and aspirations which have developed in the directions and to the extent that have made the world and the human race what they are today. If we are to understand how to introduce incentive in industry, the first principle is to deal with reality in dealing with people and understand why they are as they are, and how they got that way. We must understand what incentives spur people to develop, to cooperate and to work at greatest usefulness. If this is not understood clearly, there can be little chance for a successful plan of incentive in industry.

TRADITION HOLDS HIRED MANUAL WORK DEGRADING

The second principle that must be understood in the application of incentives in industry is that because of past history we have accepted beliefs regarding work and the worker that are entirely wrong if we are to apply incentives successfully. For instance, certain kinds of work are held to be degrading in the minds of most people, if done for hire. They are highly respected if they are done without pay. Doing housework, which perhaps is one of the most important activities that we have, is thought of as degrading if it is done for wages. It is, however, respected if we do the work ourselves in our own homes. Driving a high-priced car is a boost to anyone's ego if the car belongs to him. It is an act of the lowest form if the car belongs to someone else and we drive it for hire as a chauffeur. This stigma of being a chauffeur is gone, however, if we drive the same car as a favor to a friend. The care of a child by its mother is thought by all to be one of the most respected occupations. It is considered almost the lowest form of service if done for hire.

The reason for these diametrically opposed views is the result of ancient history. Our reactions still remain, even when the reasons for them have disappeared. We think work in the home or as personal service, if done for hire, is degrading because it was formerly done by slaves only. Now that it is done by free people for hire, we still hold it in disrepute because of this ancient history. However, when we do it for ourselves, we do not connect it with the former slavery and the stigma disappears.

In our minds, this reaction regarding manual labor's connection with the work of slaves and serfs is the source of much of the misunderstanding between labor and management. While many are not conscious of the fact, manual labor is still held in low repute in our thinking. In spite of its skills and importance, in spite of the fact that its value is often far greater than that of the white collar job, it is still thought of as degrading compared to less important work that is not associated in our minds with the

94

previous slavery.

Understanding these psychological reactions resulting from previous custom is of utmost importance in understanding incentive management, since they explain the aspirations and hatreds of human beings. We must understand these reactions if we are to succeed in introducing any successful incentive to workers in industry.

ATTITUDE TOWARDS WORK MUST CHANGE

There must be a tremendous change in man's attitude toward his work. Most wage earners think of work now as a degrading thing because of ancient custom and recent reactionary legislation. In very few cases does the worker think of work as he will in incentive management atmosphere, as a means of attaining his fondest hopes and aspirations. It is the industrialist's job to get the wage earner to see just that.

In order to do this, the industrialist must get his own thinking straight. He must stop thinking of wage earners as "masses." He must stop treating them on one hand as if they were animals or children whom he must be kind to and take care of, and on the other hand as if they were sullen and rebellious, inferior classes. He must see each one of them as a person like himself; a human being with all human needs and hopes and trouble. He must realize that human beings must cooperate in order to live on this planet and that cooperation is not a one-way street. If he does not fully and sincerely cooperate with every man on his team, he cannot honestly expect, and certainly will not get, any more cooperation than he gives.

NEED UNDERSTANDING OF SIGNIFICANCE OF INDUSTRIAL SYSTEM

The third difficulty that we are dealing with is the lack

of understanding by many people, particularly the worker, of the present industrial system. The worker does not usually think of the industrial system as the most effective means for his own progress that has been developed in our economic struggle upward from slavery and barbarism. He does not think of it as the tool that has made us the darlings of history.

He does not recognize the fact that our industrial development is the only reason why the white race is dominant compared to all other races and why the United States is in its present unique position of leadership. No, the worker in industry usually thinks of industry as the way that certain industrialists have made a lot of money. He is not alone in this. He, being human, does not like to see this because he does not like to see anyone rise above his small abilities. He will cooperate with those who wish to destroy those leaders so as to drag them to his level. Herein is the primary reason for the popularity of the New Deal and the Wagner Act.

ALL MEN HAVE GREAT POTENTIAL

The fourth fact on which incentive must be based is the tremendous possibilities of the individual. He is a hopeless clod in much thinking now, not because he was made so by the Creator, but because custom encourages him to be no more than that. Bad leadership, bad morals and crass stupidity have made man a shadow only of what he can be, what God intended him to be, and what he eventually will be.

The program of incentive based on the inherent potential greatness of man, outlined herein, will be clear to the man of vision. It will be nonsense to the creature of habit. It will be workable to those who will understand.

It will be funny to the so-called old time "practical man."

The possible progress is too great to believe by those who cannot dream. If we are not ready to see that men through cooperation can make the future as much better than the present as the present is better than savage wretchedness and cannibalism, it would be well to throw this book aside. There is nothing but foolishness in it for those who cannot see reason.

The plans and suggestions that are given here are based on the premise that the latent abilities of man, when properly developed and directed to the proper end in industry, will make possible a state as unimaginable now as the ordinary way of living today was unimaginable only eighty years ago.

It would be well also to remember that we are just starting on the road of progress. We have not arrived. The future will make the present development of incentive management seem as crude to the generations who will follow us as the state of development of the Pilgrim Fathers' industries seems to us now. The Indians then thought that all progress had already been made. There are many descendants of those Indian minds that are now in our midst and probably always will be.

The great progress of the future is not going to be primarily in machines. It will be in men. It will not be clever gadgets. It will be developed men. The possibilities of machines are limited. The possibilities of man are unlimited.

MANY INCENTIVES HAVE BEEN TRIED

There has been much written and said about various incentives in industry. There is the feeling in many places that piecework, profit sharing and various forms of paternalism will buy greater efficiency in industrial production. The outright payment of more money for more production has been tried by management in many forms. The results have been variable. The plans have succeeded and have failed in what are seemingly the same conditions. In some cases the use of these incentive plans has been disastrous. Sometimes a company trying the scheme has been forced out of business as a result of the plan and the reaction of the men to it. In other cases, greater efficiency and more contentment have been the result.

It is obvious, therefore, that money incentive for more production is not of itself necessarily the means that will get increased production. There is more to the story than paying more money for more goods produced. Money alone does not give to the American worker the incentive that he wants and eventually must get if industrial progress is to continue and the American way of life is to survive and continue constantly to grow better. Let us look further.

Perhaps the best guide to the proper answer is to find just what incentive it is that spurs us to do our best in other activities. What is the incentive that brings out our best efforts in activities other than industry? If we can find the incentive that urges us to do our utmost in other activities, perhaps it will indicate to us the incentive that would bring out man's best efforts in industry.

AMATEUR ATHLETICS PROVIDE REAL INCENTIVE

In all human experience, there is no better example of an incentive which develops a man's individual abilities and cooperation with others than the incentive in amateur athletics. No one strives harder to increase his skill and output than the amateur athlete in playing and training for a championship game. No one tries harder both at the time and in his training for preparation than a track athlete in a championship race. No man strives harder in training and in the game than does the amateur football player. Here is a guide that may answer our search as to what makes a successful incentive. Let us follow this indication to its logical conclusion.

NOT MONEY

No one pays an amateur athlete. Hence, his incentive is not money. He cannot and does not want even one cent from his efforts. He does not, in fact, ever think of money as his reward. If he were paid, his efforts would probably deteriorate. Money is the furthest thing from the player's mind when he plays a game. Hence, we can conclude that money is not necessarily an incentive. We must look further.

NOT SHORT HOURS

Short hours are not an incentive either. The athlete will strive continually to win. In fact, if he is taken out of the game so that his hours of work are shortened, he is very unhappy. If, instead of being taken out of the game he is not put into it at all, he is desolate. He wants hard work and long hours in athletics. Not only that, he will strive mightily over long weeks prior to the games to perfect himself in his playing. All of this hard work he could side-step if he wished. He does just the opposite. He wants long hours and hard work at no pay, and he will go to any extent to get just that. He obviously could spend his time at an outside relatively soft job, at money wages, with much less effort, if he chose to do so. Hence, we can conclude that short hours and a soft job are not a primary human incentive.

INCENTIVE MANAGEMENT

NOT SAFETY

Safety is not an incentive. The football player is often injured so that he never recovers the full use of his limbs for the rest of his life. Some players are killed in games or in practice. All could be free from any danger of injury if they so chose. None do. They strive mightily to expose themselves to such injury. If they do not get this chance to get injured, they are badly disappointed. Safe working conditions therefore are not an incentive.

NOT SENIORITY

Seniority is not an incentive. No one in athletics wants the oldest people to play on the team just because they have been on the squad a long time. The man who starts the game is usually taken out. In fact, the longer he plays in a game, the more apt he is to be taken out and a fresh substitute put in his place. He wants it that way and so do all the rest of the players and spectators. Seniority is not an incentive.

NOT SECURITY

Security is not an incentive in athletics. No one wants security in a game, neither the players themselves nor the spectators. If a better man comes along, the previous star is out. He wants it that way since he wants to be the one who may oust the star. The only end in view is to be the best so as to keep his job. If security were introduced into athletic teams, there would be no athletics, no players, no spectators and no interest. Job security is no incentive in itself.

NOT BARGAINING POWER

Collective bargaining through a union is not a desire of

the players in athletics and never could be. The Wagner Act is not an incentive in athletics nor any privilege legal under the Act. In fact, union activity has no place in amateur athletics in spite of the sweating of the athletes by the coach and the entire lack of grievance procedure present. In fact, the union as a means of gaining the laboring athletes' goals and protecting them from exploitation by the boss is unthinkable. No player ever thought of such a thing.

We have seen from the foregoing that the goals striven for by labor union leaders are not incentives when we actually deal with matters which call forth a man's maximum efforts. That gives us merely a negative answer to the program now followed by labor union leadership. There is no incentive in what unions do. It should, however, indicate the proper approach to a positive answer to the problem itself.

RECOGNITION IS *REAL* INCENTIVE

What, then, is the incentive that causes people to strive so mightily for success in an amateur athletic game? The answer is *recognition of our abilities by our contemporaries and ourselves.* The gaining by our skills of the feeling that we are a man among men. The feeling that we have desirable abilities that others covet. The feeling that we are different in some way or ways that others admire and wish to emulate. The feeling that we are outstanding and are so recognized by our fellows. That is the greatest incentive that is universal. That is the incentive that almost completely determines our efforts in life.

We sacrifice all other things to this deep satisfaction which comes from proving our competence to ourselves and from knowing that others recognize it. It is the incentive that has made the human race what it is; hence, it is the primary drive on which all successful effort to increase man's efficiency in any human effort must be based. Any plan that does not start from this fundamental urge is bound to fall short of best accomplishing the end desired. Let us analyze the matter on this basis.

Achievement means that we are evaluated more highly by ourselves and by our contemporaries because of our skills and abilities than we would be if we lacked these abilities. Our proved skill increases our self-respect and wins the respect of others. That makes any effort to improve a skill attractive to its possessor. It is our sense of achievement and its recognition by others that we desire most. Money is of relatively small importance. Money is an economic necessity. Beyond enough for our real needs, money itself is valued less for what it will buy than as an evidence of successful skill in achievement.

The story of Robinson Crusoe is a case in point. He took the "pieces of eight" from the wrecked ship and stored them away, only after at first concluding he would not. Money meant nothing to him on the lonely island. Money could not be used for any purpose that would make Robinson Crusoe a more eminent man in his own estimation, and, of course, in that of everyone else. However, had he been in another environment where money meant position and power, he would have been very anxious to get it and use it for that purpose.

Recognition by ourselves and others means everything to all of us. This fundamental urge shows itself in the infant as well as in the man. The baby struggles to get the attention of his mother away from his smaller brother and is desolate if he does not. The youth struggles for recognition in all his efforts. The man gauges his success by the opinion of those who know his ability and his work. That is what we strive for and we hold all else secondary.

Perhaps we do not accept this fact at first thought. If, however, we will objectively think the matter through, we can come to no other conclusion. The threat of a blackmailer, which has in many cases taken all the money from the victim, obviously is based on this one fact. The person who is blackmailed usually has nothing to lose except his standing in the estimation of his contemporaries. Often he would lose only friends and their good opinion, yet he will give the blackmailer money in large amounts to protect himself from this penalty.

The fourflusher and his boasting is another example. He will risk anything frequently to get a good opinion of a fleeting audience. He also knows usually that he is risking much to get such recognition, yet he does it enthusiastically. He also will spend money beyond his income in order to impress people, if only for the moment. Here again money is willingly and enthusiastically thrown away for a feeling of importance.

BASIS FOR SUCCESSFUL INCENTIVE MANAGEMENT

Perhaps I seem to over-stress the point when I cite so many illustrations, but it is fundamental to our theme. Incentive that succeeds in industry or any other activity is based on this primary urge of all mankind. Incentive cannot succeed largely unless this principle is followed. There has been no continued success of incentive in industry, athletics or life unless these controlling facts are firmly fixed in the program. Here is the first and most important fact in incentive management. It must have complete recognition and full understanding.

Recognition of our abilities by ourselves and our contemporaries is the chief incentive. Too often the industrialist thinks that if he puts his workers on some plan that gives them more money for more work, or if he gives his men a part of whatever profit is made, he has an incentive system. When it does not work, he can't understand why it does not. He is even shocked when the plan causes resentment among his men when he was so sure he was doing them a good turn. He will not consider that his men are exactly like himself in their aspirations. He thinks the worker is a man apart. He does not apply the plan to himself as a trial. If he did, he would understand. In the mind of the worker, mere production efficiency means only more profit to the boss who, he thinks, already has too much.

DESIRE IS PROMPTED BY RECOGNITION

The industrialist does not see that he must get the *desire* to accomplish into all those who must cooperate if high efficiency is to be obtained. This desire must be prompted by the fact that the job is the one way in which the man can raise himself in his standing relative to his fellows. That cannot be done unless the man feels that he can be important because of his skill in his job.

It is interesting to note, however, that much effort is given to doing just that in the higher brackets of management. Position and publicity are given to the outstanding performer. The results show the effectiveness of this. The principle so amply proved in top management and athletics is usually cast aside when the factory worker is considered.

Here is the answer to the problems that exist between labor and management. Anyone who follows these obvious tenets cannot fail. No one can succeed if he does not at least partially follow them.

PIECEWORK ALONE IS NOT INCENTIVE

Let us consider how we can apply this fundamental principle in an industry. The first thing to do is to encourage a man's pride in skill in his job. That can most easily be done by seeing that he earns in accordance with that skill. Piecework is a plan which can do that if it is applied accurately in the case of all workers and continues to be so applied. Then each can always earn more as his skill increases. He will always earn more than the less skillful man. His skill is then recognized by all and his pride in it is justified in his own mind and in the minds of his contemporaries.

The difficulty is that no ideal application of piecework has ever been made and perhaps never can be made. Piecework cannot be applied that accurately. No one can set prices that will differentiate according to skill, imagination and effort, between workers who are doing various jobs at the same time. No plan yet devised has made the worker feel that he is considered outstanding relatively and accurately by applying piecework. It cannot be done that well. Hence, the recognition by earnings does not so distinguish the worker. He does not become outstanding by it.

The fact that no attempt usually is made to distinguish workers shows how little we recognize this possibility of fundamental incentive in our planning. The difference between the first string and second string back's ability in a football team may be small, but it is decisive in the incentive that it carries.

If all involved in industry could judge the ability of the worker as successfully as the crowd at a baseball game does the ability of the player, the answer would be easy.

The workers do not accept the opinions of their abilities as now given, no matter how accurate their boss's judgment may be. Therefore, piecework alone cannot be the incentive we seek. It is, however, a measure that can be useful when combined with other incentives.

PROFIT SHARING ALONE IS NOT SUFFICIENT

Profit sharing in its many forms as generally applied fails and for the same fundamental reasons. Profit sharing does not distinguish the worker. He is likely to consider the share of the profit given him in the usual profit sharing split somewhat in the nature of a tip to a Pullman porter. If he by any chance feels that he is really part of the company, he loses caste in his own mind when he accepts a tip. If, however, he feels that tips are the proper way for him to be paid, then he feels that the tip was not enough. In no case can such a tip be a real incentive to induce the worker to develop his abilities and skills.

Let us now consider how to apply incentive as it is applied in the amateur athletic game. How do we get that incentive in industry? Why do we not get the same determination to win in industry, which is all-important to all of us, as we do in an athletic game that is actually of no importance to anyone? The correct answer to that question solves our problem of putting incentive in industry.

INDUSTRY MUST HAVE PROPER GOAL OF SERVICE

To get all the workers in any industrial organization to *want* the company to succeed we must have a goal that appeals to all of them as proper. That goal in the athletic game is to win the game. That appeals to all. However, in industry the goal of the company's operation that is stated in the by-laws is to make a "profit" and profit only.

There is no one outside of the stockholders who gets that profit, and few stockholders generally are workers for the company. As long as that is true, the goal of profit will engender no enthusiasm in the workers. That goal will not do; in fact, most workers feel that too much profit is already given to the stockholder.

There is, however, a goal for the company's activities that will appeal to all as proper. That goal is service to the public. A lower and lower price for a better and better product is such a service. It is obvious to all workers that they are part of the public. Such a policy will show them that they to a great extent are working for themselves. All workers would favor such a policy for obvious reasons. All can see such an end as right and proper. All can strive for such an end and never feel that they are being "played for suckers," as they do where the goal is profit only.

The worker knows that manufacturing is necessary to the consumer. He is not sure about profit. He thinks that the salary that the boss gets should satisfy him without any profit. Therefore make profit a by-product of service to the consumer, not an end in itself. That program can be sold to any group of workers as a proper goal because it is the proper goal. It is the actual end and aim of industry. It is industry's reason for existing: to produce more and more wealth for more and more people at less and less cost. When the wage earner finds that the plan of the company is service, "no kidding," private industry will at last make sense to him. He will go along.

PRIDE IN SKILL FOLLOWS REWARD PROPORTIONATE TO ABILITY

If we are to get incentive for the wage earner, we must also make his job the means of making him outstanding in the eyes of those whose admiration he covets. While a philosophy of more and more for less and less as a company goal is satisfactory to the worker in showing him the reason for his company it is no great incentive to him to increase his skill and efforts beyond those of his fellow workers. This does not introduce the necessary competition which could make him a winner.

If we return to our athletic comparison, the worker wants to be on a great team, but he also wants even more to be the star on that team. The objective of more and more for less and less produces a great team. The worker now wants to star in his membership on that team. That is the next and most important step for the industrialist to take in incentive management. He must find the way to satisfy the worker's desire to "star." In doing it, management must be sure that the man who "stars" by management's standards will also be a star by his fellow-workers' standards.

Again, it is well to take a good look at the worker. He looks just like the executive, although he is usually more healthy. He reacts to the same stimuli. He resents being fooled by economic theories about paying for the tools of production when he often sees these costs being frittered away by incompetence and selfishness in high places. He can often suggest means that will greatly increase efficiency. They are not accepted since they would stop some of the prerogatives of top management. He does not try to play the game if the rules do not apply to all alike. He is human, even as you and I. The problem we have is to put this man into a game that he believes in, so that he can show that he has outstanding ability of which he is proud. The first step in this plan to make the worker proud of his skill is to make him realize that his reward will be in proportion to his ability. As ability to produce increases, the reward will be in proportion. Piecework payment and profit sharing as generally practiced do not accomplish this for the reasons noted above. The way that these difficulties can be eliminated and the incentive made real is actually to reward each person from top to bottom in proportion to his contribution to the success of the company each year.

BONUS REWARDS CONTRIBUTIONS TOWARDS SUCCESS

The Lincoln Electric Company calls this reward a bonus. Perhaps this sounds like a gift or profit sharing. It is neither. The difference is that just being in the organization is not the measure of reward as is true in the operation of profit sharing or yearly bonus as usually handled. This bonus plan goes very much further than that. The man is rewarded for all the things he does that are of help and penalized if he does not do as well as others in all these same ways. He is a member of the team and is rewarded or penalized depending on what he can do and does do in all opportunities to win the game.

In applying this system, the man is rated by all those who have accurate knowledge of some phase of his work. On this rating he is rewarded or penalized. This program runs parallel to the write-ups following the playing of a game or the selecting of an All-American team. The best man gets the praise and the standing he warrants and craves. In the bonus plan described here, man is rewarded in direct proportion to his contribution to the success of the company. The parallel is obvious.

Each man is advanced or retarded in his standing by his current record. He is rated three times per year. The sum of these ratings determines his share in the bonus and advancement.

At the time of giving each man his rating, any question that he may want to ask as to why the rating is as it is and how it can be improved is answered in complete detail by the executives responsible. The income, advancement and standing of each man obviously are determined by this rating. He not only tries to be a more productive worker, but he has equally the incentive to be more accurate, more cooperative and more helpful in finding new methods of more efficient production. He not only will save waste and time, but also he will be a self-starter who does not need much supervision.

Because of the greater desire for production accuracy, cooperation and the resultant elimination of overhead usually needed, great reductions in cost are almost automatic. The progress in new methods and techniques flows naturally from the desire of the worker to find these progressive ideas. It is obvious that lower cost will be the outcome. It is also obvious that contentment of the worker will be greater and friction will largely disappear.

HOW BONUS IS DETERMINED

The size of the bonus referred to above, as handled in our own case, is determined as follows. At the end of a year, a dividend is paid to the stockholders. This we call the wages of capital. It usually is somewhat more than the return from safe investment in high grade bonds and somewhat more than average dividend rates. It is well to say in passing that the dividend rate is on the actual investment in the company, not on a theoretical "book value."

INCENTIVE

After the dividend is provided for, we set aside "seed money" for the future of the company. The amount of this "seed money" is determined by the directors, based on current operations. This is needed since with the present tax program of the welfare state that is developing, there will be little chance for money from the outside. The only way that money for expansion can become available will be by plowing back profits and perhaps by selling stock to workers. Seed money, however, must be the chief source of expansion or replacement, under the present attitude of government and the voter.

After these deductions from profits, all the balance is divided as a bonus among the workers and management, on the basis of the contribution of each person to the success of the company for the year in question. It has represented a total amount paid to the worker of from approximately 50% of wages and salaries per year as a minimum to a maximum of 150% per year.

This bonus is in addition to regular earnings. All workers have the same basic wage rates as those usual in Cleveland, Ohio, for comparable operations. The bonus is the extra reward that can come from cooperation, skill, development of latent ability and desire to use these abilities for the best interests of those involved, i.e., consumer, worker and owner.

EFFECTS OF RECOGNITION THROUGH BONUS

Under conditions of maximum desire for efficiency, the bonus should average more than wages. The production rate in units should be more than four times that of the factories which are operating with the friction and misunderstanding now usual between so-called labor **and** management. At least the above is the relative record in The Lincoln Electric Company and comparable industry.

It is to be noted that each worker is rewarded for his individual contribution. His skill is recognized. He is made outstanding as an individual in his own and his contemporaries' estimation. This is not cited as the best that can be done; it is the result of making a few halting steps in the right direction.

Recognition of the player's abilities by the spectators is the incentive that exists in amateur athletics. If any college football game were played in the middle of the night, far from a place where a crowd could come to see it, if no notice of the game were taken by anyone, and if the newspapers were excluded, the incentive could be self-respect only. This is a great incentive, but it would still lack the kindred incentive that is nearly as great; that is, the recognition by our fellows of our abilities. There is little chance that athletic games will from choice eliminate this great incentive as long as it can be added to that of self-respect. The parallel to industry is close and illuminating. The way is indicated. The successful program is evident.

INDUSTRIALISTS AND LABOR LEADERS SMOTHER DESIRE TO DEVELOP

There is no doubt that the present attitude of the industrialist and particularly the labor leader will completely stop the development that is latent in every person. Latent ability does not develop unless there is a burning desire to develop, to do what has heretofore been impossible. Such desire does not come from the present attitude toward work that is taught by union leadership, as now constituted. Development of our latent abilities comes only when we desire mightily to do the seemingly impossible.

The whole history of labor-management relationship shows the tendency to stifle rather than promote such development. From the relationship of the slave-master, serf-feudal lord of antiquity to the boss-worker of the present day, there has been no tendency to put the worker in a position in which he would desire even to know of his latent abilities, much less develop them. No slave, serf or union member wants to be an outstanding producer. He rather wants to see how little he can do and still get away with it. He has succeeded remarkably well under the Wagner Act as production rates now show. The worker can out-manoeuvre the boss when it comes to loafing, if he is protected from correction by law, as he is now.

NEW ATTITUDE NEEDED

A new attitude must be developed in industry. Men must be encouraged to grow. They will then develop efficient machines. No industrialist will consent to put a ten horsepower motor on a load that a one horse motor can do easily. No industrialist will use a thousand ton press to form thimbles one at a time. All industrialists use all mechanical facilities intelligently and to their capacity. They are usually sure to use the proper mechanical tools. They have no such program for eliciting and applying the abilities of the worker. This greatest of all assistance for efficient production that the manufacturer has is not even recognized in many cases. Genius in the worker is usually overlooked. Here is the greatest failure of the present industrial system. The industrialist concentrates on machines and neglects man who is the producer and developer of the machine and, obviously, has far greater

113

potentialities. He will not consider the fact that undeveloped geniuses are doing manual jobs in his plant where they have neither the opportunity nor are given the incentive to develop themselves to genius or even to normal intelligence and skill.

What a certain machine can do is reasonably easy to determine. What a man can become, no one can know completely. That he can develop greatly is proved by the history of every person. How far he can go is unknown. That he can be much greater than he usually is must be known. This development of the individual is the opportunity of all industrialists. On its completeness the success of the industrialist depends. Incentive management starts here.

HOW TO ENCOURAGE DEVELOPMENT

We know our physical skills can be greatly developed by training. We know that the development of our mental ability can also be greatly increased. Yet with all this experience, we do not encourage development of the latent abilities of the men on whom we could depend for outstanding success in industry.

After we have the incentive of recognition and belonging to the great team, the question then becomes: how shall the industrialist directly encourage the developement of the latent capabilities of the worker? The answer is rather obvious. Again, we go back to the athletic game. We should use the same methods in industry we use in athletics. The first step is to challenge the worker's ability. Put a job above his present ability before him. Give him something to do that is beyond his present ability, plus a burning desire to accomplish it. Put him into a scrimmage with his fellows and see who is best.

114

Give him the chance to beat the top man.

The second step is to make the worker know that there is no limit to his capabilities except those that are self-imposed. That is one of the great opportunities of the leader. Jesse Owens did not break the world's record for the broad jump the first time he tried. He did not come to be expert until he had given himself many challenges which had fallen far short of the world's record. He would never have approached his best had he not tried and continued to try to do what he had never done before. He challenged his ability and developed new ability. All ability that everyone has is developed in the same way.

ADVANCEMENT FROM WITHIN

The third step in this development of latent capabilities is to make all know that advancement in the organization is from within and that such advancement depends completely on ability of those chosen for advancement compared to all others and on nothing else. It is not only fair to do this, but it is very important to incentive. Don't let the good man wait for a funeral to get his proper place.

The fourth step is to put the development pressure on yourself as the leader so that you will develop your own capabilities in making yourself a great leader. You must be the inspiration to your followers. Always expect the impossible from yourself as well as from those around you. You will frequently achieve the impossible also if you will but challenge yourself.

It is in this development of yourself as a leader that your greatest challenge will come. Your followers will unconsciously pattern their behavior after your own, if you have the right to lead. The incentive system outlined

115

herein will put more pressure on you as the leader than on those of less responsibility. Your reaction when you accept this responsibility will be one of added contentment. The pressure will be a joy as it develops your own latent abilities.

GOVERNMENT DOMINANCE DESTROYS INCENTIVE

There is another question that bears on this matter of industry incentive, and that is the place of government. At the present time, government takes nearly a third of all wealth produced. Not only that, there is a growing feeling in the minds of many people that government should be even more important in the lives of all. Many want government not only to spend the present third of our incomes in making our government a welfare or socialistic state, but to go even farther in the totalitarian direction.

There is no need of discussing the pros and cons of such a state. It is doubtful if anyone who can think the matter through would be in favor of such an outcome. In any case, no successful worker under an incentive system would ever be content to give up his individual freedom to any government. Incentive management encourages men to be great. All great men will fight to the death for freedom. It is only those who are degenerating that are weak enough to give up their freedom, as all history shows.

It is well to consider here just what the dominance of government over the citizen leads to. There is no doubt that the free enterprise system presents many problems to all its workers from top to bottom. There is lack of security for the incompetent, the lazy and the unfortunate. To an extent, communism eliminates that problem. It eliminates the lazy and incompetent by death or the labor camp.

INCENTIVE

There is a wide variation in the distribution of wealth in the free enterprise system. There are many chances for the selfish to over-reach. There is a wide variation in luck. There is a chance for much disappointment and suffering. A totalitarian government could change much of this. The socialist says that it would.

The dominant reason for the free enterprise system is that it is the only known way that outstanding progress of the individual can be made. It is the only system that introduces competition in such a way as to develop the latent abilities of the individual. That reason is of sufficient importance to justify all its theoretical shortcomings listed above. We have not listed the difficulties of totalitarianism. They are many. The lack of incentive for the individual should be enough to eliminate it.

WE MUST CHOOSE

America is at the crossroads in this matter. A decision must be made, and soon. There is much lack of understanding by the people generally, yet they must choose. On their decision depends the future of the United States and of the individual.

It is rather difficult for the average citizen who has suffered because of lack of work, which he feels is not his fault, to see that governmental paternalism is bad. It is difficult for the subnormal person to feel that someone should not take care of him. It is difficult for the usual industrialist to see that governmental help in the form of a protective tariff in time of distress is not fully justified, particularly when he is competing against foreign manufacturers who pay much lower wages. However, unless we all do see that the free enterprise system is the only one so far suggested that will work, unless we so believe and act

117

accordingly, the United States will disappear and a more self-reliant nation, when it develops under adversity, will surpass us in the race for dominance. History is a continual story of the prosperous softening and dying from dry rot. They are then taken over by the tough nation, made strong by adversity.

We recognize that fact in our own experience. We know it is the overcoming of great obstacles that developed our present strength. We know that if we had not overcome them we would be weaklings, as is the case with those whom we call "mamma's boys." We know that leaning on others for those things we should do for ourselves makes us incompetents. We know that the great were the ones who overcame the greatest odds. We know that in athletics we would not tolerate any softness which would give to the weak or incompetent a place on the team which another ought to have, based on performance. However, we are apt to lose our perspective when it comes to the game of life.

The rotting out of the pampered and the rise of the hard worker has been the history of all time. The only way that the pampered can survive in competition with the self-developed is by governmental control of the economy. When they do, the government that preserves them must collapse as a result because those whom it supports can't support it. In the free enterprise system, ability will rise, incompetence will be defeated, and a free economy will support itself and its government.

The program outlined herein will produce almost unbelievable results. This is not a scheme to increase production ten percent, or to reduce labor costs by a fraction. This is a program that will revolutionize the record of any company. There is no limit to the possibilities of man. Do not underrate him.

Expect that incentive management will cut costs by half or more. Expect that it will make your company dominant in its field. Expect that there will be unlimited progress because of the plan. Expect that your company will write a new chapter in industry. Do not be satisfied with less. If you do not get such results, you have failed to understand and apply incentive management.

Chapter VII

How To Install Incentive System

The successful installation of incentive management in industry must be based on the fundamental desires of the men involved. It cannot be successfully operated unless those involved want intently to go along with the plan. It is not a formula that can be installed by a firm of industrial engineers who put it in as a plan for "efficiency." It is more accurate to say that incentive management is adopted by all the people in the organization, rather than installed in it.

INCENTIVES ARE ADOPTED, NOT INSTALLED

This point is of great importance if any incentive plan is considered. Too many people consider incentive wrongly. The incentive system of management is a speed-up if a union leader is talking. It is some form of profit sharing plan or piecework or a premium system in the usual industrialist's thinking. It is a "pain in the neck" if the Treasury Department is talking since they have not found the way to tax it successfully, as yet. It is a natural plan for men working together for a common, greatly desired, result when properly understood.

Incentive management is not a method of merely paying more for more production. In fact, the most successful incentive system in all experience pays no money at all. The amateur athletic team member gets nothing per hour, no matter how great his accomplishments. It is obvious, therefore, that the narrow conception of money reward on the basis of piecework or premium payments alone, no matter how clever in itself, or efficient in its results, is not incentive management as the term is used in this book.

Incentive management is not a new method of wage payment. It is instead a new conception of the relationship of so-called management and workers. It results in both wanting to work together for a common and very useful end. This end must be one on which both agree. In the accomplishment of this end both fulfill their basic desires for recognition and pride in their individual abilities and worth. This is far afield from "profit sharing," as now usually understood. This difference is fundamental and controlling in the ultimate success of incentive management.

Since incentive management depends on the acceptance of the plan by all the people in the organization, it can succeed only when all want it to succeed. If that desire is lacking or merely a luke-warm acceptance, there is no way known of making incentive management succeed.

MUST GET DESIRE FOR PLAN BY ALL

The primary problem in successfully installing incentive management is to get the desire for the plan in the minds of all in the organization. This cannot be done by merely telling the organization that management has decided to install it and outlining the advantages that will result. It is not that easy.

Getting acceptance of any new idea is often a long and difficult process. No new idea that upsets old habits is easily accepted. It is only necessary to cite the difficulty of getting the acceptance of the philosophy of Jesus to prove the point. No one who knows the facts doubts that the philosophy of the Sermon on the Mount would solve all our problems, both moral and economic. However, we still will not accept such philosophy and live our lives in accordance with it, in spite of the conclusive teachings of man's experience and of the Church over the last two thousand years. To accept the teaching of Jesus, it is necessary for man to break habits of thought and action developed over millions of years. He cannot break with the past quickly and easily as we see. Man, however, is prone to experiment, and will if the experiment is made attractive enough and if its acceptance does not necessitate too much sacrifice of present beliefs and habits.

ANNOUNCEMENT DOES NOT CREATE DESIRE

Merely announcing to all those in an organization what advantages will accrue to them from their adoption of incentive management principles will not usually get their enthusiastic acceptance on which such a program's success depends. In fact, it will instead usually arouse resentment in many minds in the usual organization. The men and their union leadership usually will jump to the conclusion that they are to be sweated by this plan for the benefit of their natural enemy, management. If there is no open revolt, there will at least be no enthusiasm. Such passive acceptance will make the plan fail almost as completely as open revolt.

It can be expected that the present union leaders will buck the plan in all cases. They will know that success of incentive management will eliminate them as labor leaders. As a matter of fact, it will do just that if the union leadership has the usual union philosophy of output limitation.

This opposition from the union will not be easy to handle in the usual plant. In some organizations there is perhaps enough belief by the men in their management so that the plan can be sold. This is not generally true, however. In most unionized companies the union leadership dominates the worker completely. He will follow the union leaders without question; in fact, he must. The union leader can and does have him fired if he does not obey him.

The greatest difficulty in getting acceptance of incentive management, however, will come from the ingrained skepticism of the worker, developed over long years of labor-management friction. He has had much unsatisfactory experience with the boss. This experience makes it difficult for him to believe that all at once the boss has changed from a driver who demands all and gives little, to a fellow player on a team who has a new and proper philosophy.

There are many ways that have been tried to sell the incentive idea; in fact there are at least as many ways as there are people to be sold. Many ways are partially successful; none is universally so. The getting of others to believe what is said to them is a problem that has been unsolved from the beginning of time. There is no universal answer to it. Selling is not that simple.

The following plan has met with success in some places. It is being given, therefore, because it reduces the matter to a simpler form and therefore reduces the difficulty. It is not a sure cure.

SELL PLAN TO TRIAL GROUP FIRST

Do not try to sell the whole organization at once; rather sell the plan to a small trial group. In this way the difficulty can be made much less in getting acceptance. There is still another advantage in this plan: it allows all, both management and men, to gain experience before the plan is put into final operation for the whole plant. In carrying out this idea, a single department of the plant should be chosen where a profit and loss operation can be simply installed so that records comparative with what has gone before can be accurately made and easily understood by the workers in that department.

After the possibilities of savings by cooperation and effort of those in the department have been carefully surveyed and the proper means for getting them is determined, the people in that department should be approached with a fully worked-out plan. This plan should show the possibilities of savings; how they can be obtained, and how the savings that may be made will be divided. In such an approach, the statement can be frankly made that management wants to try out the plan. Management should say that the results that can be obtained, while very attractive, are not certain. Such a program often can be made a very attractive financial arrangement for all concerned. Mistakes on either side also will not be too important, particularly if the program and benefits are fairly stated to the men at the time of starting the plan.

If the program is properly worked out and fairly put up to the men so they know they can win and how much if they are willing to put new life and skill into the doing of the job more efficiently, a real step can be taken forward.

PLAN WILL SELL ITSELF

No other attempt should be made until it is proved to all that this preliminary tryout has been successful. Then the same plan can be easily put into operation throughout the plant. Selling will not be necessary. The men in the other departments will ask for it. This makes enthusiastic acceptance simple.

The department chosen for the trial will vary, depending on the kind of industry involved. Those which are rather obvious tryout points are the following: service, repair, inspection, maintenance and sales.

This plan for acceptance is not the only possible successful approach. It is not even a sure solution. If a mistake in honesty or understanding or leadership is inherent in management, the trial will fail just as will the attempt to put it in the whole plant. The only purpose of this suggestion is to help overcome some of the difficulty that is inherent in selling the whole group. Reducing the size of the group reduces the difficulty. If the plan or the honesty or the understanding is wrong, it will fail with the small as well as with the large group. This idea for selling incentive management is not a panacea, but it is a help, perhaps.

When successful, this small group tryout will cause the rest of the organization to ask for the same incentive plan. It then will be very easy to install. In this way, incentive will in effect be installed by the workers' asking for it, rather than by having it sold to them by management. This tryout also will give management a chance to correct mistakes it might have made had it attempted to cover all workers at first.

Both labor and management will have a chance to experiment during such a tryout. It will be found that experimentation is part of any successful plan. The same experiment can be very helpful later also in trying out new phases of incentive that may be useful, for incentive is a growing activity.

EXPECT GREAT RESULTS

In general, it is difficult to get people to believe the extent of the progress that can be achieved by incentive management. Many people think of it as an expedient which will cut out some waste time and therefore increase production efficiency. This wrong idea has often condemned incentive. Management must realize what a proper goal is. There are instances where a change in lighting or addition of music or a change in the color scheme of the walls has made savings of much more than 10%. Do not go to incentive management if you are looking for such trifling progress. There is no chance for success if such small savings are all that are expected.

If incentive management is to be installed, expect a cost reduction commensurate with the abilities of man. If you do not set your sights high enough there can be no realization of what you are trying to do. You must expect to get the speed of the champion compared with that of the sleep-walker, which is the usual industrial pace. Don't underrate man. You will fail if you do.

OVERHEAD WILL BE REDUCED

The first result of incentive management is to reduce much of the present factory overhead. For example, the need for inspectors largely disappears under incentive management. The man doing the job on any operation is more expert on that job than any inspector if he wants to

be. He knows how to operate his machine better than anyone else. The only problem is to get him to *want* sufficiently TO MAKE ALL HIS WORK RIGHT. That is obviously what incentive, enthusiastically accepted, does.

There is another class of overhead people who disappear;
that is the usual foreman whose job it is to see that the
man works and does not leave the job or break up the tools
so that he can loaf or so he can show how important he is.
He is not needed since the man wants to do the best he can.
He does much better than any pusher could make him do
under any circumstances.

Now the only function of any overhead people, as far as
the producing worker is concerned, is to help him develop
his skills. Those with greater knowledge often can be useful in this way.

It will also be found that many paper records become
useless when the attitude of all workers changes from opposition or routine acceptance to enthusiastic cooperation.
The records needed in a one man factory, if that one man
is the owner, are few. There will be few also if all are as
anxious to make the job succeed as the one man in his operation is. This is particularly true when all the men in the
group have the same feeling of their responsibility for the
success of the operation.

SKILLS WILL BE INCREASED

The other great advance in efficiency is in the increased
skill of the man who is developed under the desire that incentive management gives. This can be a continuous
growth which results from the constant desire of the person himself to be a bigger man. We all know that skill increases with practice and ambition. If there is no desire
to increase it, skill does not increase. If, as is often true at

the present time, limitation of output is the desire of the worker, the only skill that develops is that of scientific loafing. This science is as frustrating to the loafer as it is costly to the buyer of the product. This elimination of frustration is one of the reasons why the workers under a system of incentive management are always more healthy and happy as well as more prosperous than their union buddies.

How great this progress under incentive management becomes depends entirely on the growth of those involved. If the desire is great enough, progress is very great. If the desire is great enough, skills far beyond what anyone believes, can and will be achieved. There is no end to progress but the limitations that man puts on himself. The first man who hit a golf ball, probably because of his lack of skill and poorness of the ball and club, did not drive it over twenty yards, if he did even that well. Now he drives it ten to fifteen times that far. His skill has developed to an extent not even imagined by the first man. The tools developed by the desires inherent in the game have also progressed to a point that was also not conceived as possible at the beginning.

This same progress in the man, the tools and the design is inherent in every manufacturing operation. Progress is only limited by lack of desire and determination.

MORE THAN AN EFFICIENCY SCHEME

The question is frequently asked: how much will incentive management increase efficiency? The answer is "without limit" with proper leadership and proper incentive acceptance. Production of ten times more than union production in shops under incentive management is common, even now. Of course, the difference depends on the lack of union efficiency as well as newly developed efficiency. Both affect the comparison.

Incentive management is not a so-called efficiency scheme alone. It is a philosophy of life and production that develops new aspirations and usefulness in all affected by it. Do not approach it from any other point of view. Incentive is not a way to get the worker to do more as an end in itself. It is a way to get him to be part of the economic team, on the excellence of which the future of our country depends. It is a way to get him to play the game in industry as a member of the economic team that has made America greater than any other nation, economically. It also opens a way toward fuller realization of the American dream and promise of a fuller, richer, happier, better life for all mankind.

RESPONSIBILITIES OF THE LEADER

The industrial manager who has the will to meet the challenge of these times and who is ready to begin the task of reforming his present methods by adopting incentive management must first answer these questions:

I.

Can he show those in positions under him that he deserves to lead them? Can he make the team, as captain?

II.

Can management respect and recognize the skill of the worker in proportion to the development in productive ability that he has made?

III.

Can management justify its salary compared with the salary of all others in the organization? Does the worker think so?

129

IV.

Can and will management put itself under development pressure that will increase its own ability and skill and make it progress and become outstanding?

V.

Can management put the worker under incentive pressure that will stimulate him to develop himself? Can management really lead?

VI.

Can management control the stockholder so he won't take for himself much of the savings made by the efficiency of the whole organization under incentive management, which savings largely belong to the consumer and the workers, including management, who did the job?

VII.

Will management advance men from within and only on their ability?

VIII.

Can management continue to lead honestly and ably after some measure of success has been achieved, or will it go soft?

IX

Is management sure it wants to be a member of the team, instead of being a boss of the old school who depends on fear to make his leadership unquestioned?

The above is the summation of management's problem. Management must be the leader. While it can still boss more or less in the old European way, it will not if it is smart enough to see the great opportunities for all men that are in America and do the job properly in an American way. Incentive management is a challenge to every ounce of ability that management has.

There is no doubt that incentive management gives to all

a new interest in life, but it also increases the responsibilities of all, since the results will be team results, not management results as now. That is a new concept and a new avenue of progress. Installing the incentive system of management is not too difficult if management can have the new concept of its position and responsibilities in the organization.

With this piecemeal program outlined above, management can get its feet on the ground and see itself in the new light as leader and co-worker. Its new place with this conception of team work is both easier and more difficult; easier because all work together; harder because it must justify its place on the team. That team is both skeptical and good. When management makes good it will be prouder of its accomplishment than anything it has ever done before, and rightly so.

Chapter VIII

Piecework in Industry

There are few ideas that will provoke as radically different and intense reactions as the word "piecework." Piecework is often thought of by labor as a little less honest than robbery. It is thought of by management as an efficient plan for reducing cost of labor and therefore a very proper economic objective. The public thinks of it as the exploiters' method of sweating profits out of workers who dare not lose their jobs. As is usually true when there is a sharp difference of opinion on any point, all the divergent views have some truth in them. None, however, is entirely accurate.

Piecework has been used for both good and bad purposes. How it is used determines its nature. Piecework installed by honest experts is a great boon to all involved, most of all to the worker and the consumer. If, however, it is dishonestly or incorrectly applied, it can arouse resentment and hatred and destroy cooperation within the industry, thus of course raising labor costs as well as creating even worse difficulties.

In piecework, as is true of all other human relations such as parenthood, marriage and friendship, great satisfaction or great disappointment can be the result. It is the purpose and ability of those involved that will determine whether piecework is a godsend, a tragedy or a "pain in the neck."

Piecework in this way is like food. It is a necessary boon when properly used. Improperly used, it can be the cause of great discomfort and when the impropriety is carried far enough, it can cause death. The final results of food and piecework depend on how they are used, not on their own inherent character. This is not unique. Most necessary things in life depend for proper results on proper use. They do not create proper results of themselves.

SUCCESS OF PIECEWORK DEPENDS ON MANAGEMENT

Piecework is good, bad or indifferent, depending on how management handles it. The fact that many workers and the public suspect and distrust it is proof that at times piecework has been improperly used. It is, of course, true that piecework has often cheated the wage earner. The fact that in such cases the boss very rarely intended to cheat him shows how unintelligently the system was applied. The industrialist is not always expert in this job of properly applying the piecework system, hence mistakes have often been made that were innocent, but they are still deadly to cooperation.

This discussion, however, has nothing to do with the errors that have been made before in applying this method of promoting efficiency. It has to do with a plan that uses piecework properly. Piecework properly handled will give higher wages, lower costs and greater satisfaction to all involved. There is no better way now known of accomplishing certain phases of efficient manufacturing. All failures that have been experienced have come from dishonesty or

133

incompetence in applying the process, not from the inherent qualities of piecework.

Fundamentally, piecework is for the sole purpose of giving to management and the worker an *accurate measure of the worker's efficiency.* Industry under incentive is a game of worker-management skills. No game can be properly played unless the score is known and accurately kept. Piecework is a means for measuring the skill and effort of all involved in winning the industrial game. Piecework can have no other useful purpose.

It is not possible to increase efficiency of production nor to develop new methods of more efficient production without some accurate measurement of progress made. Piecework is a method of keeping the score and showing the progress that new methods and skills make or do not make in the efficiencies of production. It is not a scheme for compelling men to work harder and produce more—that cannot be done to free men. Piecework is a means of measuring a man's ability.

In properly applying a piecework system, the first thing to remember is that the operator should not be the person primarily responsible for progress in methods of production. Fundamentally, that is the responsibility of management. Many managers miss this point.

The mistake made by many managements is that they think their only job in applying piecework is to time the job as it is then done by the worker and put a price on it after the obvious delays are taken out. Nothing could be further from the truth. In most cases that fail, here is the primary reason for failure of piecework.

MANAGEMENT MUST FIRST ESTABLISH EFFICIENT METHODS

It is the responsibility of management to find the most efficient way of doing any job. This is not the responsibility of the operator. If the operator continually is able to find the more efficient methods of doing the manufacturing operations, then management is uselss and should step aside in favor of the worker who has outperformed him. If management has no essential function in developing the manufacturing methods used, of what use is it? It will find difficulty in justifying its existence and salary.

When management discharges its responsibility as the deviser of more efficient methods for doing the job in question, then it is its responsibility to teach these methods to the operator. When that is done and all unnecessary movements are eliminated, only then the job is ready to be timed and a price put on it. In this arrangement the only reason for the timing is to set up the record for the operator to shoot at as he increases his skill. As the operator's skill in output increases, so must his income. Thus an incentive is given to the worker in the same way that the record for an athletic event gives the competing athlete a measure of his ability and an incentive to excel.

TIME STUDY MAN SHOULD BE EXPERT

When a time study man, armed with a stopwatch, times an operation that has been developed by the operator, obviously he contributes nothing to the operation. If the stopwatcher cannot contribute anything to the job efficiency, he is then out of place in his position. That is very obvious to the operator. He resents the authority of this dub over him as any other self-respecting, normal person would and should.

It is imperative to remember in probing incentive that the industrialist is dealing with human beings. It is well to remember that they react exactly like any other human being, including the manager. Injustice to themselves or to other workers makes them angry, as it should. They resent being in their positions of inferiority to bosses who they know are less competent than they are. Any normal person would resent such unfairness. It is well to recognize these facts in all of management's dealings with all employees. No time study man should be allowed to time a job for the determining of prices who is not at least as expert on the job as is the man who is being timed.

The obvious conclusion is that the time study man should come up from the ranks. He should be himself an operator, selected because he has shown the originality and skill to make better progress than other operators. He should also understand the reactions of those whose work he is timing. He should be able to command their respect because of his own ability and knowledge of the work.

PIECEWORK LEADS TO COMPETITION WITHIN COOPERATION

After all, the objective of incentive management is to develop in the workers themselves the desire for efficient operation. No incentive plan can be successful which is not based on such desire. No plan that develops this desire successfully can ever fail.

Let management approach the problem in the light of this conclusion. Let's think of the people in the organization as human beings whom we want on our team to help win the game of making more and more of a better and better product to sell for a lower and lower price. The approach then will be that of thinking of piecework as a method of measuring the skill of the team members so that credit can be properly given to each one. The record is set up for each to excel if he can. It measures the success of his competitive effort in this cooperative enterprise. Then piecework is not seen as a means of getting the worker to do more work for less money. This is said with full knowledge that the production now obtained in most industry can be enormously increased. Cooperation and competition within cooperation does produce this enormous increase in output. That is a by-product, however. It is not the primary objective. The objective is a better, more satisfying and fuller life for all men in industry in America; and some day in the whole world.

PROPER INCENTIVE INSTILLS DESIRE TO BE SKILLFUL

Perhaps the idea that the game spirit can be gotten into the factory worker seems impossible from the record that has so far been made in industry. It is hard to think perhaps that men who now limit an output that they can easily increase with their present skills will try to increase their skill and effort so as to get greater production. However, the facts in all instances prove they will, under proper incentive.

There is no difficulty in getting the owner of a new business to do his best and to increase his skills in his operations. In fact, he continually tries to do just that. There is no difficulty in showing that increased ability is developed when such desire to progress is present. The only problem that management has in installing incentives, is to instill the same desire in the worker as is present in the manager. That is what incentive management properly understood and applied will do.

Incentive management makes the job an activity at which the operator becomes outstanding and proud because of his skill in doing it. Incentive management makes the job important to the worker. Piecework is a way of measuring the skill that the worker develops for this desirable purpose. It is on this skill that he must depend to become outstanding.

PIECEWORK MUST NOT REDUCE EARNINGS

When we can get the operator to want to do his best, all the other problems relating to greater efficiency will disappear. Management can then, with full cooperation of the worker, set proper standards. It is obvious that these standards once set must not be changed because the worker develops his skill so that he increases his output and earnings no matter how great these earnings become.

These piecework prices should be changed only when management finds demonstrably better methods or tools or techniques. Piecework cannot and must not reduce earnings that are the result of greater skill or progress from any source developed by the man himself no matter how much he earns. Glorify and do not punish the record breaker. He is the hope of the future.

Time study men must not be spies who look for ways to cut the workers' earnings. They must truly be their friendly advisers and helpers and accepted as such. When the worker sees that the time study department is made up of experts who are developers of new methods of production that will help him to greater skill, larger income and continuous employment, the whole atmosphere changes. No longer are those in the time study department thought of as spies or thieves. They are then in their real place as manufacturing experts. They are then consultants who can and do help all to new and greater progress so greatly desired under incentive management.

COOPERATION MUST BE GENUINE FROM TOP TO BOTTOM

In the mind of the worker, generally, management

usually is of small importance. Many of its responsibilities do not loom large and seem to him unnecessary. Many luncheons, banquets, speeches and cocktail parties do not have the same world-moving weight to the man in the shop as they do to the executive who attends them. There is also the lack of understanding by the worker of the several months' vacation needed by executives, when no such need is recognized for the worker in the shop. Some workers cannot see how a five hour day during only part of the year is sufficient for the executive to do his job, when it takes all the time of every working day for the man in the shop to do his. The worker also has some difficulty in understanding how the contribution that some industrialists make to the job is worth the salaries that they get. The man in the shop keeps careful track of the doings of his bosses. He even knows some things about the boss' life and affairs that the boss himself does not know.

These facts in themselves may not be too important. Even if some executives are overpaid for their work, the amount of money involved is extremely small as compared to the total wages and salaries paid. However, the effect of the boss' daily program on the psychology of the worker is of great importance. If there is to be a game spirit in any plant, each worker must make the team. If anyone does not, be he operator, executive or owner, and the game spirit is to continue, he must be taken out of the game and replaced with someone who can and does make the team. There can be no game spirit on any other basis. Managers must be the leaders they are supposed to be. Not only that, all those in the organization must accept them as proper members of the team who have won their places as managers in open competition.

Both cooperation and competition within the team must

be genuine. No fake goes over. If managers are to get the operator's cooperation, they must earn it and keep on earning it. They cannot get an iota more than they deserve.

MANAGEMENT MUST COME THROUGH

When management does its job of setting up piecework operations, the worker expects the manager to know how to do that job much better than the worker himself could do it. If he cannot meet that challenge, the operator wonders why management is there at all. If the only way that the time study department can reduce costs is arbitrarily to cut the price (with or without some trifling change in the operation, as an excuse), the time study man deserves little respect for his ability. He will get very little. There will also be little progress in productive efficiency.

The operator is well aware of some of the possibilities involved in his job. If he is cheated by time study, he can and he will retaliate in ways that can be very serious to the plant and to his efficiency as every person in management well knows.

This statement is still true even when the cut in price is thought by management to be necessary, because a mistake of over-pricing was made when the price was first put on the job. Any fair-minded person knows that such a cut is not only dishonest, but is doubly disastrous to efficiency because it shows up the time study man as a dunce who does not know what he is doing, as well as a cheat. This loss of "face" by management merely confirms in the minds of the workers their preconceived notion that management is not holding up its end. There can be no game cooperation built up under such conditions. Management must come through.

The illustration of the amateur football team is a par-

140

allel to the industrial team. There is no chance of the line in a football team doing its job with enthusiasm if every lineman knows that the backs are "softies," chosen, not because they were best for the job, but because of personal or fraternity relationships with the coaches. Games are not won by such teams. Efficient manufacturing is not done by organizations which have the same attitude in the minds of the production workers regarding their bosses.

Perhaps it is felt that this matter is stressed more than it deserves. That is not true. This whole matter of efficiency of production ranges around this question of the workers *wanting* to produce at high efficiency. Unless the worker feels that the team he is on is one which he and all others are chosen and advanced for their skill and ability, he will give only prosaic compliance with the orders passed down to him. In the case of union control of industrial management in many ways, such as we see today, that compliance is far from satisfactory from anyone's point of view.

A successful time study man must first of all be an expert in the operations over which he is placed. He must also be an expert in handling the material involved. The operations necessary for production are always subject to more efficient methods. To find them is the job of Time Study.

POSSIBLE SAVINGS ARE TREMENDOUS

Because of management failure, it is safe to say that in the usual plant without incentive, an imaginative engineer with proper incentive could do some or all of these things to the operations as set at first: (1) cut out wasteful motions; (2) tool the job better; (3) replace hand handling with less costly mechanical handling; (4) develop new techniques that will make the job much faster; **or (5)** eliminate the job altogether, by correcting the design. No one can look over the advance that has been made in manufacturing in the last fifty years without seeing complete proof that some of these things will eventually be done to all present operations.

Henry Ford reduced the price of the Model T Ford car from $900.00 in 1914 to $290.00 in later years. The car was the same during all of that time. Raw material costs were progressively higher. Wages were nearly three times as great per hour as in 1913, yet the reduction shown above was made with great gain in profit. This demonstration, which is duplicated at least partially by all successful manufacturers during the same time, leaves no question of the possibilities inherent in any job of saving most of the cost of any or all operations. In a free economy, it is the industrial manager's job to make these savings. That is his responsibility to himself, to his co-workers in the industry, to the owners, and most of all to the consumers for whom all industry must be organized.

Those who are not closely affiliated with industry can hardly imagine the enormous savings that can be made in any manufacturing job, under conditions of genuine co-operation of all involved, with genuinely intelligent and conscientious leadership. It would be impossible to try to show here all the progress that can be made in manufacturing. However, if we compare the progress that man has made in transportation in the last 150 years we have a rough indication of what can be done in the future.

A century and a half ago the fastest means of locomotion was a horse. A man could make a maximum of seventy-five miles per day on horseback. Fifteen to twenty miles per day was good going for a loaded wagon. We now travel and transport goods at speeds of four to six hundred miles per hour.

If instead of travel we compare the speed with which a message can be sent now, as compared to a century ago, we have a still more striking example of progress that man has made. Therein is indicated the possibilities which can be made by the manufacturer in any other field. Costs of all manufactured products from their first inception to the present show great savings. There is no limit to what can still be done in all industrial production except our lack of imagination and belief in the development of the abilities of man now remaining latent because of lack of proper incentive.

Summarizing:

1. Time Study is one of the most important activities that manufacturing has. Put men of the proper ability and background in it.
2. The worker must himself accept the price set as proper. He is an expert also.
3. A price once made is a contract. Do not break a contract.
4. Remember that all methods now used are wrong. The job of Time Study is to find a method that is more nearly right.
5. There is no limit to the progress that can be made, nor to the latent ability of all the men involved to make progress. It is the job of the industrialist to see that he and all of his co-workers develop their abilities and gain such progress.
6. It is Time Study's job first to find a better method of doing a given job, then to time that method accurately and then to teach that method at that speed to the operator.

7. Manpower costs approximately ten dollars per kilo-
   watt hour. Electric power costs approximately one
   cent. Time Study should see that manpower is used
   only when the work requires that the brain power of
   the worker is also necessary to do the job. Modern
   industrial methods have already made human life too
   valuable even in its lowest terms of cash to be used
   as no more than mindless mechanical power.
8. The better way of doing all operations is looking management and operator in the eye at all times. As a
   matter of fact, that better way is rather hurt and
   shocked that it is not recognized and accepted.

The following specifications for a Time Study man are
basic.

He must:

1. Be frankly honest.
2. Have knowledge of the job he is timing.
3. Keep an open mind that recognizes that progress is
   unlimited.
4. Follow a program of study that will keep him progressing in ability.
5. Develop tact which allows him to get along with people. This is part of honesty.
6. Keep the feeling of importance of his job.
7. Have good health and habits.
8. Have ambition that will drive him to do his best at
   all times.
9. Believe in himself and his company.
10. Show leadership that will make these characteristics
    valued.

MANAGEMENT MUST SET NEW STANDARDS FOR TIME STUDY

Time Study has not been thought of in the way it should
and must be for proper progress. The chief reason is that

144

it has not done the job that it can and should do. The time study man has not functioned as an inventive industrial engineer; he has been more nearly a clever clerk. The time study man was a person who timed a job as it was already being done, not a man who found new and betters ways of doing it. Industry can and must make a great stride here. This is perhaps a new conception to many manufacturers.

As is often the case, if this new conception of incentive management is to be adopted, the greatest change will occur in the development of management of itself. This may seem a responsibility that managers will hesitate to assume. The old way did not demand such ability and concentration.

The important fact is that when both management and men assume a higher standard of responsibility, both will have greater satisfactions from these new standards of performance. We glory in accomplishment, we are uneasy in mediocrity. No man ever got much joy in being an "also ran." He gets all his satisfaction from winning, even at the cost of trying much harder and longer. The same holds for his accomplishment in his industrial job and for the same reason. Here is another secret of success in manufacturing. Here is the opportunity and one of the many reasons for incentive management.

CHAPTER IX

Why Incentive Systems Fail

A review of profit sharing systems by the National Industrial Conference Board shows that nearly sixty percent of them have failed or have been abandoned. This is a very disturbing fact. In the light of that survey, the question should be asked anyone interested in incentive management, "Why these failures?"

A still more provocative question naturally follows: "Why do forty percent succeed?" The answer to these two questions will be very useful to anyone considering incentive management, since profit sharing in some form is a usual part of any incentive system.

If sharing of profit were an answer in itself, all profit sharing attempts would succeed. It is obvious, therefore, that profit sharing as an incentive is not a complete answer in itself to a workable incentive plan. We must look further.

The fact that forty percent of the profit sharing attempts succeed in giving a satisfactory incentive shows that there is usefulness in profit sharing under certain conditions. With the incentive schemes of various kinds as now used, what causes success in some cases and failure in others, when the plan in detail of its reward seemingly is the same?

SUCCESS OF PLAN DEPENDS ON ACCEPTANCE BY ALL

Success or failure of any incentive plan depends not on the plan itself but on its acceptance by all those involved. The mere fact that money is to be given to the workers involved does not mean that they will work harder, more intelligently or be more nearly self-starters and very willing cooperators with management. The mere fact that we in management think that the wage earner should jump to do his best because he will by so doing get a profit split will make little difference in the attitude of most workers.

It is true that every worker would like to get more money —who wouldn't?—but there are many possibilities of increased income that anyone can get that few would accept. Few people will steal. The reward is thought of as far less than the penalties, both legal and personal. Few women are prostitutes. The reward is far less than the penalties, both legal and spiritual.

If a profit split is to create an incentive to the worker, he must feel that the advantages of the profit split to him are greater than the price that he must pay in effort and his other reactions necessary to get the split. The worker is human in all his reactions. There are profit sharing plans which fail because there is no relationship between the worker's efforts and his reward. He does not see where he is involved at all except that he has been paid some money by management for which management seemingly expects him to give up his ability to fight management under the present collective bargaining war.

The worker's reaction is completely human. If his future advantages are greater than what labor union domination will give him, he is tempted to go along with the proposal. The worker has no tie-in that he can see with many of the plans now tried. There is only the attempt by management to make him give up his union-given power for the offered bribe. Such a bribe he will question. He will be very suspicious that if he accepts the money and gives up his power over management, the bribe in later years will disappear and he will be left with neither power or money. He is very suspicious, since profit sharing has to him many suspicious angles.

It is obvious that the cause of failure in many cases is the lack of understanding by the worker of what management intends to do. Under such conditions, the worker is loath to expose himself to a program that may turn out badly for himself. He likes his present power. Therefore, the question that is always in the worker's mind is this; "Is management actually trying to put in a program that will be beneficial to me?" While past experience with many managements leaves the usual worker hard to convince, the job of instituting and operating a plan of successful incentive management is easy when we recognize and eliminate the causes of failure.

THREE CAUSES OF FAILURE

The reason why incentive plans fail are three. All are the result of the failure of leadership. These suspicions that usually cause failure may be greater or less in various cases because of past experience or because of strength of leadership of the unions involved. These difficulties may complicate the problem. They are not necessarily decisive.

The causes of failure of incentive plans are these:

First: Lack of understanding on the part of management of the human urges involved.

Second: Lack of honesty of purpose on the part of management.

Third: Lack of ability on the part of management to make the team and do its part to the extent that the worker accepts management as a teammate.

GULF BETWEEN MANAGEMENT AND WORKER
MUST BE BRIDGED

Let us consider these problems in order. If management is to get the best possible results from every person in the organization, the managers must understand the incentives that make men strive to accomplish a desired result. They must realize that a man's own will and desire control that man's actions. Nothing external to a man can make him strive to do better unless he really wants to do so.

Telling him he will get a part of the profit of the company, when the making of that profit is far beyond his power to control, will not stir him to action. He will like more money—who doesn't? He likes sunshine, but forecast fair weather tomorrow, he won't do anything about it. Management seems to him as much beyond his control as the weather. He sees his work as of very small importance compared to many things that have a far greater effect on profit than anything he can do.

He knows that an error of judgment by any one of many people can and does destroy many times more profit than his work can ever make. Those errors are numerous in his sight and, as far as he can see, the managers do not bother about them. He does not see himself as important to the company's success or profit. He cannot see where he has any necessary part in its operation. He could quit tomorrow and never be missed.

This is a part of the basic problem in getting acceptance by the worker of any incentive system. *He does not believe what management tells him,* or he does not understand completely.

There has always been a great gulf fixed between labor and management by long standing custom. This is because custom has always made manual labor the lowest form of employment, even when great skill is necessary. A white collar job which requires far less skill and ability is usually thought of as a higher position for those doing it.

The reason for this is the fact that all manual labor was previously done by slaves. No boss then would think of getting his hands dirty in such work. That division between classes still remains in our thinking, in spite of the skills often greater than some management jobs, now needed for such manual labor.

In any case, because of the gulf that has always existed between the manual worker and his boss there is great difficulty in getting the worker to understand the boss's attitude when he approaches the worker with any plan that will make for cooperation. The boss has always been considered a man apart, who has no community or common interest with the worker and cannot be accepted as a teammate except after considerable hesitation and soul searching. This gulf is hard to span.

As a matter of fact, the conditions that management now must deal with have radically changed. The worker and the boss are in very much different positions than they were a century ago. Cooperation now is a must. Cooperation a hundred years ago was not. Industry now and then are and were far from the same things.

Industry now has to do with many complicated machines operated by experts. A century ago, the worker produced by hand. Management of industrial operations now, because of this change in the character of these operations, makes cooperation far more of a must than before. No manager can boss the expert, whose skill and knowledge of his particular operation is far beyond those of the manager, in the old way that the feudal lord bossed his serfs. The possibilities of both production excellence and machine destruction is too much in the hands of the operator to do otherwise than court his cooperation. While this change may not be too obvious to all management, its truth is becoming understood and accepted progressively.

RESPECT AS CO-WORKER MUST BE EARNED THROUGH HONESTY

The second cause of failure is lack of honesty on the part of management. This usually is the result of the manager's ignorance of all the facts involved. No successful industrialist plans to be dishonest in any of his dealings. He could not be and have any chance for success in the operating of any industry. Honesty is the first essential in business, as all practical business men know. There is a dishonest result possible without a dishonest intention, however. Such dishonesty may take one or more of various forms.

The cutting of piecework prices when a man earns more than a certain amount is often done on the theory that the price is a mistake and was set too high. Cutting such a price does not disturb the boss, as he thinks it is honest to correct a mistake. The production worker knows differently, however. He has been cheated of his honest earnings and he knows it.

It does little good for management to try to justify its act by showing how far out of line the piecework price is. The man will still think he has been cheated, no matter how well justified in his action the boss thinks he is. Progress toward efficiency is out. The man will limit production from then on. He will also consider the boss a thief and will carry that idea to his grave with him.

Until recently, the worker has been in a very subordinate position compared to the boss. He had no rights that the boss had to respect. He, therefore, being human, will always suspect many things that actually are far from the thinking and planning of any boss but are very real to him. The boss should and must live up to the standard of honesty that the man sets for him if he is to be accepted as a team mate. Put another way, the man must accept the boss as his fellow worker without mental reservations. That is hard for the man to do when the boss has unquestioned authority and seems to act as he pleases with no limit set on his arbitrary orders.

Yet if there is to be successful incentive management, the wage earner absolutely must regard the boss as a trusted, reliable co-worker on and for the team. The boss can win this acceptance in only one way. He must deserve it. He must hold himself under sterner discipline; he must demand more of himself; he must try harder to measure up to higher standards of honesty, fair play and achievement; he must care more and work more earnestly for the team's victory than he expects anyone else to do. He is the leader and captain. His responsibility demands more from him. If he can't deliver, he should step out and let a better man take his place. His team work must be genuine. There is no other way for him to earn the respect and confidence of the wage earners who in actual fact are his co-workers, whether they know it or not. He must earn their trust and respect or he won't have them. He must have them if he is to do what he can do for his company, for American industry, for his country and the future.

MANAGEMENT MUST EARN ITS WAGES

The third reason for failure of present incentive plans is the failure of the manager to show the ability that makes him accepted by his co-workers as an adequately producing member on the team. The boss fails to make good on his job in the eyes of the men. To most managements, this may seem to be a silly statement. It is not. If we industrialists are to have real cooperation within our industries, the wage earner must feel that management has the ability to win in competition with all other managements.

As the wage earner sees it, profit depends on management's leadership far more than on his own efforts. The part that management plays does in fact determine to a very great extent whether his work can be of maximum profit or any profit at all. He knows this. In any profit sharing scheme, the manager must be able to hold up his end in the eyes of the worker if he is to be fully accepted as a star member of the team.

Any fair consideration of the facts will show that the worker is justified in his thinking. Management cannot expect cooperation or much interest unless the worker knows that it is doing an outstanding job. If management cannot or will not do this, there is little chance for teamwork. The man in the shop knows that his efforts probably would be wasted by top management's lack of ability or accomplishment. Top management must show that it can and does earn its wages by ability that is commensurate with its salary and responsibility.

This may be nonsense to old line management. It is a fact, however. Before starting on the new and unlimited enterprise of incentive methods, management should consider carefully if it wants to put itself under this pressure.

If profits are to be shared, maximum profits must be made if there is to be incentive from the sharing. Management's part in this plan is of prime importance, obviously. This the wage earner knows. He will not enthusiastically accept any management except one that can make good in an open and free for all competition. As a matter of fact, he should not accept less. Perhaps short hours, long vacations, less pressure and less need for accomplishment will be more attractive to many managements than meeting such a challenge to man's power of achievement.

NO FAILURE WHEN MANAGEMENT PAYS THE PRICE

These shortcomings in management in the application of incentive to their workers are the reasons for failure of all incentive systems that have failed. Where there is ability and willingness of management to pay the price in effort, honesty and understanding, there never has been and never will be any failure. All men respond in the same way to the same stimuli and always will.

The attitude of union labor leadership may at first make any approach to the men looking toward cooperation difficult, but it can never make it impossible. The honesty and ability of any management can always overcome such resistance. When it is overcome, the trust in a management that overcomes this resistance will make the standing of such management that much greater in the eyes of the men. Thus the opposition of labor union leadership is an incident, not a crisis. It should and can be taken in stride.

It is well to remember that incentive methods will be universal in American industry at some time if Americans are to remain free men. It is not a question merely of an incidental method of production of goods. The question for every manager is, "Will I put in a successful system soon enough to hold my place in top management of the only nearly free economy left on earth?" The time is ample to accomplish the job, but delay is dangerous, both because of present low efficiency and also lack of stable labor-management relationships, added to the political invasions of the economy. Union organization came fast. Incentive can come even faster.

<h2 style="text-align:center">WHERE SHOULD PROFITS GO?</h2>

There is another question in incentive management that requires careful consideration here. That is the profit split. What is done by management with the profits? It is a difficult thing to get the worker to go along enthusiastically with any plan of profit sharing unless he feels that the division of profit is a fair one. If increased profit made by greater cooperation and skill is largely given to the stockholder or top management, the worker will suspect he is being played for a sucker. He sees no contribution that the stockholder has made to the better result. He can therefore see no justification for the stockholder's large share of any saving resulting from labor management cooperation.

The worker will question also giving all of the increased profit to the consumer in lower prices, but he will have an entirely different reaction to such a move. He resents the greater income to the stockholder, but he understands and does not resent many reasons for lower prices to the consumer.

He may rather have all added saving come to himself, but he does not resent the consumer's split as he resents the increased profit to the stockholder. Lower prices make sense to him; higher dividends do not. He will always feel that the stockholder already gets too much for no effort.

Talk about risk capital is apt to leave the worker cold. He has bet and won or lost on the horses or dice; why should not the stockholder do the same? I am not arguing the rightness of this idea. I am only relating it. Make the worker a stockholder and he will then understand.

It is true that the worker will more or less willingly go along with a large split to the consumer on savings made by cooperation. Good management will have no great difficulty here. He will have real trouble if the stockholder is highly rewarded from any profit increase that incentive management gives when the worker knows the stockholder did nothing to produce such profit. Complete fairness and understanding on the part of management here is essential. Let management carefully put itself in the worker's shoes before making this decision.

Incentive profit that is not given to the worker or the customer should be used for expansion or new tools, rather than for greater dividends, if a proper dividend is being paid already. Expansion and better tools increase the efficiency of the operation. They make the company more stable as a profit maker. Such action will not be questioned by the worker if intelligently done.

This profit split suggested above will be justified in the minds of the workers even when they are stockholders, which most of them should be under incentive management. The worker regards stock he holds as an investment which he wants to be safe and to pay the income that he expected when he made the purchase. He did not and should not buy it as a gamble. He, of course, will be glad to get a windfall, but he is content to have a sound investment. It is made more sound by giving the customer more and more for less and less, and advancing the efficiency of the operation. It is not helped by paying larger dividends.

SUMMARY

The matter can be summed up in this way. Failure of incentive management stems from the wage earner's lack of trust in top management's honesty, ability and understanding. The worker is accustomed to these lacks in the usual industrial operation. Incentive management is not customary operation, however. The manager who expects to succeed in this new departure from custom must recognize wholly the new environment and atmosphere into which he and all those in the operation will be advancing. This is a challenge and a great opportunity. It will require new thinking, however. Management will, of necessity, have to take the lead here as in all other programs. That is what management is for. It cannot justify itself otherwise.

CHAPTER **X**

Security

Security has a new meaning in America since the advent of the New Deal. The word now means economic security and this has changed from a much desired reward for ability and application of work and thrift to an inherent human right. At least that is the belief of those who listen to the clap trap of many of the present politicians and so-called intellectuals. There are many who wish to believe even when they suspect the present and past dealers, both New and Fair. They suspect that they are fooling themselves but wouldn't it be wonderful if it were true, so why not believe the story, even if it is only a politician's promise and hope for the best?

THE VALUE OF INSECURITY

The human race has been made by insecurity. It was the threat and the reality of insecurity that developed the completely necessary latent abilities that now make it possible to produce some degree of security for at least part of the human race.

Any security was an impossibility for all human beings ten thousand years ago. Man then was no more secure than

158

is the rabbit today. He had enemies, both animal and man, who ruthlessly took his life either for the food his body supplied or the food he had in his possession. Life was a gamble that free humans played to the usually quiet and natural end.

Two hundred years ago sickness took a toll that we do not even know of now, so far has medical science advanced our security in health. Starvation then killed multitudes in famines. Famines now are practically unknown. Now the elements also have been almost subdued and put to the use of man. Nature now has been turned to advance security, not threaten it as it did previously. The only threat to man's security now is man himself. The competition of man with his fellows for the good things of life often seems to threaten his security. He therefore again tries to advance his security by taking it from others by force, legal or illegal, as he previously did.

This does not mean to imply in any way that security is not desirable. It is. Security of life and liberty, however, is far more essential to man than economic security. Given life and liberty, man can and should produce his economic needs. By fixing his attention on economic security, as the politician now does, man risks losing these more essential securities left unguarded.

THE PROBLEMS OF ECONOMIC SECURITY

To most Americans today, however, the word "security" means economic security. No one would say that this is not desirable. In regard to it, however, the problems are these: does the economic security obtained by one tend to adversely affect the economic or other securities of others? How can economic security be a properly distributed reward?

159

To begin with, there are many who receive economic security from others than themselves and properly so. The child receives such security from his parents. This is entirely natural and proper. However, we look askance at the parents who have more children than they have the ability to care for properly. We question their reliability. The old who cannot support themselves are cared for by the public in the absence of family or friends to care for them. This is perhaps necessary. However, we have more respect for the people who have had the foresight and character to earn economic security for their own future. We do not want to live in a country in which all older people are parasites on the younger ones. Such an economy would probably fail eventually, from the lack of self-reliance, responsibility and prudence that would be universal. The insane, the physically handicapped and the criminal are given security provided by the rest of the economy, and properly so. We do not want such people to increase in number, however. Such an increase, if carried far enough, would wreck the nation both from lack of supporters and deterioration of the race itself.

It is not into these catagories that those who now crave economic security wish to be placed. The present craver after security wants it as a right of citizenship. He expects it in the same way that he expects air to breathe and room to move about. He feels he should be born with security. When it is not forthcoming he turns to the politician for it. The politician will do anything that he thinks will be immediately popular. This reaction of the politicians to popular and selfish appeal was the fear that our Founding Fathers had, to a great degree, regarding our government. Madison wrote: "All democracies destroy the economy and themselves. They are as short in their lives as they are violent in their deaths."

The Constitution as at first adopted guarded against the ill-considered will of the masses by providing an Electoral College, to pick a proper man as President. The Senate also was elected by the state governments, not by the voter. Both these safeguards, by custom or amendment to the Constitution, now have been eliminated. The result has not been too encouraging so far. The dangers prophesied by Macaulay, Madison and all others who had carefully considered the matter, are evident now or are in the making, as our drift to Socialism so plainly shows. The question that vexes any thinking man in the light of this drift is, can representative government succeed? Can the power to exploit the minority be safely given to the majority? The answers so far given by our experience here are far from encouraging.

THE PRODUCTIVE SUPPORT THE NON-PRODUCTIVE

The problem of security is not that it is not desirable, but what happens when government takes it from Peter to give to Paul, rather than letting Paul earn it for himself if he can. There is the rub. If government is to guarantee to all everything that each should get to live a desirable life, we would have a government that could not long survive. Robbing productive Peter to support unproductive Paul has always ruined every government that has tried it, from ancient Rome to modern Germany. The reasons are obvious. Meanwhile, Americans seemingly are willing to take such security with the consequent loss of freedom. Any right thinking person values freedom far more than security. In fact, desire for freedom was why America was founded. Our forebears wanted to rid themselves of security to gain freedom. That was why the Pilgrim Fathers came to these shores.

The security as now promised under the various deals, New and Fair, has only one thing wrong with it. That is that it is given to the seeker by government after being taken from someone else who has produced it for himself. This causes all the trouble. The producer produced it for himself. If it is taken away from him and given to the non-producer, two things happen. The producer will quit producing since he is being "played for a sucker" by the non-producer by the power of government. This will make him one more seeker of government-given security for someone else to support. Secondly, the non-producer will be assured by the gift security that work is a mistake. He will do no more of it. In this way both the previous producer and non-producer are continuing charges of the taxpayer.

POLITICAL ECONOMIC SECURITY LEADS TO SLAVERY

It is obvious that before long there will be too many supported for the dwindling number of supporters to support. That brings the crisis. Government must step in then and make at least some of the developed loafers work. That is called a totalitarian state. It is also called slavery. That is when individual freedom goes and government takes over. We Americans still say we do not want that, in spite of the fact that we are anxious to go in the direction that can only end in such totalitarianism.

It is well to remember now that there will be no objection, when we do trade freedom for security, to government taking over, since the people will have deteriorated to the extent that they will be glad to trade their freedom to anyone who will assume their responsibilities for their security. Their manhood will have disappeared. They will have rotted out as has every other civilization from the beginning of history under the same conditions. Freedom will be a memory.

SECURITY MUST BE EARNED

Economic security is desirable. Any normal person in America can obtain it by effort. When so obtained, it becomes a boon. Let it be the goal that will be obtained as one of the rewards in incentive management. Let it be a proper reward for excellence in the worker, be he sweeper or president, or anyone between. Under no conditions, however, should the loafer be allowed to live on the efforts of the worker. That immediately upsets all natural incentive.

The problem of economic security for the unfortunate, the insane, the old and the loafer is a problem that cannot be easily solved. So far, the attitude of most people is to cover all with charity no matter why they want such help. We do not want to face up to the problem and solve it properly. We are not sufficiently interested to put the necessary effort into the problem. We therefore tax the worker sufficiently to take care of all and sundry who will ask sufficiently often for help.

This is the easy way out, but it is national suicide, as all history shows. It is the usual indication of dry rot in the character of the people. It is the forerunner of the conditions which force dictatorship. It is the indication and warning that loss of individual liberty is on the way and that the end of that civilization is approaching.

Every nation that has disappeared has gone through that same sequence and with the same result: first, softening of the people's ambition with its lessening of incentive; second, increase in the number of people who fail to try to develop themselves or their latent abilities; third, helplessness of such people to the point that destitution faces them; fourth, public support for all who ask for it since they cannot or will not support themselves; fifth, still further destitution of the economy as fewer will work both from exploitation to care for the careless and also from the same softening process that caused the problem; sixth, taking over of such a nation by a virile race which has not yet gone soft.

If economic security is a gift, neither the recipient nor the nation providing it can long survive. This does not mean that economic security is not a prize of great worth. It cannot be given, however, it must be earned. Only so can it be safely won or long continued. This problem of earned security is fundamental in incentive management. It is a fundamental part of its philosophy.

INCENTIVE MANAGEMENT CAN PROVIDE CONTINUOUS EMPLOYMENT

The maximum efficiency in industry cannot be obtained without producing job security as a by-product for all workers. The salary worker already usually has security of employment. He is seldom thrown out on the street when business slackens. That only happens to the hourly worker who can least afford unemployment. Obviously, if the salary worker can be continuously employed, the hourly worker can be also, under proper understanding and handling of the problem. Let us approach the problem in this light.

How can we assure security of employment to all workers under incentive management? How can continuous employment be obtained?

Unemployment results in industry when the product which is being made is not sold. Yet there is always an unlimited market for any useful product if the price is low enough. We can conclude therefore that if the price is reduced sufficiently during slack times the product will be sold and employment will continue, and a boom will result.

Price reductions can be made by reducing wages, increasing efficiency or running at a loss. Incentive management should not plan to operate at a loss. Therefore, price reductions should be obtained by increasing efficiency or reducing wages. Both are generally necessary. It should be borne in mind, however, that when wages are reduced the reduction should affect all in the organization. Those who can best afford it, that is, top management, should be willing and anxious to take the largest cut in income. Only so can the greatest cost reduction be made. No team can work together without all doing their proper part in winning the game.

Incentive management always recognizes that any cost can be reduced by any amount that the skill and imagination of the producers will provide. Cost reduction can be made without end. We only need to look at the progress that has been made in industry in the last generation to prove that such progress can and should be continuous. Cost reduction during a slump to increase the market is therefore a normal and natural development. It is also obviously most needed then and hence will be a source of great incentive with proper understanding. When both labor and management recognize and fulfill their responsibility in cost reductions, there will be little unemployment. Prices will be so low that the buyer will buy. That is what eventually ends all slumps.

If an industry continually reduces its cost and selling price, it will have as a result an ever-expanding market, not a slump. Slumps will have little effect on such a business. Any slump will merely inspire greater progress in such a company's normal program.

To further insure continuous employment, industry should have available additional lines which can be added to its standard products if and when needed. These may be products that are used as their raw materials, these products being ones that are usually bought outside. They may be, also, end products for other than normal markets that are not usually covered. Export can be one of these which under proper conditions can be made a limitless market. There is no end to the market when a better and better product is sold at continuously lower prices.

WORKERS EQUALLY RESPONSIBLE FOR CONTINUOUS EMPLOYMENT

While it is management's responsibility to plan for the future and guard against what will cause trouble, it is not solely the responsibility of management to get the answer. The wage earner under incentive management has a great responsibility also. When the slump comes, threatening unemployment, all in the incentive-managed organization must rise to it. It is, of course, management's job to chart the plan for continuing employment in such a crisis, but it is the worker's responsibility to do his part in quick cost reduction. All in the organization may have new demands made on them to meet the crisis. All must rise to the occasion. Incentive management produces an organization that will and can so rise.

Management's plan will call for more efficiency to make lower costs and prices. All will respond to the call. Management may need new skills to produce new products. All will respond strongly and put forth their utmost efforts, because incentive management produces such a spirit.

Incentive management produces better and smarter men because it develops their latent abilities, left dormant by usual management. During a crisis produced by a slump, these developed men can and will show their greater stature by answering the challenge in ways that the usual organization cannot do and could not even imagine.

It is obvious that the bickering, featherbedding and lack of cooperation introduced into labor-management relationships by collective bargaining would be fatal to any such program as outlined above. Such cooperation is now impossible with a Lewis or a Murray.

SLUMPS WILL BE MINIMIZED

As is true of all progress in any direction, each step not only is good in its own results, but it also encourages and promotes other progress. An illustration of this will be seen in the result of guaranteeing employment to the industrial worker. The fact that the worker has the assurance of being continuously employed will mean that there will be fewer ups and downs in his buying. He will have no need of such variation. Because of this, there will be fewer slumps. What slumps there are will be less deep. In the same way, there will be few booms. Normal economic life will be a boom. Whatever other booms there may be, will be of less duration and also much more restrained. There will be small encouragement for anything except continuous progress of the economy.

OTHER AIDS TO CONTINUOUS EMPLOYMENT

In approaching the problems that guaranteed employment introduces, management has at hand several aids in getting a solution. It can vary to a considerable extent the weekly hours of labor. Suppose management concludes that thirty-two hours (four days at eight hours) per week is a minimum work week needed. It could go to fifty hours a week as a maximum six-day week. Here is a variation in capacity of thirty-six percent. This of itself will produce a cushion that will greatly reduce the monetary responsibility of the guarantee. The worker, however, will still be well protected against unemployment. In periods of low demand, management can also build up its stocks which will help it over a peak demand. In periods of slump, costs are lower. Whatever is made for stock at such a time will eventually be sold at a greater profit than production made during periods of peak demand.

All companies have at all times the problem of product development. This can be speeded up at times of slump since more help is then available to promote such programs.

New methods in production can be worked out in slack times much more easily than when the going is fast. New tools can be planned for and their use developed at slack periods much better than when production is at the top. There are many helpful programs that can be developed during slump conditions. Use them.

SLUMPS CAN BE AN ASSET

The chief threat to continuous employment is perhaps the feeling on the part of management that a slump is going to last forever and be the end of all things. It feels that no such slump ever happened before and that it is in the midst of a new problem on which no previous experience is available. Many managements feel at such times that they have a crisis to handle rather than an obvious and routine problem which has occurred in about the same cycle from the beginning of the industrial revolution. They are very apt to read into the slump many dangers which do not or need not exist.

If we will consider history, we shall see that in all

industrial history there have been booms and slumps. If the industrial manager will consider such industrial history, he will see that he is handling a routine matter only. His problems may be different from those of normal business, but problems of management are always different. If they were not, there would be no reason for the manager. The only reason he is there is to handle the unusual.

Slump problems are different but they should, because of their difference, be very helpful to the manager. If he will use the slump as a trial period to help weed out his own and his organization's bad habits that a boom always introduces, he will find the slump very helpful. If he will use the slump as a testing period of himself and his men, both he and they will develop new abilities that can come only during a slump since such pressures come at no other time.

Industrial history has always been plagued by booms and slumps. All those who took both in their stride came through them with progress being made in both conditions. It is obvious that booms and busts therefore should be expected as a matter of routine and should be so met. They should be capitalized, not feared.

There should be another principle obvious to the modern manager. If business should continue on a dead level at all times, stagnation would be much more usual than it is now. We must have the stirring effect of crises to shake us out of our rut of lethargy. Any unusual occurrence always has some good results in it. It is safe to say that if every company should have a fire or an earthquake that would completely destroy its plant, so that a new start would be necessary every twenty years, there would be enormously greater progress and prosperity in industry.

Change is the life blood of the industrial system of

free enterprise. Anything that forces change in our thinking can be made a great boon. Stagnation is the greatest threat to success in industry and man. Change in our industrial pace is one way to encourage progress and combat stagnation. Booms and busts are good in much they do if we will but meet them as we should.

ONLY MANAGEMENT CAN AND MUST GIVE JOB SECURITY

It is management's duty to make the worker secure in his job. Only so can the worker feel that he can develop the skill and apply the imagination that will do his job more efficiently, without fear of unemployment from the progress he makes. If a man is threatened with loss of his job by a better way of producing, which eliminates the need for his service, he cannot do his best. Don't punish progress, as our income tax laws do.

Only management can protect the worker in matters of this kind. The fact that the usual management will fire the worker when he runs out of work has had more to do with production limitation than any other circumstance. No man will willingly work to throw himself out of his job, nor should he.

This attitude that the unprotected worker has toward progress will limit his usefulness to the company. There may even be no conscious effort on the part of the worker to hold back progress. However, in his subconscious mind there is the fear of the consequences that come from job elimination unless there is assurance that if the job he is doing is eliminated for any reason there will be another one equally attractive awaiting him. Only so can any man cooperate to the full both by mind and body in the progress so necessary in a free economy.

170

UNEXPECTED PROGRESS WILL RESULT

This whole idea of guaranteed employment is not only a boon to the worker. As a result of his safety in his job, it is a much greater boon to the progress of industrial operation. As is always true, a right principle, properly applied, will not only answer the problem in hand, it will also promote other progress unthought of at the time of its adoption.

Guaranteed employment will change the whole approach to the job that both men and management now have. It is not just a guarantee that eliminates the man's fear of the future, it also, by so doing, opens new opportunities to great industrial progress.

A great difficulty that holds back much incentive in industry is our wrong approach to the problem resulting from our lack of understanding of our workers.

The usual manager does not try for the interest of his men. He thinks of them as merely workers paid to do the bidding of management. He does not see them as members of a team playing a championship game. He does not think a game can be arranged.

Few managers even consider the possibility of any need to make the job that his men do something of which they should or can be proud. The position of the men therefore in their own minds is that of paid servants who do only what they are told by their boss. That makes work that can be an inspiration under proper conditions, a hated routine that leads only to frustration and continual bickering, instead of progress. This eliminates any possibility of a game spirit. This stops all interest that should be found in the work. That makes work drudgery and hence hateful.

The stimulus of competition is absent in such occupation.

171

The fear of being outdistanced by our fellows is lacking. The spur of work of importance well done is lost. The possibility of rising above our fellows by means of skill or imagination is not there. Why should anyone try to make the operation efficient? Both the incentives and fears that should exist are absent. It is only to be expected that efficiency will be at a low ebb and decreasing as boredom and frustrations increase.

A NEW DIRECTION FOR MANAGEMENT

Perhaps management will feel that I am pointing to an impossible standard. That is not true. What is shown is a new direction in which management's thinking and planning must go and eventually will go. No one feels that the continual bickering we have now under enforced collective bargaining can be either satisfactory or permanent. There is certain to be a change made. It can be new progress or it can be regression back to the pattern of socialism, stagnation and dull submission to the state. It must be one or the other. Time and man do not stand still.

Incentive management points a new direction. It uses the new competitions and rewards inherent in this system so that the natural aspirations of man will be naturally used. Man will grow and be content. That is a great step forward, not because the forces brought into play by incentive management are new; they are as old as man. It is a step forward because it inspires the changeless, natural aspirations of man. It makes man what his Maker intended and what he aspires to be.

In passing, it is well to note that acceptance of the leadership of management under incentive management is much less difficult than under the usual collective bargaining battle. Management then is also far more attractive and satisfying to the manager.

Security, as given by government, is an end for which many ignorant people hope. So far it has made political preferment automatic. It is, however, as we will find after more experience, in the same general category as several stiff drinks of whiskey; the drinker feels at the time much better than he ever felt without it. If this feeling could be permanent, whiskey would be the world's greatest boon. Unfortunately, the pleasant first reaction is only temporary and the total effect is far worse than going without.

Security is like good health. It must be deserved and earned, under which conditions it is man's greatest boon. It can't be stolen continually or delivered as a gift. Incentive management makes security a deserved and a very real reward for those who have earned it. It then is not a gift to the beneficiary taken from the earnings of others.

We will find, as did our Founding Fathers, that liberty is priceless. Let us so recognize it before it is gone. There is no chance to trade security back for liberty after we have bartered our liberty away for security and have found it an impossible bargain.

CHAPTER XI

How Big Is Too Big?

When starting its operation, any manufacturing company will usually have a plan as to what products it will produce. Manufacturing plants are generally started with that particular end in view. If success is achieved, there will always be the temptation to expand into new lines of production. What these new lines will be is a problem, the answer to which is one of the most important that the industrialist will ever have to face. This decision will largely determine the success of the company.

The reason why this question is so important is because no new line of production can be added to any plant's operation without affecting the cost of all the other products then being made. The real question is not whether a new line shall or shall not be added; that question is relatively easy. The real problem is accurately measuring the interference that the new products will exert on the production of the products which are standards. Along with this is the second question, will the new line as it can be made with the facilities at hand be attractive to the customer in competition with the competitive products already on the market? If all the facts on both these points

174

are objectively considered, the decision would generally be, not to make the new product. Instead, perfect what is now being built.

NEW PRODUCTS AFFECT COSTS OF STANDARD PRODUCTS

The manufacturing of any new product in any plant cannot help but affect the cost of products then being made by the same organization in the same plant. Not only that, the effect cannot be accurately measured. Therein is the danger involved. The time and attention of the top executives will always, to a great extent, be put on any new product. Since that is true, their attention will be taken from the products already in production. If the new product is the center of attraction for these men, as it must be, obviously the lines already in production will have relatively less attention. Because of this, the reductions in cost, the progress in perfecting the new methods of production of these products will, to that extent, cease.

This elimination of progress often will cost more than any possible profit that the new contemplated lines can give. Not only that, when once management starts flitting to one new line, there will be the tendency to continue to flit to some still newer product with progressively greater stagnation in the progress of what is being produced.

It is obvious that success of any manufacturing company depends on making its products progressively better and more economical than competition goods. If this progress stops for any great length of time, competition will overtake and pass the company's efforts.

No company can spread its efforts without lessening the effort on each product produced. This usually will be true even if additional people are taken on in the effort to maintain full attention to all activities. Top management's attention, which to a great extent determines how and where progress will be made, cannot do otherwise than direct itself to the new products with the lessening attention to ones already produced.

It is well to state here that if management knew the costs and the complications involved in the new, and, at first glance, attractive devices, it would not be attracted. Competition is looking at the same attractions, but often with experience that is more complete. Competition is awake and will produce any product that actually has unusual attractions. That is what competition is.

It is well therefore to conclude that there are no products that in themselves have any possibilities that competition has not exploited. If your organization is to make them successfully, it is necessary that the new product as produced be better than what has been made before. That is not always easy.

NEW THINKING NECESSARY

There are no gold nuggets lying around for anyone to pick up. The point is, that to be successful in making established products, new thinking must be done. New thinking about a new product usually seems easier. This is an illusion. The fact is that creative thinking about the present product is easier because you know that product more thoroughly. Progress therefore will be easier even if it seems at first to be less exciting.

It is necessary to have a definite policy on this matter and follow it. There will be many temptations to change that must be resisted. The appearance of some one else's backyard always seems better than our own. It actually is not as good as it seems, however. Our salesmen will often bring in orders for special products which are departures from our standard line, and seem very attractive because the price they bring seems high. These orders will be either the result of the enthusiasm of the buyer, who thinks he has a new brainwave that will revolutionize the future, or the cleverness of the salesman who has suggested a new departure, believing he has a brainwave himself.

Again, the policy adopted must be founded on a well-considered plan that is far removed from guessing or chance or a temporary expedient. The industrialist is dealing with fundamentals in these cases and a decision based on fundamentals must be made. If we follow any will-of-the-wisp we will get the usual will-of-the-wisp penalty.

MUST DO BETTER JOB THAN COMPETITION

What are the factors that should determine the decision in these cases? The first factor, and the one that is of primary importance in making the decision is, "Can these new products be made more efficiently than the competition which is now established?" In other words, "Can we make this a better product at a lower price?" Secondly, "Can the new product, if we make it, be made a natural expansion of our present activity? Is this direction also the best direction in which to grow?"

It is obvious that if the present plant and organization cannot make the product better or more economically than it can be made by competition, there can be little chance of success. If a basic change is necessary in plant or personnel to make the new product, then in effect a new company is being started. If the job is to be done by a new organization of men and plant, then the problems are the same as those involved in starting any other new company. It will give any executive a proper point of view

177

to approach the matter in this way. His thinking then will be based on fundamentals.

If it is obvious that a new organization for doing the job would not be justified, a very great likelihood exists that putting the same new production into the present plant, with the present organization, will be equally difficult to justify.

Properly fitting new products into the plant and into the abilities of the organization is a task of the industrialist that has generally received far too little attention compared to its importance.

The chief reason for failure of industries is their inability to meet competition. This failure usually stems from the attempt of management to spread the company's abilities too thin. We cannot expect to do a better job than competition unless we are more expert at doing it. We therefore must specialize and concentrate if we are to exert expert ability. We should not expect to win a hundred yard dash merely because we are good shotputters. No other field is actually as green as we think it is when we look at it from afar.

DIFFUSION OF EFFORT BREEDS INCOMPETENCE

The primary reason for failure in industry is incompetence, often the result of diffusion of effort. We see continually the successful concern and the unsuccessful side by side. They produce the same products for like consumers under seemingly the same conditions. One succeeds; the other fails. Why? The answer is generally found in the relative ability of management in its direction of the operations in the two concerns. The expert will always beat the less expert.

All managers have ability. Some have more than others.

If the manager of small ability sticks to a job that does not go beyond this ability, he will succeed. If he goes beyond it, he is almost sure to fail, since his relatively small ability disappears in competition, unless it is concentrated.

The wrecks in industry are usually the organizations that spread out too much. They were not sufficiently expert in their jobs to meet competition. They went beyond their expert field. They tried to do the things in which they had insufficient expert ability. They thought of ease of selling instead of cost reduction of their product as their goal.

SIZE SHOULD BE CONTROLLED BY MANAGERIAL ABILITY

The above is the measure in the expansion of any industry. Expansion can be done safely only when expert ability is available to make a better product at a lower price than competition. Not only that, it should only be done when that expert ability is available after the jobs already in process are being done successfully in competition.

The proper size of any manufacturing company can be stated as follows: no manufacturing organization should be larger than one which can be sufficiently understood so as to be expertly directed by its manager. Size, complication and managerial ability are interdependent.

It is obvious that proper size of any manufacturing organization is therefore a variable, depending on the ability of the leader. It is obvious that the man who has greater ability can operate a larger and more involved organization than the man of less ability. The amount of effort that the leader willingly puts into the company will also have an effect on how large the company can be successfully. Expert knowledge can be acquired in any direction if leadership will strive enough to gain it. Industrial leadership can grow in the same way that any other skill can grow. Leadership in industry is no different from any other skill that man develops. Its development depends on the incentive and ambition of the leader as well as on his latent ability. Development of latent ability can take place in any man.

There is another factor that bears on the subject. Some activities can be larger because of their simplicity. A tool and die shop needs much abler management than does a warehouse of the same ground area. Size depends on ability, of course, but also on the complication of the operation handled. Correct size is the ratio between available ability and the complexity of the operation.

There is a limit at any given time to the ability of the individual. Therefore, there is a complexity of industry beyond which any management, no matter how able, will fail. The converse of this is equally true. If any unsuccessful organization should cut down its field to one commensurate in size and complexity with the ability and knowledge of its management, such an enterprise would usually succeed.

SIMPLIFY THROUGH SPECIALIZATION

There are many ways that have been tried to overcome this handicap of limited ability of management and its limitation of size. One is departmentalization of a company by which separate products are made in different departments or separate plants. Another is division into independent production units, which is something of the same nature. Either expedient overcomes some of the difficulties; neither is entirely successful.

It is true that dividing a company into units which are autonomous, theoretically, eliminates the need for over-all understanding of all operations by a single management. However, no organization can be split up into units so that each unit is completely independent. Management must still determine the overall policy no matter how much it wishes to give complete authority to a division manager.

In all companies there must be over-all financing, over-all labor policies and over-all manufacturing philosophies. The primary thinking of the top management will still be controlling. Full understanding of fundamentals is still necessary by top management. Splitting up into autonomous units will not answer all managerial problems of great size. It does, however, mitigate them.

The General Motors Company has been most successful in dividing its activity into units. Each unit is largely autonomous. To the extent that such unit is independent, General Motors eliminates the difficulty of the complicated organization dominated from the top.

This concentration of production of many things in one company, however, also has certain advantages. The publicity advantage of great size is helpful. The development of unified research has great possibilities of progress. The development of certain manufacturing methods that could not be developed in a small organization can be done by large organizations. The difficulty is that the people in the management of each of the units are often still held in grooves by top management, out of which the subordinate manager will not, and probably cannot, escape. This restricts his outlook and by so doing also restricts his growth. Henry Ford could not have been the leader he was had he not built and directed the Ford Motor Company. This tremendous responsibility developed him. A lesser responsibility, such as being a superintendent under some management, would never have done so.

There is no doubt that the problems of the industrial leader are most difficult. He must not only deal successfully with things, he must also deal successfully with people. He must deal with people not only as his customers, but also as workers in his plant. There is no other job that is as involved as that of industrial management. Those who succeed are not usually properly evaluated by people generally. They do not see in the successful industrial leader a genius, a man in a million, a champion who has successfully met the challenge of thousands of others who were striving for such a top place in our economy.

WHAT SHALL WE MAKE?

There are two general philosophies that can be followed in answering this question of, "What shall we make?" The one is to make one thing and do it outstandingly well; so well that competition cannot meet it. The other is to make all types of product in a certain field. The first plan makes an outstanding product, constantly improving in quality and lowering in cost and selling price. The second plan makes distribution easier and often cheaper when the making of many products is combined with the fame that the resulting size may give the company.

There are advantages in both programs. A parallel case is the specialist and the general practitioner in medicine. It is well to note that the progress that is made in medicine mostly comes from the specialist. The general practitioner has a greater area of usefulness and experience. His patients call on him for all medical services, while they go to the specialist for the answer to one specific problem. Both have their usefulness.

182

The industrialist can go in either direction. He can be a general practitioner and serve a group in all their needs in a large field, or he can specialize in a certain product and make it better than any general practitioner can do it. He can be the outstanding expert in a certain field or he can supply all related products in some field. Both are useful and both can succeed when properly approached.

FOLLOW A PLAN

The decision must be made and a plan followed to its logical conclusion. Where most industrialists fail who do fail is in starting to follow one path and then diverging over into the other. There is the danger and the danger is real.

What has been said above should not be construed to mean that manufacturing methods should ever be static. Such a conclusion is completely at variance with the policy of successful manufacturing as outlined herein. Change in methods of production must be continuous. The point made is that the plan of the operation once started must not be changed unless the whole program is adjusted to the new plan. It is not possible to change from a specialist to a general practitioner and then back again without a severe penalty resulting.

Perhaps the following will illustrate the above point. Suppose we form a company to make automobile bumpers. If we are successful, we must make the bumper good enough and sell it at a low enough price to have the automobile makers buy it in competition. Suppose now our salesman comes back with an order for windshield wipers from the same company to which we sell the bumpers. We must at that time determine what our policy is to be. Are we going to remain the bumper manufacturer, or are we going into the new line of windshield wipers? The future of the company rests on our decision.

The problem is not one of making windshield wipers or bumpers per se. The problem is: shall we distract our minds with this new problem when we have, or should have, a hundred suggested ways in which we can make better and cheaper bumpers? Where can we use our abilities to the best advantage? We know the problems in the production of bumpers. We do not know the problems of making windshield wipers, and, hence, our outlook for manufacturing them is probably too rosy. Not only that, we must get new ideas if we are to go into this new field. We must also get new tools since the present ones will not make the new product. The greatest problem is this: who in the organization, as it now exists, can take over the new job without interfering with our present progress in production of bumpers?

Of course, there would be no one available if the present organization is properly organized and directed in making the present product. If we are to make windshield wipers, new people must be taken on and organized to do the job. The difficulty comes in the reduction of attention to the present job of making bumpers that will result in top management if we are to make windshield wipers. How much less progress in bumper manufacturing will result from this making of windshield wipers?

The answer to this question cannot be a rule. That is obvious. The closest approach to the answer is that present production will be affected greatly if we take on the new product.

This illustrates one of the problems that the industrialist must solve if he is to succeed. He cannot expect that the new line will be any more profitable than his present line unless made more efficiently. When products are equally efficiently made, related products have about the same profit. That is the result of our system of free enterprise which regulates profit by the efficiency of the producer.

MAKE INSTEAD OF BUY

There is another way that branching out in industry can be taken with less danger and often more profit than by taking on new lines. That way is producing rather than buying more of the materials used in making the present product. Here is often a very profitable program since it will produce a greater scope for the organization, reduce costs, and still not require a new end product for the company.

There is increasing pressure in this direction because of changing economic forces. The selling price of any product is cost of material, plus labor, plus overhead, plus distribution cost, plus profit, plus tax. This total is generally at least twice the bare cost of labor and material. This margin tends to increase as taxation and necessary profit because of taxes increases. Profit must be more now than prior to the New Deal. Taxation makes money for expansion or replacement available safely only from profit of the company. Taxes take more than half the profit of industry, therefore industrial profit must be at least three times greater than in the days of lower taxes.

Because of these facts, most organizations can profitably make many things they previously bought. If the product is made as efficiently as the seller now makes it, at least half of the present cost of such product can be saved by making it. This is the first direction to go if expansion of manufacturing is considered. There is far more profit here generally than in putting a new product on the market. Most manufacturers add only a small part of the productive work necessary in making their finished product. The materials that all manufacturers buy are the finished products that are made by others. The final product is the accumulation of these efforts. There are many advantages, therefore, in going back further in producing those materials which were formerly bought to make any finished product.

If we are good manufacturers, we can often make these products as efficiently as our suppliers. If we do, we will save their distribution overhead, all of the sales cost, all taxes which were part of their costs, and all of the profit that we had formerly paid to these other manufacturers.

There is still a second possibility in such substitutions. We may find that when we make the product formerly procured from our supplier, that it can be redesigned in shape or in material that will make it not only cheaper, but also better for our purpose. When we buy such products from the outside, we are very apt to accept what is listed as standard because nothing else is offered. When we make the product for ourselves, we can usually find changes that did not occur to us before that will make the product so produced by ourselves better or cheaper or both. Such possibilities of substitution have great usefulness, both in cost reduction and exciting new vision in our operation.

If we are thinking of going into new lines of endeavor, this direction should get first and very careful study. The chances of success here are much greater than in making a new finished product.

As an example of the above program, if we are bumper manufacturers, perhaps we can form the steel from the billet in making a bumper instead of buying the finished strip for the purpose. This may effect a large saving. Perhaps we can do our own plating instead of farming it out. Perhaps we can develop new shapes that will save material, as well as make a better bumper. In general, it is best to exhaust all our ideas in these directions and on our supplier's products before reaching out for new products that we will offer to the public.

SPECIALIST HAS BETTER CHANCE FOR SUCCESS

Success in industry is founded on doing a useful job at a lower cost than anyone has yet done it. The diversifier will have a harder time doing that on his many products than the specialist.

There is limitless progress to be made in the design and manufacture of any product as all industrial history shows. The specialist is the one most likely to make such progress. The specialist will always have the greatest chance to concentrate on the development of his product, his methods, or his materials. The diversifier has too many problems in everyday operation to develop many of these opportunities.

It is well to think of this problem in the same way as one would plan an expedition of exploration. What the party has in the way of equipment and experience should determine where it can go. Certainly if we have only tropical clothes, we should not plan a trip to the Arctic regions. If our operations are chemical, we should not branch off into mechanical products.

There is too much indecision in much of our planning in these matters. Getting an order often upsets policies that should be controlling. This should never be allowed. Orders are not hard to get if we build a better product at a lower cost and selling price. If we make the ease of getting an order the controlling factor, we may not be around long to either get or fill orders. Therefore, follow the plan that is determined by your ability and equipment. Only so can real progress be made.

IS LARGE SIZE GOOD OR BAD?

There is much discussion by the public generally as to the proper size of a manufacturing company. What should be the proper size? In the minds of the public now great size itself is suspect. This is the natural urge of the "small" to tear down the "big" so as to make the large less important. This is a fundamental urge in all men.

It is not the plan of the writer to discuss size here, other than its effect on efficiency. There has already been much discussion of size in the press and by government. The snap judgment of many is that great size in private industry is dangerous monopoly, and therefore wrong, but enormous size in government monopoly is good.

No one who knows the facts and considers them objectively agrees with such a conclusion. History and our experience in America as well as in the rest of the world, shows that the abuses of big government are much worse and far more dangerous to mankind than any possible abuses by industrial organizations in a free competitive economy. Monopoly in private enterprise eventually destroys itself. It always dies of dry rot, just as does the individual who does not have to try.

This is one fact that all history has proved completely. Big government unfortunately does not destroy itself. It destroys its citizens instead.

There is always a new organization that takes the place of the industrial monopoly that rots out. Such disappearance gives new opportunity to the economy. Large government, however, destroys the economy.

Private monopoly is subject to law and investigation. Government monopoly is not. Theoretically, Congress can investigate and control government. Actually as we now see, it can do neither. Look at the difference of opinion regarding all governmental monopolies such as the Tennessee Valley Authority. The believers in big government tell us that it has cut power costs. Those who believe in private enterprise say that its costs are far above those in private enterprise. Obviously, no definite facts can be forthcoming, since government keeps its own records in its own way.

Laws that will restrict industry in its desire to expand healthily will not solve the question of monopoly. There is much more danger to the economy in present governmental restriction than from industrial monopoly. Monopoly can be best controlled by little law and much competition. No monopoly can stand up in the American system of a free enterprise in a free country, where any industry is allowed to make its own way up if the obvious abuses are stopped by law.

Competition introduces many problems to free people. As competition increases, fewer can succeed. For example, there are far more successful players in the minor leagues in baseball than in the majors. In the same way, there are many who can run a corner grocery; however, there was only one Henry Ford. He could hold the marvellous pace that made the Ford Company famous for only part of his life.

INTERFERENCE WITH INDUSTRY INCREASES
COST TO CONSUMER

The greatest threat to American industry and to America, (since America depends on its industry to keep it the dominant nation it now is) is the pitiful lack of understanding of industry. Few understand what makes free enterprise succeed. Because of that, there are many obstacles placed in the way of the industrialist by government and the people generally that needlessly hamper operation and efficiency. Perhaps it would be more accurate to say it this way: there are many restrictions placed in the way of the industrialist that needlessly increase the difficulty of operation so that he can function only at greatly reduced efficiency and, hence, at greatly increased prices for the product that the public must pay.

Present labor legislation illustrates this fact. The effect of our labor laws is to largely increase interference with industrial operation. This does not benefit the wage earner as supposed. He gets more dollars only, not more meat.

These regulations mean continuous bickering regarding real or imagined grievances. These require the time and attention of much of top management which should be doing things of real importance and benefit to the American economy. It cannot, however, since the law makes the union dominant and if grievances are not handled to the satisfaction of the union management, output stops or greatly decreases. As of now, management cannot manage. The consumer pays the cost of this in continually higher prices.

I am fully aware that there are grievances that need attention. The fact is, however, that most grievances are gripes that have no basis in fact or justice. If either party to any industrial operation is given the power, it can have a continuous string of grievances that will interfere with production and will never end. That tendency is fundamental in man. It is only necessary to see the bickering between husband and wife when both are tired to see that fact illustrated. Did any teacher satisfy all students in any school? Do all people agree on anything, be it religion, government or baseball? Can anyone outside of an insane asylum expect that with the present power that labor union leaders have, they will feel that conditions in industry are satisfactory? The answer is obvious. However, in the face of these facts, the industrialist is by present law forced to placate every whim of the worker, plus the attacks from government, plus manufactured grievances by the leader of the union. Is it any wonder that costs have skyrocketed? It is well to note here that the industry affected does not pay for this scandalous waste. The consumer of course does, as he does all other costs of all kinds, when he buys any product.

DO WE WANT FREEDOM?

This whole matter of union power over the wage earner and industrial management, which is now sponsored by our government, needs careful consideration if we are not to be forced into totalitarian control of all people. This problem is part of the question, "Can representative government in the United States succeed and remain?" Stated another way, "Will the average person exercise his responsibility as a citizen of a representative government so that the freedom on which our future depends will continue?" Our experience under Roosevelt and Truman answers this question with a definite NO. The majority of the voters cannot or will not produce a government that can continue. This majority cannot or will not think governmental problems through. They will instead follow the self-seeking demagogue. The experience of the last twenty years illustrates these facts.

The wage earner must by representative government law in most cases belong to a union to be able to hold a job. In belonging he gives up his freedom of action and choice in his daily life in his job. He cannot express his opinion either by voice or vote. For example, a coal miner expressed his poor opinion of John L. Lewis. Lewis forced the employer to fire him when Lewis threw the man out of the United Mine Workers' Union. The majority of Americans still want such lack of freedom of the citizen as their voting record shows.

The wage earner under present representative government law cannot handle his own wages. Government forces the employer to extract from the wages of each man a sum determined by the bureaucrat without any reference to the man who earned it in spite of the fact that the sum deducted and collected from the pay envelope has little relationship to the tax levied by the government. It may be much more or much less and usually is. The majority by their votes show that they o.k. that infringement on their liberties.

The only person who had the courage to challenge this iniquity was Vivien Kellems of Stonington, Connecticut. She was kicked around by the bureaucrats and her own bank account illegally taken over by them. The final outcome is still uncertain to the extent only of how far she will be punished. That she will be punished by loss of her freedom of action is already proved. A government that will allow such crime cannot long remain even in name free or representative. Obviously it is not now. The form must go, as the substance has already gone.

The prediction of all thinking men when our government was formed that the majority cannot rule themselves, is being proved by our present experience. The demagogue was obvious to them then. Experience has proved the accuracy of their predictions. The majority of the voters do not want freedom. They want instead the rule of a hoped for benevolent dictator.

LEADERSHIP IS KEY TO SIZE

It is obvious that the reason why the United States leads in industry is the ability of its industrial leadership. This leadership is so far ahead of the rest of the world that it can accept the handicaps of much higher wages and governmental interference and still win by a great margin. Every handicap that is placed on our industrialists, however, closes the gap. If the handicaps are carried far enough in the direction now headed, the lead will soon disappear. America's dominance as a nation obviously will disappear with it.

The importance in the above digression lies in the fact that every item with which management must deal, which takes its time and attention from its job as a manufacturer, reduces its ability as a manufacturer and also reduces the size of job that it can accomplish as a manufacturer.

In judging how large an organization can efficiently become, we must take into consideration all these factors. This restriction will disappear immediately if the public will accept the facts regarding the free enterprise system and incentive management. The chance of its doing this is now remote. The facts do not agree with the dreams that have already been sold to the public by the politician. Too many people think that under proper restrictions of industry by government the worker can have an assured living with little or no effort. It is only necessary to think up the right law.

Efficient size is still dependent on the ability of management. The restrictions that are introduced from without change the answer, but do not change the fundamental facts regarding it.

Efficient size is still the size at which an organization can be successfully guided by one man. The idea that much responsibility can be handed on to subordinates is, of course, true. The fact still remains that before the handing on is done the chief executive must find out what it is he is going to hand on, and why and what will be done with it when handed on. The fundamental plan of the company can only be correctly determined by one man. He, only, can tell the direction and the goal to be achieved. When that is done, the various people who are to carry out the plan can go to work with understanding. No one can tell where he is going, however, until a goal is set.

THE EXPERT ACHIEVES SUCCESS

It is not necessary to make many things to succeed outstandingly well. It is only necessary to make something that is outstanding. It is unnecessary to be big to be outstanding. It is only necessary to be the best in the field and continue to be so. Babe Ruth could not play football, tennis or hockey. He could not run fast or far. He was not physically strong. He was, however, the greatest home run batter that has ever played professional baseball. He is and until surpassed will be outstanding for that reason. He needed nothing more. We hear more about the record breaker in one event than the winner of the decathlon, and properly so. That is a good guide for the industrialist to follow in his thinking.

THE TRUE MEASURE OF SIZE IS SERVICE

There has been much said about the law of diminishing returns as size increases. That is true only when size has not been properly based on efficiency. There is no case of diminishing returns when the products are rightly conceived and progressively more efficiently produced. There are no diminishing returns if the standards mentioned above are followed. The reason for diminishing returns is the increasing of size without increasing usefulness. When size is the natural outcome of demand for a product that is made at an ever-decreasing price and ever-increasing worth, there are no diminishing returns.

The industrialist who is a leader in any field will never be attracted to a product already on the market unless new progress can be made in its manufacture by his company in cost or usefulness. Progress cannot be made by copying what is now produced; it is made by producing the new, the better, the cheaper. An industrialist who has this basic philosophy will not be connected with a concern which could be affected by the so-called law of diminishing returns.

The idea that size itself is a help or a handicap is wrong. Size of itself is no measure of success. A large plant can be very efficient. It can be made more efficient than a small one. The fact is that in general it is much less so. That is often because the leadership has allowed himself to be enticed into fields to which is contributes nothing. Any industry in such circumstances, no matter what its size is, is too large. The true measure of size is service given the public. That may mean that any plant may be too large or too small.

The greatest difficulty that the industrialist has in considering this matter of size is to continue to deal with reality. The products that he builds may at one time have been the best in the field. The temptation is to then become static and dwell in the past. Often such an industrialist does not awaken until after he has been passed by a wide awake competitor. He has not seen the progress that competition has made because he has been lulled to sleep by continuing demand for the old product that people buy as a habit from him because of his past reputation. When demand drops off in such a case the company probably is too far gone to catch up, at least under such management.

CHAPTER XII

The Place of the Union

The philosophy of the Wagner Act, if it is to remain on the Statute Books, will change our whole concept regarding the reason for and the responsibilities of industry. Perhaps what was believed before was wrong. In any case, what we now must believe, as directed by federal legislation as to the responsibilities and rights of labor, management and the consumer, has undergone a complete revolution. It is obvious that a change must be made from the present resulting civil war between labor union leadership and industrial management ordered by the present labor legislation. We can scarcely continue to go on as we now are. The only question is, in what direction we shall go. On this decision will rest to a great extent the future of our economy and, as a result, the future of the nation.

INDUSTRY CANNOT CONTROL COST

The theory behind the Wagner Act is that the power of labor union leadership over industrial management must be increased so that union labor leadership can force certain advantages for itself. Labor union leadership has been given power to eliminate the authority of industrial man· agement in its direction of the worker. Industrial management now is permitted only to suggest. It can no longer direct the worker. This revolutionary change has been in effect for a sufficient time so that its results can now be judged.

The union executive under this Act has the power to raise wages generally to any extent that the union leadership determines. He can limit the worker's output in any of many ways. Production costs therefore are no longer under industrial management's control. Labor union leadership can also decide who will work or not work at any job in many plants. Such power completely changes the operation of industry. It eliminates many of the possibilities of cost reduction that management's direction could give and stops growth in many directions possible before.

Labor union management also does not come under the laws that regulate industrial management. Such laws treat industrial management and labor union management in completely different ways. Acts that fine or jail the industrial manager do not even apply to the labor union manager who does exactly the same things.

This philosophy in its eventualities can not now be completely foreseen; however, the effects that are now obvious are sufficiently disturbing. For example, wages have more than doubled in the last ten years while the efficiency of production has been reduced. Costs therefore have more than doubled. This perhaps does not disturb the industrial worker whose wages have kept pace with increased costs. Such people, however, are in the minority. Most people have a fixed or nearly fixed income. They are being crucified by this rising cost resulting from the decreased production per dollar of wages.

DISCRIMINATORY LEGISLATION LEADS TO REVOLUTION
Perhaps this result is not too serious. Perhaps the inde-

pendent person earning a fixed salary or unable to increase profits from a little shop should be crucified. Perhaps all should belong to unions, including housewives, then all could unite in this merry-go-round of increased wages, less efficiency and increased prices. The matter of greatest moment to the American people resulting from this labor union legislation is the fact that the law of the land as now enforced is different for the union leader than it is for anyone else. Such legal favoritism will eventually lead to revolution as it always has. For legislative acts that do not apply in all circumstances to all persons equally and without distinction between persons may be legal, but they are not proper American law.

This abandonment of fairness in law does not disturb the present thinking of many people. Most agree, for instance, that the man of small income should be taxed entirely differently from the man of larger income. In fact, the application of the laws written for each are not only widely discriminatory but also are by plan differently applied. For example, the application of the income tax law is not only taxation at a different rate for different incomes, but it is enforced in an entirely different way for each. No tax dodger whose income is less than ten thousand dollars ever went to jail, although there is no doubt that 99.9% of all tax dodgers are in this lower income group.

The eventual outcome of this policy of discriminatory laws and different application of those laws to different classes is in the future. It is interesting to note, however, that it was this unfairness in tax laws and their application that caused the French Revolution and that we Americans claimed caused our own Revolution.

We at the time of the American Revolution advanced the claim that taxation without representation infringed the

American's natural right of ownership of property; i.e., that *any* taxation without the taxpayer's willing consent is robbery. We now have departed far from our Founding Fathers' love of liberty and willingness to pay the price always needed to get and keep it.

LIBERTY IS LOST WHEN LAW IS FLOUTED

The complete softness in our attitude toward John L. Lewis, who has continually flouted law, liberty and fair dealing in his domination over government and his union members, only shows in a striking manner how far we have gone in this softening process. We do not even care to object to the complete surrender of our elected representatives in their dealing not only with Lewis, but with all other union labor leaders. What would have caused immediate impeachment or removal a hundred years ago now elicits only a tolerant smile by our citizenry.

We can be sure that when Americans are willing to accept the flouting of laws because we hope that such acts will benefit our set, other laws will be flouted by another set that will handicap us as we handicapped others. When such action becomes common, we call that chaos, or revolution, or an uprising. The final result is the same: our liberty goes—a dictator takes over.

John L. Lewis has demonstrated that he can force any wage he desires. All that is necessary is for him to stop coal production long enough to upset the whole American economy or entirely shut it down. There is no answer that can now be given by government that is decisive. All that the people can do is grant labor union management's demands if they wish to live.

It is of course true that the present Fair Deal administration is so completely dominated by the union leaders that government makes no move to eliminate the difficulty. If government did use its power, it could not force the miners back to work. Coal must be mined by miners. It cannot be mined by soldiers. So far has gone this Frankenstein monster developed by political quacks.

Labor leaders are not the ones at fault. They do not follow their judgment in making their demands. They are not allowed to do so. Competition between labor leaders determines what is to be demanded of the public in wages and security. This has nothing to do with justice, fair dealing or efficiency. It has only to do with each union leader's continuance in his job.

Lack of enforcement of present laws covering monopoly allow the union leader to do as he wishes. If one leader gets a wage increase, his competitor in another union must get more or "holler uncle." So far no labor leaders have shrunk from the competitive struggle.

If a mere manufacturer should adopt the labor leader's formula he would be indicted immediately, charged with monopoly and restraint of trade and sent to jail. His company would be so restricted that failure would be imminent.

OUR HIGH STANDARD OF LIVING HAS NO SECURITY

The primary cause of our present dilemma comes from the lack of understanding by the people of the economics of the industrial setup. The usual concept is that the owners of industry are taking too much money from the workers' earnings. The feeling is general that the industrialist is a selfish and wealthy man who pays as little in wages as he can so that he will have a greater profit for himself. The fact that industrial profits have increased as rapidly as wages increased makes no difference, seemingly, in our thinking.

Since the Wagner Act has raised dollar wages and made the worker largely dominant in his relationship with his previous boss, the feeling is fairly general in the minds of the unthinking that labor legislation has succeeded in its purpose.

There is no doubt that the Wagner Act has completely changed the relationship of so-called management and men. There is no doubt that industrial management's control over the worker has largely disappeared. There is no doubt that money wages are being raised continuously by the power given to union leadership. To that extent at least the Act has succeeded in its announced purpose.

The point that is primary is whether it has made the average person better off by so doing. Are the workers themselves better off? If this question were put to a poll there is no doubt that the present answer would be "yes." There is no doubt that most of the people in the United States now generally have the highest standard of living of all time. If we can continue our present high standard, we shall be very fortunate. The difficulty is that we cannot.

Rising wages and decreased output that union leadership domination have forced on the economy will have far reaching and extremely serious results. At the present time, the wage rates in terms of dollars in all foreign countries are a small fraction of ours. If the foreign manufacturer tried to do so, he could shut down every factory in the United States because of his relatively low wage rate and greater production because of lack of union restriction on output.

The only reason why we are now fully employed is because of our war preparations and the chaotic conditions in industry abroad resulting from the last war. However, we are seeing the beginning of what is in store for us. In spite of our giving many billions of dollars to many foreign countries so that they can buy war products, we last year (1950) imported more than we exported for the first time in eleven years. Ships, steel, machine tools, electrical equipment and almost all other manufactured products can be bought abroad for much less than they can be here. The end is in sight. We have priced ourselves out of the world market.

The fact that money buys less than half what it did ten years ago is another indication of our trouble. The fact that each family has a bill of over $8,000, its part of the national debt, which it must pay in some way, is a further indication of future trouble. The present seeming prosperity is the result of inflation. Such pseudo-prosperity is always evident in the first years of any inflationary period. The check we have to pay for our economic excesses will be presented later.

There is much difference of opinion in this matter of inflation. Even the union leaders are unanimous in saying that wages have trailed behind the cost of living and that the worker is badly off. Inflation always follows this pattern. Wages are a consequence of prices. Inflation gives more pieces of paper to all people. This paper is called money. In our minds we think of what we got for these pieces of paper when we last spent them, which gives us an inflated idea of their value since we could not get the same purchase for the same number of dollars again. That is the first deceit of inflation.

The next vice stemming from inflation is that it forces us to spend not save. Since the money we have will be worth less tomorrow and worthless eventually, we must spend it as soon as we get it. Economy is an automatic vice.

Another result of inflation is that no one can catch up with it. Wages today cannot buy the product tomorrow that the wages today produced. The buyer is always behind and always must be.

There is one fact of which there can be no doubt during inflation. The standard of living of all those on fixed income is lower than before and will rapidly be getting lower still. This same result must happen to all, even those who have some flexibility of income for the reasons cited above.

THE CONSUMER PAYS THE BILL

If the consumer is satisfied with the cost of inflated wages and taxes and deflated efficiency of production, which state and federal policies have produced, there is no personal worry that the manufacturer can have. He does not pay the higher cost or taxes. All that must of course come from the consumer when he buys the inefficiently made product. However, every manufacturer knows the buying habits and prejudices of the purchasers of his product. He knows the facts of life even if the consumer now seemingly does not. He knows that his future is controlled by one decisive fact. That fact is that selling price determines the size of his market. He knows that every cent that is added to price, be it increased wages, taxes, inefficiency, profit, or inflation, reduces the size of his market. He also knows that every cent that is taken off the price by any means increases the market. Here is the only selfish interest he has in wages, taxes or waste. Here is his only selfish reason to strive for lower price for his product by reducing any or all items of cost.

LAW MADE THE SITUATION INEVITABLE

The labor union leader has no cinch in our present economic friction; he is caught in the toils. He must get wages and conditions of employment better than those of rival union managers or he loses his prestige and job. He cannot follow the dictates of his reason. He cannot do what is best for the country or even what is best in the long run for his own union men. He must get more right now than his competitor got. Only so can his future career be assured.

Our dilemma is only to be expected. That we should be faced by some such threat was obvious when the Wagner Act was passed. Every wrong step builds up penalties that eventually must be faced. Every thinking man warned against giving the unfair power to the union labor leader. The politician, however, was too eager to reap the benefits of political preferment inherent in such legislation to follow a reasoned judgment. He knew that someone else would reap the penalty for his error. He himself could not lose. The penalty would be delayed while he cashed in on the political boost that the law would get from the unthinking majority. Politically, the reason was most sound. Roosevelt and Truman have cashed in tremendously. The country now is beginning to pay the price of its selfish attempt at over-reaching. The final penalty is yet to come.

RETURN TO COMPETITION OR GO TO SOCIALISM

There are two avenues open to us to solve this problem. The first is to return to competition as a means of regulating wages, prices, efficiency and taxes. In other words, let the worker compete through his company for the dollars of the consumer with all other competitors making the same product. This is the only known way a free economy can remain free.. The objection that labor will be beaten down under this system of free competition in

205

wages and prices is not true as our advancing standard of living for everyone including the wage earner showed over the last hundred and fifty years of free enterprise prior to the present governmental interference.

The second way out is to do what has been done in every totalitarian state. Put the power of the state over the operation of industry. That is called socialism by some, communism by others. It is actually totalitarian government in which the citizen is a serf of government directed by bureaucracy.

The machine gun and the political prison added to the threat of starvation make most people singularly eager to do what they are told by the bureaucrat. That is true in Russia and in fifteen Russian-subjugated countries. That was true in Italy and Germany. That will soon be true in the United States under our present program.

It is obvious that one or the other means of regulating the economy must be followed. There is no other way that has ever been known or suggested. We must either regulate the economy by competition or we must go to regulation by the bureaucrat. Both methods have been used long enough to show in a way that leaves no chance for any misunderstanding as to what to expect as a result of either method.

NO ONE CAN OPERATE ALL INDUSTRY

Control of all people by bureaucracy has been the method used by government from the beginning of history. It is only in the last two hundred years that much deviation from this method of government has occurred in any nation. The American Revolution of 1776 was the first real step toward freedom of the individual.

No bureaucrat can operate any industry successfully. Experts are needed there. No one expert industrialist could successfully operate all business. The job is much too large and too involved. The expert would be the first to acknowledge this fact. The only man who thinks that he can control all industry is the bureaucrat with no manufacturing experience. Because he knows nothing about industry, he does not know its problems and hence, the difficulties involved do not disturb him.

The intricacy of industry is so great that the inexperienced outsiders do not see the problems the industrialist must handle any more than the man in the grandstand sees why his ideas are not the best in playing a ball game.

It is the trying and failing in free enterprise that eventually develops the new and better process. While the successful industrialist is an expert, yet his methods and processes must continuously develop into new and better ones. That means trying and failing before eventual success. That is how a better and better product is made at a lower and lower cost.

BUREAUCRACY HAS NO OPPORTUNITY TO PROGRESS THROUGH EXPERIMENT

No bureaucrat could or would even attempt to develop products the only way that development can take place. He would have no chance to experiment nor recover from failure. Governmental planning is a process that fastens on the whole economy the old and well known programs and processes in the belief that if all do the same thing that has been determined by experience, that no mistake will be made and no losses encountered.

There is no doubt that if all acts have been based on past experience the result can be predetermined. The only trouble with this program is that no progress can then be made. Man is not willing to stand still, particularly when his contemporaries are moving forward and outdistancing him. No one is content with last year's newspapers, clothes, automobiles or baseball scores. We insist on being up-to-date even when no one can say exactly what up-to-date is. In any case, we want to keep up with or, better, ahead of the Joneses. We are not content to see the Joneses leave us behind. No governmental bureaucracy can make progress, since progress is not in governmental planning, nor can it result from governmental operation.

COMPETITION MAKES PROGRESS

Control by competition, not by bureaucrats, is the only successful method that has ever been devised to make progress. First of all, competition develops the abilities of individuals in the fierce fire of competitive effort. The champion is then selected from the mass by this same competition. When this champion is selected and developed, he is the leader with the necessary abilities to direct successfully free industry. Control of industry by the bureaucrat means selection of that bureaucrat by political maneuvering, not by competition in actual operation of industry. The man skilled in political maneuvering is never skilled in industrial management.

What is more to the point, if he were skilled in industrial management, he could not succeed in a planned economy, since the job is too big to be handled by any single human being or single management. Not only that, political considerations would eliminate any truly economic management. New ideas could not be tried by the bureaucrat. Only new ideas can make the economy advance. Furthermore, government policy is forced on industry while modern economy depends for its existence upon the free choices and voluntary actions of free persons. Nobody, collared by a policeman, is in a state of mind or affairs to act according to his personal choice. Whatever his personal judgment, he will defer to the policeman's requests.

In this control of industry by the bureaucrat, we have set up a law to promote so-called collective bargaining. This is a perfect illustration of the fuzzy thinking in government on industrial control. This decision to make so-called collective bargaining a must, was the result of desire for political preferment, not the desire to help the wage earner. All bureaucratic decisions in an otherwise free economy will be made the same way. Such judgments cannot make a successful production operation.

Labor union management comes to the bargaining table with two primary objects: first, to assert and prove its power; second, to get higher wages. The asserting of its authority is necessary to give the worker the feeling of self-importance which is the greatest reward that the labor union has to give to its workers.

The second object that the union has is to get higher wages for its men. Obviously, over the whole economy, arbitrary higher wages are not possible. If wages are raised and efficiency is not proportionally increased at the same time, industry must hand on the raise in wages to the customer as an increase in price. This raise in price lowers the purchasing power of money including the money paid as wages, so the wage raise cancels itself out.

In spite of this completely obvious fact, the public generally think that wage increases are proper and usually applaud the increase. They, however, damn the industry as a thieving group when the increase is handed on to the consumer in increased prices, as it must be, since it can come from no other source.

In spite of all the nonsense talked by labor union management as to the freeing of the wage slave by union action, the consumer is finding that all that the union is doing is to raise the cost of all things that he, the consumer and the worker, buys. While the worker is perhaps able to increase the number of dollars he gets in his own pay envelope by union action, it continues to cost him still more dollars to get the things he needs according to labor union management's own statement. Inflation penalizes all people.

RESTRICTION OF SKILL WILL BE FATAL

There is only one way that any person can have a contented life. That is by gaining the stature that a job well done, which requires and displays an admired skill, can give. Union labor philosophy despises work. Every way that work can be ridculed is part of the union program. Feather-bedding is only one of the ways that has been developed by the union. Work instead of being an expression of the skill of the worker is a nuisance to be endured, stretched out and escaped from at every opportunity. Is there any wonder that the union man is frustrated, irritated, blinded, resentful, quick to take offense and act on an angry impulse? Are "wild cat" strikes, set off by trifles, at all surprising?

If a union should put on the professional baseball player the same limitations that the union does on the worker, the spectator would run such labor leader out of the country. The player also would rebel for the same reasons. The player's skill and its exhibition are the first desire of both the player and spectator. Is it not equally true that the same urge must be given to the worker since his skill is much more necessary to the economy than any ball player's skill.

This restriction on the skill and ability of the worker is the most damnable act that the present labor-union management has to account for to the wronged consumer, and so he will shortly find.

There is also the spector in the air of ultimate defeat of the whole system of union domination. What will happen when the present entirely artificial prosperity disappears? How will the union leader and his union fare when there is no work to do because the companies, forced to price themselves out of the market, are gone? Who will he then exploit for more wages for less production? Who will he then tell to "go to hell?"

THE CONSUMER IS CRUCIFIED

It is perhaps a truism that man does not learn much by precept. He learns everything that he does not like to learn by bitter experience only. This fact is now being illustrated. We will learn by bitter experience, perhaps when it is too late, that the present civil war between union management and industrial management is industrial suicide. They are allies, not enemies. If there is any real bargaining in industry, it is between labor and management on one side and the consumer on the other. It is the consumer that is being crucified in so-called collective bargaining.

This discussion is not for the purpose of condemning labor unions as such. I am a very great believer in workers uniting for their betterment. I am very sure that this is the direction of progress. I am, however, very much against stupid selfishness. I have seen the destruction, the dominance of the dumb over the intelligent, the waste and the heartbreak that comes from such stupidity. Both sides lose in every labor war as they do in military wars. The innocent bystander, however, is the chief sufferer always.

There is no reason why war should be the result of labor uniting. Workers can get much more than union management can get for them if they will only deal with reality

211

in their united action.

The point is that this better lot of union labor cannot be had by exploitation of the consumer. Every worker is a consumer. Up to date no way has been found, nor any plan, whereby a man can get prosperous by taking money from himself. That is the trouble with the present plans of labor leadership; they are exploiting their own members by continually increasing the cost of what they must buy.

Now let us approach the matter from another angle. Let us make the plan of the labor union that of giving the customer, who actually pays his wages, more for his money. Let us make the labor organization a means of increasing efficiency of production and so lowering costs. Let us have labor accept its responsibility to the consumer. Let us see what would happen then.

In adopting a program such as that, the labor union must change its present philosophy. Wage earners and union managers must see that they are not beings apart whose sole responsibility is to force advantages for themselves as union members and from themselves as consumers. The employer obviously is merely a middle man of expert ability, who can, because of his genius, machinery and factory organization, take the skill of the worker and transform it into a standard of living for the whole economy, which is largely the worker himself. The consumer, not the employer pays all wages. The worker can get that desired higher standard of living only by using his skill combined with the direction of the industrialist to make a cheaper product.

UNION LEADERS AND INDUSTRIAL LEADERS MUST COOPERATE

There have been attempts by labor union managers to

use the workers' skill under the union's direction for their profit without the direction of the middleman, called here the industrialist. All such attempts have failed. These companies could not meet competition. Industrial leadership was lacking.

This fact should receive the attention it deserves. The worker alone, without direction of the expert industrialist, fails to get a standard of living he desires. This is true even when the union can eliminate most of the handicaps it imposes on the industrialist. No union ever succeeded in operating an industry in competition with the industrialist, even when its wages, working conditions and so-called fringe benefits can be determined with no friction, strikes or slowdowns which it now imposes on the manufacturer. Labor as shown by this experience must have the direction of the industrialist.

Since that is true, labor must accept its responsibility to the public in cooperation with industrial management. It cannot resist such cooperation without threatening its existence. The same responsibility devolves on industrial management. The problem facing both, therefore, is this: how can we both so organize our efforts so as to be of maximum benefit to the economy? This will also answer the question: how can each worker have a progressively higher standard of living?

In carrying out this program, obviously the present philosophy of labor leadership must be completely revised. Cooperation with industrial management is completely out of any planning by the present labor leadership, completely necessary as it is. Its program is in the directly opposite direction—that of interference with management and reduction of efficiency.

WHAT CAN THE UNIONS CONTRIBUTE?

When labor accepts its responsibility to the public, what can be done for the benefit of all, including labor?

First: The union can make the skill of its members progressively greater and therefore make the worker more valuable to the economy if it will make skill a necessary and valued quality of its membership. The medical, dental, engineering and agricultural professions, to mention a few, have made greater and greater skill the primary desire of their members. Great progress has resulted. Certainly labor unions can do the same. This is the first step.

Second: The responsibility of labor to the public should be and must be accepted as a primary responsibility of the labor leader. If all other professions can make such service to the public desirable, there is no reason why labor leadership should not do the same. If it does not, or cannot, it must be replaced eventually by leadership that can and will.

Third: Labor has tremendous abilities and opportunities because of its experience and environment to make progress in efficiency of production that would assist and increase the effectiveness of all plans of management. The desire to assist in the development and adoption of these new methods should be the religion of labor leadership. The doubling of output efficiency could occur immediately if the desire to double it was in the minds of all workers. That efficiency could then be doubled many times again if latent ability were developed also.

Fourth: The union should introduce the desire on the part of the workers to protect and more efficiently operate, instead of destroy, the tools of production. With this desire would be coupled the desire to make present tools work

214

instead of fail. Such failure is now part of the teaching and philosophy of much labor leadership. This is only another object of cooperation which includes all programs that will make production more efficient and less costly.

THE RESULTS WILL JUSTIFY UNION'S POSITION IN ECONOMY

What would happen if both union and industrial management accepted their mutual responsibility to the public as has been outlined in this book and as has been done to a considerable extent at The Lincoln Electric Company? Reduction to less than fifty percent of the previous cost of all manufactured products would be almost immediate. Increase of wages to more than double the present rates would occur, as has been demonstrated at the same plant. Decrease of selling price to less than half the present price would result. Living standards would therefore quadruple immediately for all. Of course, some such plan must eventually be universal. Delay, however, is dangerous.

This mutual responsibility for cooperation of so-called worker and management is the place in which the labor union could be of decisive help. It is here that it can develop and function with safety and profit for all. It is only by some such program that the labor union can justify itself and safely look to the future. It is only by changing to this program that it can continue to be allowed to remain in the economy.

The union must teach the worker where his actual interests lie. It cannot take the position that more money for less production is the end sought. What is actually desired is a continually higher standard of living for all. That can be obtained only by more efficient production of goods. Higher money wages per hour cannot obtain a higher standard of living unless efficiency of production goes up faster than wages per hour. That obvious fact must change all the present plans followed by union labor leadership.

The higher efficiency of production can be obtained by greater skill of the operator, by better tools of production or by improved management. It is the development of both the skill and the better tools that can be made by a proper program of the union in its cooperation with management.

After the worker knows that his real goal is greater efficiency of production, his desire to increase his skill will be automatic, particularly if the union encourages him in that direction. New skills, new methods and new strengths for the job can and should be the developments made by the man in his training given by the union. Union membership should be dependent on great skill as well as proper understanding of the industrial economy. Such organizations would make a higher living standard for all its members automatic and would also raise the standard of living of everyone else. This result must be the goal of the union as well as the goal of the industrialist and government. All three must accept this as their responsibility.

Chapter XIII

How To Finance the Company

There is now much discussion of the financing of industrial companies. The statement is often made that present tax laws eliminate the risk capital that is needed. There is little doubt that this criticism is probably one of the least warranted of the many that could be made of the present tax laws. It is about on a par with the condemning of murder only because it is apt to be messy.

Taxation on the present scale based on punishing the able for his ability and his use in the economy is suicide in its eventual effect, but the reason is not that such taxation eliminates risk capital. The decisive argument against our present tax policy is that such taxation eliminates incentive, with sorry consequences. Under such pressures and punishments as our present taxation gives, ability will not be developed in the individual. The able men of the past who created the American economy of abundance and the able men of today who are punished for ability and achievement, will have no one to replace them in the future.

Capital for the development of any business should usually come from the workers in it. Capital to start any company is usually a contribution from the founder or founders. After the enterprise has been put on a paying basis, further capital should and could in the same way come from those who are employed in the business and from its profits. Outside capital for the building of any industry is less desirable than the capital put in by those who make the company succeed. Capital from the insider is much more understanding than capital from those who are employed elsewhere or not employed at all. If the workers own a large part of a company, many of the problems that so often plague the outside-owned company disappear.

The difficulties that will be cited against financing from within are visionary. The only healthy way that any industry can grow is by financing and development from within. As a matter of record, almost all successful industry starts that way. It is only when such an industry gets large and prosperous that any attempt is made for capitalization by the public. It is then that most trouble starts. The outside stockholder has only dividends as his reason for owning stock. There are many other and more important reasons for stock ownership that should be present.

The greatest corporation of all time was financed entirely from its own profits. It could not have made the record it did if the stock had been publicly held. Henry Ford recognized that at an early date and bought the outstanding stock at a thousand times the original investment made by these stockholders. Only so could he have gone forward as he did. Only so could he have applied the philosophy that made the Ford Motor Company so outstandingly successful. He saw the opportunity of modern industry and adopted the proper program. Outside stockholders can only be interested in greater dividends. The tax authorities encourage them in this demand since only so can they collect a maximum tax. Otherwise, government can tax profits only once. That is why dividends are by law made large compared to what can legally be retained in the business.

All business starts from a man with an idea. If he develops the company successfully from this start on his own, as is true of most industry, the activity is obviously then financed from within. That is always true during the early life of the organization when money is hardest to get and most needed. When success of the activity is assured, money can be gotten from many sources closed to it when its future was in the balance. If the preliminary period can be financed from within, as is done in almost all cases, surely in the later period when the firm is successful there will be no difficulty in financing from within.

PUBLIC STOCK OWNERSHIP WEAKENS TEAM SPIRIT

Much stock selling to the public by successful industrialists is to allow them to cash in on their holdings. They want to have money rather than to own a going and successful business. This is often the beginning of the end for both the business and its founders.

Another reason for public selling of stock is to make possible rapid expansion. Such rapid expansion, as history shows, usually is not justified as compared with the more orderly growth that can be financed from within the company itself. This restraint on too rapid growth is often a very healthy control.

Actually, if the company can carry on at first there is every reason for continuing to keep it self-supporting. This not only keeps the control where it belongs, in the hands of proved, successful leaders and cooperative workers, it also makes the company more self-reliant, self-sufficient, cooperative and hence more efficient.

As has been stated many times before, the success of any industrial organization depends on the attitude of those in it. If they are mutually anxious to make it succeed, the future of the company is bright. If they do not care, as is often true of companies owned by the outside stockholder, success will be certainly less marked.

THE INCENTIVE OF OWNERSHIP

Ownership of the company by those in it is of prime importance in getting the company's personnel to work as a team. There are other useful incentives mentioned in this book, but the feeling of ownership by those in any company will be a very useful and continuing incentive that obviously will make such organizations more cooperative.

There is no doubt that if those in any company have the feeling that they own the company, many advantages are automatic. First, there is no question as to interest in the job. This will be as true of the worker as it is of the boss. There will then be the same responsibility of ownership felt by the worker in handling his tools that every owner of property feels. Up to date there has been little difficulty in getting the owner of anything to take an interest in it. As a matter of fact, there is much objection by many incompetents because the worker-owner takes too much interest in his job and therefore gets too much income. The point has often been made that the workers at The Lincoln Electric Company are too highly paid, in spite of the record that they have made, which proves just the opposite. Their productivity is more than four times that of competition. They are paid only slightly more than twice the wages of competitors. The rest of the earnings from their great efficiency is passed on to the customer in lower prices.

It is obvious that if the same feeling is universal in all organizations, the first step in making any organization a team in its operation is accomplished. Stock ownership by those who work in a company will automatically put them on the team with the team spirit and interest.

OWNERSHIP IS EDUCATIONAL

The second advantage that flows from worker ownership is that all owners will know the facts of life. They will know how profits are made and lost; how success is won and lost. They will therefore be more diligent, more cooperative and much more understanding workers. They will know the responsibility of ownership. That is a very helpful education.

There have been few stockholders in any company who ever believed in communism or any other form of government that takes freedom or punitive taxes from the individual. There are few socialists in the lists of stockholders of the nation's industries. This educational result of such stock ownership is important. Free enterprise exists nowhere at the present time; however, the United States still comes closer to allowing it than most other nations.

If free enterprise and its necessary freedom disappear here, we will go into a period of Dark Ages in which freedom and the new economy of abundance will disappear. If that occurs, man will regress as greatly as he did after the fall of Rome. Any plan that will save the world from that is of utmost importance to all Americans.

Stock ownership for those who work in an industry is therefore a very important development. It is of great importance not only for the industry involved, but for the economy of the country generally and for the preservation of our freedom.

CAPITAL AVAILABLE FROM WITHIN CONTROLS EXPANSION

The question that is most generally asked is this: "How is it possible to get enough money by profit and stock sale to the workers to finance expansion?" The answer is rather obvious. No expansion should be undertaken if it cannot be financed in that way.

If a company can be started by the founder from his resources of pocket and mind, there is no difficulty in expanding the company from the pockets and minds of a group most interested when the success of the plan is assured. If this source will not provide enough capital to expand the company, the plans for expansion are probably unjustified by solid facts.

Capital from absentee stockholders always represents a threat. The only interest that outside capital can usually have is to produce the largest income possible to himself. For that reason, the consumer of the product, whose interest should be paramount, can only be thought of by the absentee stockholder as his competitor for the gain he put up his money to get. The latter's interest, therefore, must be in the direction of "all the traffic will bear."

The worker in the plant also will resent such an attitude, as he does now. He cannot receive such a stockholder as a teammate. For these reasons, outside capital is a constant threat, the size of the threat being measured by the percentage of outside holdings and the attitude that management takes because of its influence.

STOCK OWNERSHIP NOT A MEANS OF GAMBLING

As has been indicated, stock should be sold only to those employed in the company. This provides a great incentive for the stockholders in their job, as well as protecting the company from trouble inherent in absentee owner-

222

ship. It is sound in all phases. Since it is so important in its effect, careful consideration should be given to the method of doing it.

There is nothing that will wreck any organization's spirit more quickly than the selling of stock to its employees which is over-valued or unsound.

The usual workers in factories are not expert financiers. They can be, therefore, easily misled. All men under incentive management always will believe their leader. If he should use this trust to get his men to make a wrong decision on stock ownership, he will quickly end his usefulness and his plan of incentive management.

There should be little difficulty for the leader in guiding his men properly. Industry under incentive management can greatly reduce costs and increase profits. Such profits are inevitable in the efficiency that incentive management produces. The proper distribution controlled by the philosophy already outlined, therefore, is necessary.

The stock selling plan must be properly conceived. When that is done, there is little chance of failure. It is necessary, however, that the stock be placed on a proper basis so that growth of the business will add properly to the value of such stock.

The details of the plan for selling stock to the worker need to be well thought out. The worker may not have the cash to put up all that is needed at once, yet he should be a stockholder. A plan that will allow him time to pay for the stock over a period of time is proper. The stock should be paid for within a definite time, however, or it may take on some of the earmarks of a gift. That is always bad.

Under some conditions, the buyer may see a chance to call the turn on the fluctuations of the stock's price. Such gambling should be discouraged by not allowing the stock to be sold for such market turns. Stock ownership is for the purpose of making the stockholder part of the organization. It must not be a means of gambling.

STOCK OWNERSHIP PLAN

The following plan has worked in case of The Lincoln Electric Company over many years with success. It may have some features that can be useful to others.

First: The dividend paid is generally somewhat more than the average dividend paid by industry and is based on the actual value of the company's assets each year.

Second: The dividend is paid quarterly.

Third: Only those employed in the company for at least one year can buy the company's stock. If for any reason they cease to be employed by the company, they must offer to sell the stock back to the company. As a matter of policy, the company always buys stock so offered. This makes stock always available to those employed. The whole plan is based on the idea that only those who have the greatest interest in the company shall be the stockholders. Only by selling back the stock to the company on leaving can such ownership be continued.

Fourth: The employee can take a year to pay for the stock and no more. He gets the dividend as a credit on his purchase as soon as his application is approved by the directors, but if he does not complete the payments in a year's time or less he gets back only the money he actually paid.

Fifth: He can borrow on his stock at normal interest to about 65% of its value for projects that are proper. He cannot buy additional stock as long as he has a loan on the stock he possesses.

Sixth: The selling price and the buying price is the same and is set by the Board of Directors each year for a year.

Seventh: The stock increases in value and dividend rate

as the net worth of the company increases.

Eighth: Do not try to sell the stock. Stock should sell itself.

Ninth: When stock is sold to the worker under this plan, it is purely a business proposition. It is not paternalistic in any way. These safeguards are solely to protect the interests of the buyer so that there never can be the feeling that he has been rooked. Do not try to control the doings of the stockholders outside of protecting their interests. One of the greatest benefits that comes from this plan of stock ownership is the self-development of the men in their understanding of the operation of industry.

Tenth: The reason for the stock selling plan is to get money for expansion and to develop men of the proper calibre to operate the expanded company. Men are made by responsibility. Stock ownership is one way to give them responsibility. Money for the company can be gotten in many ways, but men can develop only when properly inspired. Stock ownership under proper conditions helps to solve this great problem of individual development.

OWNERSHIP AN INCENTIVE TO DEVELOP

There are certain conclusions that can safely be drawn from the above discussion that are of utmost importance to the free enterprise system and our whole economy. If most workers held stock in the company for which they worked, there would be no threat of totalitarianism, in any of its forms.

The present interference in industry by government, both by taxation and by foolish laws attempting to control the governmentally-sponsored, labor-management war, would completely disappear. The worker would then be a capitalist. He would make short work of present political self-seeking interference either by government or labor leaders. The greatest advantage would be the development of the individual worker. Under the incentive of owner-ship, he would become a greater man.

It would be well perhaps at this point to discuss the problem that management faces in its so-called labor relations. It is not understood generally, even by industrial leaders who have made great records in manufacturing, why the industrial worker is continually bucking management.

He is the highest paid of all workers. He has the easiest work physically. He has the highest standard of living and the greatest amount of leisure of any worker in the world. In spite of all this, he is continually rebelling against the industrial leadership that makes all this possible. Why is this true? The answer is that industry as now organized does not give the worker the chance to develop the pride in himself that we all crave far above any other reward. No worker will go along willingly with an organization that disregards his human dignity and has no recognition for his personal pride and self-respect that should be inherent in a job well done.

He may not even recognize these facts himself. He would in most cases insist that his trouble with management is something else. The facts are, however, that he does not get the opportunity to be a respected man because of the ability he has in doing his job. He will resent and resist such management even when the reason is not too clear to himself.

There is the problem that industrial management must solve. Incentive management does just that. That is the reason for its success. We Americans regard equality of treatment, individual liberty, the recognition of individual ability and the right to own property as natural rights. Incentive management must and does recognize all these natural rights in every worker and to the extent that his development and worth will warrant.

Industry as usually organized at the present time, exercises dictatorial power over the worker. He has no control over his future in his work except that given by his union. The union, however, now submerges his individuality. Industrial management puts him on work with methods and tools about which he has no choice. The more efficient the plant, the less influence he will have on anything that is being done. His personality as a man is submerged. So far as his personality is concerned, he is little more than his Social Security number. His position relative to the boss is also that of servant to master. There is a great gulf, therefore, developed between boss and man because of their relative positions.

Custom in this matter is the result of centuries of owner-slave and serf-feudal lord relationship. It is true that this is the land of liberty where men were set free, but industrial organizations are still set in the old pattern of class societies. The lord of the industry may be a stern master or a kindly, patronizing one, caring for his workers' welfare, but he is still the lord, far above those in inferior station. This was natural and proper to a European worker not long ago. His American grandson endures it but hates it. This is the hurdle that management must eliminate before much progress in the desire of man to excel as a worker and develop as a man can be made.

The greatest hold that the union has on its members is its power over the boss, not its ability to increase wages and shorten hours. The union's appeal to the worker is its challenge to the boss. The union defies the boss, threatens him. It is his equal and more. It overpowers him, makes him yield and obey its will. The union revenges the worker's ignored personality. It asserts for him his equal stakes with the highest boss. The union, however, does not give to the man the feeling of importance of himself as a worker. The union also simply makes the man a number.

OWNERSHIP BRIDGES GULF BETWEEN WORKER AND MANAGEMENT

Any industrial organization must be a dictatorship in the old and still usual view. Managers in all successful departments of industry must have complete power. They must control all the operations if any industry is to succeed. Incentive management must have this power and at the same time there must be universal confidence that this supreme power will not at anytime overlook or fail to recognize the complete need and essentiality of the worker. He must be recognized equally as essential as management, which he is even when he is completely at the direction of management. Management is the coach who must be obeyed. The men, however, are the players who alone can win the game.

Stock ownership is one of the steps that can be taken that will make the worker feel that there is less of a gulf between him and the boss, but it will not completely bridge the gulf. It is only one of the things that will help the worker to feel his importance and his interest in the game that is being played. Stock ownership will help the worker to recognize his responsibility in the game and the importance of victory. This feeling is very important and very lacking in industry generally When it is achieved, as incentive management can bring it to achievement, the results are miraculous.

CHAPTER XIV

Conclusion

Incentive management is a new approach to human relationships in industry. It is obvious that what has gone before leaves much to be desired. Our former attitudes did not recognize what man can become. Because of this lack of recognition, he did not have the opportunity nor the desire to develop to the marvelous stature that he can, will and does when the natural spurs are present. Incentive management is a means of supplying these lacks in present industrial management.

This program of incentive would be equally effective in any other action which requires group cooperation. It is a fundamental philosophy, since man is the individual he is. It is progressively more important to the economy, because industry is absorbing a progressively larger proportion of all workers. All people also depend progressively more and more on the products of industry to live a satisfactory life.

Because of this progressively greater importance of industry to the worker in it and to the buyer of its products, some form of satisfactory labor-management cooperation is essential. Failing that, we must go to some form of police state that will force some degree of cooperation by its power. It is not possible for America to continue in a muddle wherein one man can shut the economy down at his order and only at his order can resumption of production be had. It is obvious that such power must be curbed. It is fairly obvious that it cannot be stopped under our present representative form of government. It will therefore force a dictatorship with all its dismal consequences, unless some other means that is effective is developed. Incentive management is that means.

INCENTIVE MANAGEMENT ENCOURAGES CHANGE

Incentive management does not force cooperation, since cooperation cannot be forced. It invites it. Incentive management is a profitable answer for all people. Incentive management is not a law. It is a way of life that all will gladly follow if they are given the understanding and the opportunity. Incentive management has always been a basic desire of all. It has been held back because of age-old custom. We would not, because of custom, accept the inherent greatness of man and his insistent desire for such recognition. Incentive management encourages us to change this notion.

It is perhaps hard to accept any new concept, no matter how logical, if it disturbs our present habits of thought. We shall always resist change. The plea of the poet or the objection of the "practical" man is always the same, as given in the quotation:

"Change and decay in all around I see:
O Thou who changeth not, Abide with me."

Classing change with decay is not unusual in much thinking. The only trouble with this plea is that even the pleader is not satisfied to keep from change after the change has become universal. He then insists on it, no matter how hard he bucked it before. The most stand pat horseman at first ridiculed, but now worships the automobile. We all want change after it has become accepted, no matter how much we ridiculed and resisted it at first.

This very human trait is one of the most difficult problems for the leader to solve in developing incentive management. It is the basic problem. It is so difficult for the average person to recognize the possibilities of man, whom he had always underrated. It is so difficult to believe the assertion of the psalmist that man is only "a little lower than the angels."

In the same way it is very difficult for us to believe the endless progress that can be made by developed man. We here also are apt in our thinking to identify change with decay. We will not recognize that any man can make great progress by developing himself; but when he does, we at first are apt to insist that no progress has been made. It is little wonder, therefore, that man has had little encouragement in self-development and in his consequent usefulness to the economy. It is surprising that he has caused so little trouble heretofore because of his frustration under our previous thinking.

THE DEVELOPMENT OF MAN—WHY AND ITS IMPORTANCE

No one can look back through history without recognizing many facts that it will be valuable to review here because of their indication of the possibilities facing us in industry.

First: The industrial revolution is only two centuries old. The progress that has been made during that time in science and industry is almost unbelievable in the light of previous history. There is no doubt that progress in science, even during the last fifty years, is greater than all previous progress combined.

All progress is made by man. Hence, man now is progressing faster scientifically than at any previous time. He is developing useful things faster. We know, however, that man as a creature has not changed. He has merely developed. The development of man's latent ability is the reason for the progress of science. That also is the reason why more progress will undoubtedly be made.

The question may well be asked: "Why has man developed only in the last few generations to produce the marvelous results that we are now seeing? Why did not this all happen long ago?" The reason is that only lately has man had the freedom and incentive to develop in the directions he is now going. Only recently have the freedom of opportunity and the incentive been present to make man what he now has developed into. Most men were serfs, slaves or "lower class" up to a few generations ago.

Had the opportunity and incentive occurred before, man would have developed then. The geniuses who have made our economy the wonderful thing it is, could have developed at any previous time in the world's history. There have been millions of Edisons, Watts, Ketterings and Einsteins who lived in previous generations, who did not develop their abilities and hence were not recognized. Some were inherently greater than anyone we now know about. They lived, but they did not have the opportunity nor the incentive to develop their latent genius. They went to their graves without themselves or anyone else knowing of their great abilities. Their abilities remained latent; hence useless.

Gray in his Elegy puts it thus:

"Perhaps in this neglected spot is laid
Some heart once pregnant with celestial fire

Hands that the rod of empire might have swayed
Or waked to ecstasy the living lyre.

But knowledge to their eyes her ample page
Rich with its spoils of time did ne'er unroll
Chill penury repressed their noble rage
And froze the genial current of the soul."

Second: The direction of development taken depends on what genius is developed and how it is directed. New development obviously can go unlimited distances and in any direction. Science is in its infancy. Great genius can develop science, therefore, in any direction and to any extent. Progress will be made in the direction that genius is directed and to the extent that genius is developed.

Atomic power will be a useful thing for man's use very soon only because genius has been directed in that direction. It would have been discovered years ago, had the incentive existed to develop the latent genius that was needed. Perhaps the human race would have been destroyed then, rather than waiting until now. That also is a problem, posed by our progress.

Had metallurgical genius been developed and directed toward the gas turbine before the steam or gas engine, we should have had a different kind of power plant with much greater efficiency than we have now.

No one can know how future development will take place. That depends on the direction that an idea takes in the mind of the genius who happens to think in that direction. There is no end to the new ideas that eventually will completely change the course of our existence. Our program of day to day life is changing continually and radically. Where it will lead, no one knows. No one can possibly imagine the future, since it will be the result of the diverse imaginations of many people. We can be sure, however, that we can not recognize now the world they will produce a century hence.

Third: The nation that develops the greatest genius will be the dominant power. This is not the result of birth; it is the result of the development of the individual's latent ability. Every nation has enough latent genius to make it dominant if sufficient development takes place. Most nations now largely eliminate such growth by their frustration of the individual.

The reason for the favorable position of the United States in the nations of the world has been the freedom of opportunity and incentive for development of genius here and its direction toward useful things. Other nations could have outdistanced us had they given their people the freedom that allowed our country to develop the geniuses that have made us great. All Americans were foreigners a few years or at most a few generations ago. When these foreigners came to America with its freedom of opportunity, they grew to genius in enough cases to make them and America the leader of the world.

Such development is being stopped now. We will lose our dominant position as we progressively punish genius by the frustrations that dominant government always places on any man of genius and his accomplishments.

The drive toward any new accomplishment can always be stopped by sufficient opposition. That is why freedom of opportunity is so important. No one can tell at first how any development can be accomplished. If he could, the development would have taken place long ago.

The reason why America has progressed so far is the freedom of opportunity that at first existed here and did not exist in the foreign countries from which all Americans originally came. Had that freedom existed abroad, the development would not have taken place here. Present Americans would have stayed at home rather than have come here. Those nations, therefore, would now lead the world.

If America is now to eliminate that freedom of opportunity, which it is doing by the program of punitive taxation of the successful and encouragement of the loafer, we can be sure that progress will stop here and we will stagnate as all other nations have who have adopted the same restrictions.

We fear Russia and its totalitarian rule. We should, since Communism destroys the freedom of opportunity that would wreck our progress if we adopted its philosophy. We seemingly do not fear, however, the enormous strides we are taking toward Communism that is implicit in our present program.

Our present governmental program of restriction will be even more destructive, since Russia, while eliminating liberty, does reward handsomely the progress that the individual makes; while we punish the same individual by progressively steeper taxation and ridicule of his success.

Fourth: Putting people in grooves stops their development. They must be free and individually responsible. Only so can development take place.

Universal military training stops all progress of those in the ranks. They will be good soldiers, but they will not be good or imaginative thinkers.

The history of Germany, Austria and all other universally militarily trained populations shows the truth of this statement. After any person has been forbidden to use his mind for long enough time, he will have no mind of his own to use. He will have no chance to develop such a mind. The German people have paid an outlandish price for Germany's military policy.

NEW ATTITUDES NEEDED

The philosophy of incentive management is not generally followed because it is new. No one questions its basic rightness nor its results. The difficulty is that it is too new to be accepted. It is difficult for the usual industrialist to believe that man can become as great as he can. He therefore will not accept the incentive philosophy. He is looking for the catch instead.

New progress means new methods. Therefore, we should be as prone to accept new concepts of men as we are new concepts in science. In fact, we should be more so, since man has far greater possibilities. The machine has relatively few. This conception of man is completely necessary to leadership that wishes to adopt incentive management.

Management under incentive has a radically different role than management under the present warring program necessary under collective bargaining. Productive work as now viewed by union leaders and by government regulation is something to shun. Labor to them is abhorrent. To produce as little as possible is a virtue. Efficient production is ruled out. The skill of the worker and its development are frowned on and boycotted.

The result of this policy is of course to increase the cost of living, as we now see. That increased cost is decried by government and the labor leaders who caused it, but the blame is placed on industrial management's selfishness instead of on the present restrictions. Seemingly, the public is satisfied to have the blame so placed and to pay the bill in higher costs. So far have we missed the point.

This result is no doubt serious, but it is of relatively small importance compared to the lack of progress of the worker and his development which is the natural result of the present program. That is the real tragedy.

No union man under present labor leadership can develop himself nor can he have satisfaction in his work. He is doomed to a life of frustration since his skill is decried and his progress is stopped by his own leaders. Such a man can never be content.

No man can be happy if the ability on which he must depend for recognition is decried. He cannot be proud of such skill nor can he feel his importance as a man. He is ripe for any program that will upset the existing economy. Revolutions are made by such frustrated people.

Markham expresses it thus:
"O Masters, lords and rulers in all lands,
How will the future reckon with this man?
How answer his brute question in that hour
When whirlwinds of rebellion shake all shores?
How will it be with kingdoms and with kings
With those who shaped him to the thing he is,
When this dumb terror shall rise to judge the world,
After the silence of centuries?"

The only reason why there is no revolution in the union ranks is because management has been equally negligent in its understanding and recognition of man and his dignity. The worker has no chance for contentment under present union leadership. He also has the same lack of opportunity under much present industrial leadership.

LEADERSHIP'S MAGNIFICENT OPPORTUNITY

The above facts show the direction to go. The industrialist can be sure that if his leadership will develop his men in the way that incentive management develops men, any labor leadership or government that attempted to get in the way would be immediately kicked in the teeth.

The present concept of the relationship that should exist between labor and management as exemplified by New Deal labor legislation gives the industrial leader all the ammunition he needs to combat it. It is obvious that government has missed the point as completely as has present management, both union and industrial.

Incentive management is as different from our present concept of industrial relationships as the Sermon on the Mount is from present armament programs. That is its strength and its opportunity.

The domination of the labor leader is not the desire of the worker to make union labor leadership dominant over himself. It is instead the result of the frustration that usual industrial operations give to the worker when he has no means of making his job one that will express his personality. The power of the union over his boss to some extent eliminates this frustration because the worker then feels that he has regained some degree of self-respect because of this power over a previously dominant power. He therefore gives up his freedom to the union leader or to governmental domination, since this power eliminates the still more hated domination of the usual industrial boss.

THE EVIL OF DOMINANT GOVERNMENT

The American concept of government at first was far from that of any other nation's concept. We have always before the New Deal, held government in check, while most nations have been under a dominant bureaucracy. It is our freedom from governmental domination that has made America the place to which all other peoples were drawn.

Because we have not seen the result of dominant bureaucracy, except in time of war, we do not fear it. We still think of big government as virtuous, not evil. We still think that dominant power in government is satisfactory, yet we know from past experience that domination by any group in any field is outrageous in its selfishness. We do not see that the dishonesty met with in other groups would be multiplied many times when a dominant governmental bureaucracy takes over.

We do not see that the small wastes of industry, so evident to us, would be infinitesimal compared to the wastes of a dominant government. We think perhaps that people change when they work for government. The fact is of course that the vices that man has as an individual are often multiplied many times when he is entrenched in government and can force the taxpayer to support him in any program he may elect.

Dominant government eliminates freedom from all its citizens. It must, since only so can it accomplish the purposes that a dominant government is established to perform. If government is to give security, the citizen must first make dominant government secure. Only so can the caretaker take care. Government can produce nothing. It can only get the necessary money for its dominance by extracting it from the citizens, the only wealth producers.

That is the reason why progress, prosperity, individual development and contentment go when government takes over. History is full of the miseries that dominant government causes. In spite of this long record, we seemingly cannot or will not believe the facts.

Man has always in all history, however, turned to government for security when he got soft. His disappearance as a free citizen occurs shortly thereafter. We must be self-reliant if we are to be free. Security is only sure and lasting for the soft in a penitentiary.

Governmental domination grows as the citizen shrinks. The two go together. Which is cause and which is effect is anyone's guess. The final result is the same, however.

There has been much discussion by many people as to just what powers and restrictions government can and must have in a country where the citizen retains his freedom and individuality. It is evident that government must have certain powers over the citizen if he is to be free. It is also certain that there are certain jobs that government can do better than anyone else. These will have to be done by a central government even with its waste and lack of ability in the doing. It is obviously better to have certain jobs done, no matter how inefficiently, than not to have them done at all. What, therefore, should be the responsibilities and limitations of government of a free people?

The primary purpose of a proper government is to make its citizens free. The secondary purpose is to do the things that government only can do. The third and most important government job then is to keep out of the way of a free people, no matter what crises occur in the economy. Government cannot go beyond these limits without damage to the citizens' freedom.

Every nation that disappears goes to government when economic difficulty occurs. Slumps in business that pinch part or all of the citizens have been the usual time when freedom was sacrificed for governmental help extracted by taxation from the rest.

We do not perhaps believe in individual robbery. We overcome our qualms by having government take the necessary money from those who have it, by taxation, or steal it from the next generations by deficit financing. Seemingly, we feel better about the matter that way. We feel then that we are not robbers personally.

240

The cycle of civilian decay has always been the same in all civilizations. First, a nation of self-reliant people, because of their freedom and development, become wealthy. Second, because of their wealth, they begin to grow soft. Third, because of their softness they become lazy; then they cannot support themselves; then they turn to government for support. Fourth, government must eliminate individual freedom by sweeping taxation to do the supporting that these soft people ask government to do. Fifth, the consequent loss of freedom and ambition that results from progressively higher taxation of the producer eliminates incentive. The labor camp and the bullet then are necessary to produce even a minimum standard of living. Sixth, a virile country that has not frittered away its strength and freedom takes them over. Every nation in all history has followed this pattern.

THE PROPER FUNCTIONS OF GOVERNMENT

Let us now outline the powers of government that would keep a people free and virile. Government of a free people must have as its primary object the preserving of its people's freedom. It therefore protects the citizen from any aggression by a police force, by courts of law, by a constitution that guarantees freedom from any restraint that will not infringe the freedom of others, by an army that will guarantee freedom from any outside power. Lastly it guarantees freedom from a selfish majority that may attempt to infringe the rights of any minority. That is the reason for and responsibility of government of a free people.

It is evident that such a government can do other things that will be helpful and which would not infringe the freedom of the citizen. These are various. The coining of money is one. The doing of certain research or development work that private industry would not normally follow is another. Such programs as controlled weather and controlled erosion of soil are samples of such work. There would have to be a definite limit on this, however, so that results would be universally valuable, not to the advantage of one group only.

Whether handling of the mail would remain a governmental function is questionable. Private industry could do this job for less than half of what it now costs the taxpayer. The organizing and controlling of a company for this purpose would be a large and difficult problem, but the advantages are far greater than the probable penalties.

All the needed functions of such a government as outlined above could be paid for with less than one percent of the income of a free country, except in case of attack from without by some enemy. Such an attack would be very improbable, since a free country would be so valuable because of its products to all other countries that cooperation would be automatic. The relationships with all other nations would be similar to that now existing between the United States and Canada. Each is indispensable to the other. War between them now is impossible.

Before Canada and the United States became indispensable to each other economically, however, we fought two wars with Britain, of which Canada is a part. Each got a bloody nose and much jealousy as a result of these wars. After that, we started to deal commercially with each other. Now no one could imagine another war occurring. That obviously is the only sure cure for war. No dominant government, however, could recognize this fact, much less act on it. This is one of the most dangerous features of big government. It always tries to dominate all peoples. That alone is enough reason for eliminating it.

The domination of the individual by government, now willingly given to political hacks by the average American voter, is not due to his desire to be subservient to a strong central government. All people hate to be subservient to anyone. We all will, however, try to pick a better dictator than the one we have when we are forced to be under someone's domination in any case.

Incentive management will not come of itself except after many years of bitter experience. It can come soon if we will but believe and act.

INCENTIVE MANAGEMENT AND FREEDOM

Incentive management is of great importance in promoting labor management cooperation. It is potentially vastly more important in its effect on the whole economy. The most pressing questions now before this nation and to a great extent before all nations, are these: how much freedom is the citizen to have? How much power is government to have over the individual? *Is government made for man, or is man made for government?* The answer to these questions will determine the future of every American and also whether any American is to have any future as an individual.

We perhaps feel that such a statement is far overdrawn. We cannot believe that anyone, least of all our own government, can make us anything else than free. We have been accustomed always to thinking that our government is primarily for the purpose of maintaining our freedom. We cannot believe that it can do otherwise than continue in this role.

The difficulty is not that government plans to make us anything else than free people. The difficulty is that a very large number of Americans now want government to assume responsibilities that can only be assumed by a government which greatly restricts or entirely eliminates freedom of the individual.

I am enough of a believer in the desire for freedom that is inherent in Americans to be sure that if we all could see the necessary restrictions that government must put on all of us, if it is to accomplish the requested ends, that the majority now want government to assume, we should stop at once and go back to the small government of small powers that we had up to twenty years ago; i.e., the government the Founding Fathers planned.

We do not want serfdom to an all-powerful government. We do want, however, the promised security in a soft life that an all-powerful government can promise to give.

THE CHOICE IS BEFORE US NOW

All Americans must answer this problem and now, as the power to change our program will disappear as an all-powerful government takes over.

So far, this fear of a powerful government is not well developed in Americans. Since we have never before had such a government, we therefore do not know how it would affect us individually.

Government control over the economy can only mean economic stasis. Progress cannot be made under such conditions because the individuals who can make progress cannot then have the necessary freedom of opportunity. They are cast in the mold that government forms. This mold recognizes only what has been done, not progress.

Can anyone imagine the automobile, the airplane or the Golden Rule being developed by government bureaucracy? No such progress could be made by dominant government.

The conception that everything we do now is wrong and will be changed could not exist in a governmental bureaucracy.

If the citizen is primarily for the purpose of paying taxes for bureaucracy to spend, he cannot spend his earnings himself on his possibly progressive ideas and experiments. If he is bound by government regulations that restrict his free will and earnings he will not try the experiments that eventually spell progress.

While that would be serious in its effects, it is not the most serious of our problems with an all-powerful government. The greatest evil will be the lack of development by the individual of his latent abilities.

No person can develop his latent abilities except in the white heat of competition. Government domination eliminates competition. Government domination therefore dooms any nation to mediocrity. Mediocrity dooms any nation to disappearance in competition with the nation whose economy by competition develops the individual.

Our willingness to accept governmental domination was for the first time shown in the depression of the early thirties. For the first time in our history, we went to government for a solution when a slump struck.

We had had slumps fully as serious many times before, but we faced them ourselves. Our developed softness in the thirties caused us to hope that government could and should bail us out. Many still think government did. We have not seen the final results of the government's bailing as yet, however. We have not as yet paid the final price.

Depression is the normal and continual condition of a country whose economy is under governmental domination. Note Russia, England, Spain and pre-war Japan. They were continually in a slump compared to the normal economic conditions here. A boom is the normal upsurging of an economy that is free.

There will be booms and busts here as there always have been. The booms will be obtained because of the leadership of free genius. The slumps are normal and a continual condition in any government-dominated people. No one could notice a slump in Russia, since slumps are continuous there.

EVERYBODY CANNOT BE A WINNER

There is another problem that we must answer if we are to have the advantages and progress given by incentive management. That problem is the place of the incompetent, the lazy and the unfortunate. Much of our drift to governmental domination stems from our desire to help them. We are so apt to picture ourselves as in their shoes that we want to make personal security a reality for them with the thought that we may in the future need it ourselves.

In following out this program, we spend money and effort without limit to cure the incurable, to encourage the lazy, and to care for the careless, all at the expense of the worker who has often overcome these same handicaps to become the producer that he is.

There must be a review of our attitudes and responsibilities. If we support without their effort the lazy, the incompetent and the diseased, we merely defeat nature's method of improving the human race. If the poor specimens are not to be eliminated by nature's method, as has been the case from the beginning of time, we shall become a progressively weaker nation, as the lazy and incompetent replace the virile and ambitious.

A very good case can be made for the virtue of pity for

the unfortunate; but if we do not allow competition to continue as it always has to work out its normal results, we shall run out of caretakers for the carefree. We cannot safely penalize the producer to promote the nonproducer.

We recognize this need to eliminate the poor specimens in animals, in marriage, in the criminal and the enemy. We must also recognize it in ourselves. We cannot make all winners in the game of life. Competition is still the life-blood of progress.

The above discussion does not decry the fact that we must make the lives of the unfortunate as peaceful as is reasonable. That is an obvious program. The point that is made is that nature's elimination of the unfit by competition with the fit must not be defeated. Industry must not be forced to support the incompetent by unearned wages, merely because he happens to belong to a union. Color of the skin must not determine who gets what job. Citizenship or religion must not determine who makes what progress in any job.

Eventually, the strong and virile will replace the weak and lazy. The problem that we in America must solve is to make sure such replacement is done by us. If we do not, a more virile nation which has allowed natural competition to determine the winners and losers in the game of life and industry, will take us over.

THERE MUST BE INCENTIVES

There must always be incentives in some form. There have been many attempts to install them in industry. The fact that some attempts for an incentive plan have been made does not mean that the people involved have the actual spur of incentive.

Paying more money for more production only is not a

very great or long lasting incentive. Such payment may succeed in getting greater production. This, however, does not prove its soundness. The reason for greater production resulting from profit sharing usually is that efficiency was so low before that any change in the attitude of the men would result in greatly increased production.

Such a result has been thought by many to prove the efficiency of some particular scheme that has been tried. The results that have been so secured would look entirely different were they to be compared to the results that are obtained under incentive management when everyone in the organization *wants* to make a record.

Do not evaluate any accomplishment except as it compares to the world's record. Only so can an accurate estimate be obtained.

The psychologist tells us that under present urges, man has never yet developed half his latent abilities. There is therefore a vast untapped field of ability remaining for future leadership to make actual.

There is no reason yet known why more than one-half of our latent abilities should remain dormant. Since we have these latent abilities, it is obvious that they can be developed from their latent state. The fundamental philosophy of incentive management will develop new ways and means whereby this so far unaccomplished development will become real. No one can believe that this present waste of individual progress will always remain. No such conclusion can be possible in the light of the progress made by man even over the last five thousand years, which is an infinitely small time in the total history and probable future of man.

The heroes we pick out of our acquaintance or from history show how man has developed in many cases. Who can question that this inherent greatness will be progressively greater as man still further develops his abilities?

The progress that we have made compared to our forefathers demonstrates conclusively what the future can be if we continue to progress. It is well, therefore, now to ask the question, "What would happen if incentive management were developed to the point that man would normally develop all of his latent abilities? What would the world be then?" That is the inspiration for the new industrial leader. That is the vision that he will ever keep before himself. Eventually, man will be only "a little lower than the angels."

Appendix

In the foregoing text, theories are developed regarding efficient production resulting from cooperation of developed men. Some indications have been made as to the progress that such people have made in manufacturing operations. In this Appendix, figures are given which support the generalizations given in the text.

The Lincoln Electric Company manufactures arc welding equipment and arc welding electrodes. In doing this, the Company is in competition with the largest electrical manufacturers in the United States. Abroad, they are in competition with the largest electrical manufacturers in all foreign countries. This Company has successfully met this competition here and abroad. It sells more than half of all arc welding machines used in the United States and as an average nearly half of all arc welding electrodes.

The following charts and supporting data are given to show these relative results of The Lincoln Electric Company's operations under incentive management compared to that of other industry, which is now struggling under government-sponsored, industrial civil war, known as "collective bargaining."

251

The difference in efficiency is the direct result of cooperative desire of developed men in The Lincoln Electric Company, compared to the careless operation and output limitation practices, the result of the present friction between labor union and industrial managements.

While these results are startling in their comparison, they are only an indication of the eventual results that will be obtained when incentive management is universally adopted, as it must be, eventually.

It is well to remember in examining these charts, that the selling prices in the case of The Lincoln Electric Company are regulated by cost, not by what the consumer will pay. Since prices of Lincoln products are governed by this policy, they are very much lower than the prices of like products sold for other purposes. Lincoln sales dollar volume is therefore much less for the same amount of product.

If sales figures were accurately comparable, the record shown would be far more striking. The dollar volume of Lincoln products would be more than twice that shown.

Gas welding and arc welding electrodes are both made of similar steel rods. The gas welding electrode is merely copper plated, but the arc welding electrode is covered by an extruded coating of relatively high priced chemicals. The extruding process is a far more costly process than copper plating, yet gas welding electrodes sell for about twice the price of arc welding electrodes made by incentive management.

Arc welding machines are motor generator sets exactly similar to motor generator sets used for other purposes except in wiring and connections, which have no effects on cost. Arc welding sets, however, sell for less than half the price charged for similar sets used for other purposes not made under incentive management.

Because of these facts, in reviewing the charts shown herein, the sales dollars of The Lincoln Electric Company should be at least doubled, when compared with the sales figures of other manufacturers.

It is obvious that what is produced by a manufacturing plant is pieces of product, rather than dollars of sales. The manufacturing operations for producing a ton of electrode or a 300 ampere welder is the same, whether the product made is sold for $500.00 or twice that amount.

The reader may hesitate to believe the enormous difference in efficiency that these charts will show. It would be well, therefore, for him to compare the difference between the speed of the athlete when he is running a championship race and when he may be walking in his sleep. Incentive management and "collective bargaining" produce comparable results in the worker and his production rates.

INCENTIVE MANAGEMENT

The following charts, with their supporting factual evidence, show the results of incentive management in The Lincoln Electric Company over the past seventeen years. It is obvious that the progress made in incentive management is continuous, so that these results will be progressively better.

CHART I.

The selling price of a standard, 3/16" electrode is shown herewith, over the period from the beginning of the incentive system through 1949. The selling price of this electrode was about half that of gas welding rod which is made of the same kind of steel but without the coating of the arc welding electrode, which coating makes this electrode much more expensive to produce.

It will be noted that the price shown is less than half of that charged when the incentive system started. This price began to increase only when the price of steel core wire from which it is made more than doubled after 1945.

This pattern is followed by all products made by The Lincoln Electric Company under incentive management.

UNDER INCENTIVE MANAGEMENT SELLING PRICES OF 3/16" ELECTRODE NO. 5 AND NO. 7 BY THE LINCOLN ELECTRIC COMPANY IN RELATION TO INDEXES OF WHOLESALE PRICES OF SEMIMANUFACTURED PRODUCTS AND STEEL WIRE RODS, UNITED STATES 1933 - 1949

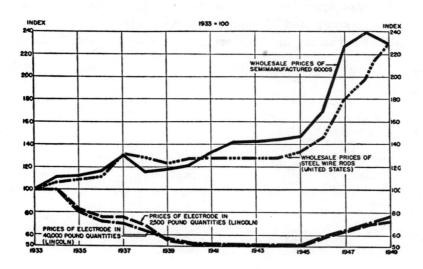

Supporting data on next page

254

CHART I (Continued)

| Year | No. 5 and No. 7—3/16 Inch Electrode—Price Per Pound in Specified Quantities (Cents)[1] | | | | | | Semimanufactured Products[2] | Steel Wire Rods[3] | |
| | Less than 50 Pounds | | 2,500 Pounds | | 40,000 Pounds | | 1926 = 100 / 1933 = 100 | | |
	Price	Index	Price	Index	Price	Index	1926 = 100	1933 = 100	Price	Index
1933	23.75c	100.0	12.00c	100.0	11.00c	100.0	65.4	100.0	$35.160	100.0
1934	23.06	97.1	12.00	100.0	11.00	100.0	72.8	111.3	37.385	106.3
1935	18.41	77.5	9.87	82.2	8.87	80.6	73.6	112.5	38.226	108.7
1936	17.62	74.2	9.02	75.2	7.92	72.0	75.9	116.1	39.173	111.4
1937	18.00**	75.8	9.10**	75.8	7.70**	70.0	85.3	130.4	46.308	131.7
1938	16.29	68.6	8.18	68.2	6.99	63.5	75.4	115.3	44.923	127.8
1939	14.00	58.9	6.60	55.0	6.20	56.4	77.0	117.7	43.139	122.7
1940	13.25	55.8	6.22	51.8	5.82	52.9	79.1	120.9	44.800	127.4
1941	13.00	54.7	6.10	50.8	5.70	51.8	86.9	132.9	44.800	127.4
1942	13.00	54.7	6.07	50.6	5.67	51.5	92.6	141.6	44.800	127.4
1943	13.00	54.7	6.00	50.0	5.60	50.9	92.9	142.0	44.800	127.4
1944	13.00	54.7	6.00	50.0	5.60	50.9	94.1	143.9	44.800	127.4
1945	13.00	54.7	6.00	50.0	5.60	50.9	95.9	146.6	46.803	133.1
1946	14.50	61.1	6.83	56.9	6.43	58.5	110.8	169.4	51.288	145.9
1947	15.75	66.3	7.55	62.9	7.08	64.4	148.5	227.1	64.960	184.7
1948	17.19	72.4	8.29	69.1	7.79	70.8	156.6	239.4	77.056	219.1
1949	19.53	82.2	8.64	72.0	8.38	76.2	150.2	229.7	79.468	226.0
Per cent Change 1949 from 1933	—11.8		—28.0		—23.8		+129.7		+126.0	

*Average annual prices were computed by weighing each existing price during a given year by the number of months during which it prevailed, in line with the data on price changes shown in Petitioner's Exhibit 39, p. 743 and data on price changes for later years submitted per covering letter dated February 23, 1950 and signed G. F. Clipsham.

**As of October 1, 1936 the Company started to pay transportation charges on shipments and instituted zone prices. All prices used in this table refer to Zone No. 1 and applied to all customers other than railroads, dealers and agents. This comprises 20 states and three metropolitan districts in as many additional states.

Sources: 1. For the years 1933-1941 from Petitioner's Exhibit 57, *The Lincoln Electric Company v. Commissioner of Internal Revenue*, United States Circuit Court of Appeals for the Sixth Circuit, No. 10,333, Transcript of Record, Vol. III, p. 799; for the years 1942-1949 computed from data on price changes shown in Petitioner's Exhibit 39, p. 743 and other data on price changes referred to above.

2. For the years 1933-1941, in terms of 1933 base, from Petitioner's Exhibit 59, *The Lincoln Electric Company v. Commissioner of Internal Revenue*, United States Circuit Court of Appeals for the Sixth Circuit, No. 10,333, Transcript of Record, Vol. III, p. 783; from indexes (in terms of 1926 base) published in the various issues of the *Survey of Current Business*, U.S. Department of Commerce, which were then converted to a 1933 base.

3. United States Department of Labor, Bureau of Labor Statistics, "Wholesale Prices," various bulletins for the years specified in the table. The prices as reported by the Bureau are for "Rods, wire, per gross ton, Pittsburgh" and are average monthly prices for the year.

255

CHART II

The following chart shows the comparative selling prices of welding machines manufactured by The Lincoln Electric Company compared to comparable products. The increase of welding machine prices after 1945 is the result of the very rapid price increase of materials which are procured from other manufacturers. Much of this material cost increase has been eliminated by reduced labor and overhead costs, as is shown.

SELLING PRICES OF ELECTRIC MOTOR DRIVEN WELDERS BY THE LINCOLN ELECTRIC COMPANY IN RELATION TO INDEXES OF WHOLESALE PRICES OF SPECIFIED GROUPS OF COMMODITIES UNITED STATES 1933 - 1949

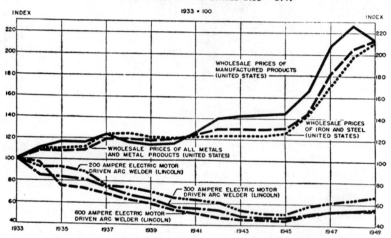

AVERAGE ANNUAL* SELLING PRICES OF SPECIFIED ELECTRIC MOTOR DRIVEN WELDERS, THE LINCOLN ELECTRIC COMPANY, 1933-1949
(1933 = 100)

Year	200 Ampere—Horizontal		300 Ampere		600 Ampere	
	Price[2]	Index	Price[1]	Index	Price[1]	Index
1933	$590.00	100.0	$770.00	100.0	$1,288.25	100.0
1934	550.00	93.2	655.42	85.1	1,254.17	97.4
1935	550.00	93.2	645.00	83.8	970.00	75.3
1936	525.00	89.0	626.25	81.3	947.50	73.5
1937	447.50	75.8	570.00	74.0	880.00	68.3
1938	440.00	74.6	520.00	67.5	810.00	62.9
1939	420.00	71.2	490.00	63.6	765.00	59.4
1940	385.00	65.3	441.25	57.3	693.75	53.9
1941	375.00	63.6	430.00	55.8	652.50	50.7
1942	360.00	61.0	415.00	53.9	610.00	47.4
1943	317.50	53.8	371.67	48.3	581.67	45.2
1944	300.00	50.8	360.00	46.8	570.00	44.2
1945	300.00	50.8	360.00	46.8	570.00	44.2
1946	340.00	57.6	386.25	50.2	632.50	49.1
1947	360.00	61.0	405.00	52.6	680.00	52.8
1948	376.67	63.8	417.50	54.2	692.50	53.8
1949	392.50	66.5	430.00	55.8	695.00	53.9

Per cent decline:
1933-1949	33.5		44.2		46.1	

CHART II (Continued)

*Average prices were computed by weighing each existing price during a given year by the number of months during which it prevailed, in line with the data on price changes shown in Petitioner's Exhibit 36, p. 737, and for later years from data on price changes submitted per covering letter dated February 15, 1950 and signed G. F. Clipsham.

Source: For the years 1933-1941 the data from Petitioner's Exhibit 58, *The Lincoln Electric Company v. Commissioner of Internal Revenue*, United States Circuit Court of Appeals for the Sixth Circuit, No. 10,333, Transcript of Record, Vol. III, p. 781; for the years 1942-1949 computed from data on price changes shown in Petitioner's Exhibit 36, p. 737 and other data on price changes referred to above.

INDEXES OF WHOLESALE PRICES OF SPECIFIED GROUPS OF COMMODITIES, UNITED STATES 1933 - 1949

Year	Manufactured Products		All Metals and Metal Products		Iron and Steel	
	1926 = 100	1933 = 100	1926 = 100	1933 = 100	1926 = 100	1933 = 100
1933	70.5	100.0	79.8	100.0	78.6	100.0
1934	78.2	110.9	86.9	108.9	86.7	110.3
1935	82.2	116.6	86.4	108.3	86.7	110.3
1936	82.0	116.3	87.0	109.0	87.6	111.5
1937	87.2	123.7	95.7	119.9	98.2	124.9
1938	82.2	116.6	95.7	119.9	98.6	125.4
1939	80.4	114.0	94.4	118.3	95.8	121.9
1940	81.6	115.7	95.8	120.1	95.1	121.0
1941	89.1	126.4	99.4	124.6	96.4	122.6
1942	98.6	140.0	103.8	130.1	97.2	123.7
1943	100.1	142.0	103.8	130.1	97.2	123.7
1944	100.8	143.0	103.8	130.1	97.2	123.7
1945	101.8	144.4	104.7	131.2	99.2	126.2
1946	116.1	164.7	115.5	144.7	110.3	140.3
1947	146.0	207.1	145.0	181.7	133.7	170.1
1948	159.4	226.1	163.6	205.0	155.2	197.5
1949	151.2	214.5	170.2	213.3	165.6	210.7

Sources: The basic data are published by the Bureau of Labor Statistics of the United States Department of Labor, using the base 1926 = 100. For purposes of this tabulation they were taken from various issues of the *Survey of Current Business* of the United States Department of Commerce and have been converted to a 1933 base. The converted indexes for the years 1934-1941 appear in Petitioner's Exhibit 59, *The Lincoln Electric Company v. Commissioner of Internal Revenue*, United States Circuit Court of Appeals for the Sixth Circuit, No. 10,333, Transcript of Record, Vol. III, p. 783.

CHART III

The comparative compensation of the workers in The Lincoln Electric Company compared to the workers in six major corporations in the United States.

It will be noted that as the incentive system became better understood, the wage reward increased. There is no end to this progress.

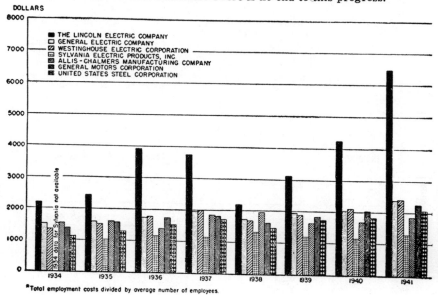

*Total employment costs divided by average number of employees.

Supporting Data for Chart III

TOTAL COMPENSATION* PER EMPLOYEE, THE LINCOLN ELECTRIC COMPANY AND OTHER SPECIFIED COMPANIES, 1934-1950

Year	Average number of employes	Employment Costs*	
		Amount	Per Employee
THE LINCOLN ELECTRIC COMPANY[1]			
1934	404	$ 884,028	$2,188
1935	485	1,183,965	2,441
1936	535	2,103,681	3,932
1937	666	2,488,634	3,736
1938	650	1,411,049	2,170
1939	637	1,988,660	3,122
1940	740	3,136,914	4,239
1941	979	6,315,790	6,451
1942	1,222	6,938,023	5,678
1943	1,245	7,443,883	5,979
1944	1,115	6,952,741	6,235
1945	1,110	6,427,868	5,791
1946	1,167	6,251,149	5,357
1947	1,157	7,561,752	6,536
1948	1,099	7,967,572	7,250
1949	1,026	6,372,832	6,211
1950	1,005	7,739,652	7,701

CHART III (Continued)

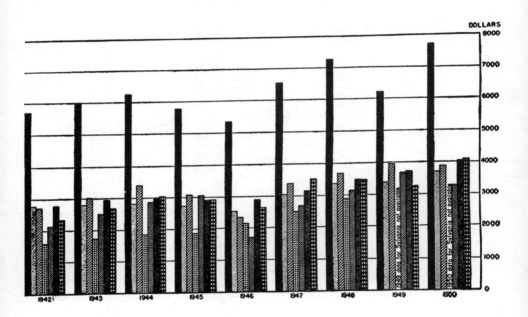

THE GENERAL ELECTRIC COMPANY²

1934	49,642	$ 76,152,292	$1,534
1935	55,706	89,837,576	1,613
1936	61,781	108,097,443	1,750
1937	75,212	147,173,236	1,957
1938	59,917	102,759,585	1,715
1939	62,797	121,607,599	1,937
1940	76,314	155,385,013	2,036
1941	109,689	260,529,577	2,375
1942	139,939	386,738,080	2,764
1943	171,133	477,451,295	2,790
1944	167,212	469,266,032	2,806
1945	148,233	404,435,154	2,728
1946	143,766	363,719,300	2,530
1947	185,696	566,640,999	3,051
1948	196,798	662,665,000	3,367
1949	179,300	606,685,000	3,384
1950	183,800	681,040,000	3,705

Supporting data for chart continued on next page

WESTINGHOUSE ELECTRIC CORPORATION[2]

1934	36,918	$ 50,175,038	$1,359
1935	36,284	55,332,684	1,525
1936	41,490	74,198,987	1,788
1937	52,249	104,287,277	1,996
1938	42,402	71,064,363	1,676
1939	43,732	81,823,273	1,871
1940	52,723	110,973,895	2,105
1941	71,073	170,125,276	2,394
1942	88,945	240,849,749	2,708
1943	105,702	318,108,808	3,009
1944	115,425	389,320,398	3,373
1945	103,333	318,343,664	3,081
1946	93,049	217,726,856	2,340
1947	102,065	344,157,341	3,372
1948	105,812	390,106,615	3,687
1949	94,729	375,917,652	3,968
1950	98,279	382,498,398	3,892

SYLVANIA ELECTRIC PRODUCTS, INC.[3]

1934	3,099	n.a.	n.a.
1935	2,970	$ 3,000,000	$1,010
1936	3,207	3,788,000	1,181
1937	3,393	3,925,000	1,157
1938	2,074	2,776,816	1,339
1939	3,261	3,886,677	1,192
1940	4,247	5,013,575	1,180
1941	5,264	6,892,078	1,309
1942	8,073	12,786,425	1,584
1943	13,683	23,766,999	1,737
1944	20,672	38,223,779	1,849
1945	22,521	42,078,916	1,868
1946	15,349	32,892,103	2,143
1947	15,450a	38,608,485	2,499
1948	14,000a	40,236,999	2,874
1949	n.a.	n.a.	n.a.
1950	n.a.	n.a.	n.a.

ALLIS-CHALMERS MANUFACTURING COMPANY[2]

1934	5,750b	$ 9,000,000	$1,565
1935	7,740	12,500,000	1,615
1936	12,736	18,000,000	1,413
1937	15,470	28,500,000	1,842
1938	11,511	22,720,054	1,974
1939	14,456	23,450,005	1,622
1940	16,908	28,670,004	1,696
1941	22,168	41,044,674	1,852
1942	31,120	66,802,605	2,147
1943	35,974	90,006,843	2,502
1944	36,832	106,185,084	2,883
1945	28,515	87,217,834	3,059
1946	28,827	49,357,069c	1,712c
1947	31,667	84,591,922	2,671
1948	33,663	105,925,073	3,147
1949	27,146	99,888,251	3,680
1950	31,086	101,948,468	3,280

GENERAL MOTORS CORPORATION[4]

1934	191,157	$ 267,179,680	$1,398
1935	211,712	334,752,385	1,581
1936	230,572	402,847,482	1,747
1937	261,977	474,359,501	1,811
1938	189,039	304,398,611	1,610
1939	220,434	397,843,717	1,805
1940	249,386	503,633,027	2,019
1941	303,827	682,131,349	2,245
1942	314,144	864,587,712	2,752
1943	448,848	1,329,250,416	2,961
1944	465,617	1,389,120,721	2,983
1945	345,940	1,018,339,589	2,944
1946	300,634	870,215,992	2,895
1947	375,689	1,184,500,638	3,153
1948	380,329	1,332,792,780	3,504
1949	401,326	1,500,690,450	3,739
1950	465,239	1,876,818,043	4,034

UNITED STATES STEEL CORPORATION[c]			
1934	189,881	$ 214,800,000	$1,131
1935	194,820	253,900,000	1,303
1936	222,372	339,000.000	1,524
1937	261,293	447,100.000	1,711
1938	202,108	294,400,000	1,457
1939	223,844	386,500,000	1,727
1940	254,393	464,300,000	1,825
1941	304,248	628,300,000	2,065
1942	335,866	782,700,000	2,330
1943	340,498	912,900,000	2,681
1944	314,888	957,200,000	3,040
1945	279,274	825,500,000	2,956
1946	266,835	704,500,000	2,640
1947	256,316	903,600,000	3,525
1948	296,785	1,035,700,000	3,490
1949	291,163	945,900,000	3,249
1950	288,265	1,179,400,000	4,091

*For the Lincoln Electric Company, total compensation or employment costs include wages, salaries, commissions, bonuses, annuity premiums, and profit sharing trust, including unemployment and federal old age benefit taxes. The same types of costs are included for all other companies. For example, in the case of the United States Steel Corporation employment costs include, in addition to payrolls, pension costs, social security taxes, insurance taxes, and payments to industry welfare and retirement funds for other employee benefits.

n.a. Not available.

a. Average of number of employees at beginning and end of the year.

b. As of December 31 of the year in question, not average number.

c. Not comparable, due to prolonged strikes during the year.

SOURCES:
1. For The Lincoln Electric Company the basic data were obtained from the company's records.
2. From annual issues of "Moody's Manual of Investments—Industrials," Moody's Investors Service, 65 Broadway, New York and from data and other information on extra compensation plans, etc., from "Standard Corporation Records," Feb.-Mar. 1950. Standard & Poor's Corporation, Publishers, 345 Hudson St., New York. For the year 1950 for Westinghouse from company's annual report, pages 1, 16, and 17. For Allis-Chalmers for 1950 from the company's annual report to stockholders, pages 4 and 12.
3. Data on employees for the years 1934 and 1935 from "Moody's Manual of Investments—Industrials;" for the years 1936-1946 from the company's annual report for 1946, p. 8 and for the years 1947 and 1948 from the two respective annual reports.
   Data on payroll were not readily available and were obtained as follows: for the year 1935 they were approximated from a chart on page 17 of the company's annual report for 1945; for the years 1936-1946 they were obtained from the annual report for 1946, p. 8 and for the years 1947 and 1948 from the annual reports to stockholders for the two years, pages 13 and 15, respectively; no later reports were readily available.
4. For the years 1934 and 1935 from the annual issues of "Moody's Manual of Investments—Industrials," Moody's Investors Service; for the years 1936-1949 from the company's annual report for 1949, pp. 41-42 and for the year 1950 from the company's annual report for 1950, pp. 49-50.
5. Basic data from the company's annual report for 1950, pp. 28-29.

CHART IV

The sales value of the product per individual in the organization. This sales value is in dollars rather than units of product. If it were in units of product, which it should be for accurate comparison, the production of The Lincoln Electric Company's employees would be more than doubled as can be seen from the comparison in Chart I and II. This is also a progressive matter as people develop in ability and skill.

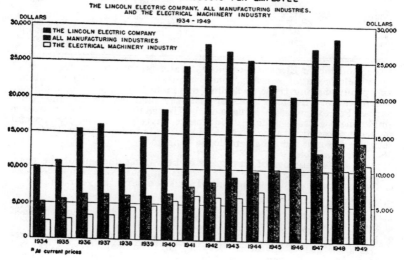

SALES VALUE* OF PRODUCTS PER EMPLOYEE
THE LINCOLN ELECTRIC COMPANY, ALL MANUFACTURING INDUSTRIES, AND THE ELECTRICAL MACHINERY INDUSTRY
1934 - 1949
* At current prices

Year	Number of Employees (Average)[1] (Col. 1)	Net Sales[2] (Col. 2)	Sales Per Employee[3] (Col. 3)
	THE LINCOLN ELECTRIC COMPANY		
1934	404	$ 4,064,820	$10,061.44
1935	485	5,262,473	10,850.46
1936	535	8,290,876	15,496.96
1937	666	10,709,084	16,079.71
1938	650	6,791,433	10,448.36
1939	637	9,257,613	14,533.14
1940	740	13,570,320	18,338.27
1941	979	24,024,095	24,539.42
1942	1,222	33,515,445	27,426.71
1943	1,245	32,987,734	26,496.17
1944	1,115	28,190,452	25,282.92
1945	1,110	24,306,430	21,897.68
1946	1,167	23,717,156	20,323.18
1947	1,157	31,297,319	27,050.41
1948	1,099	31,162,119	28,354.98
1949	1,026	25,662,744	25,012.42

CHART IV (Continued)
ALL MANUFACTURING INDUSTRIES

1934	8,364,000	$ 42,916,000,000	$ 5,131.04
1935	8,904,000	50,028,000,000	5,618.60
1936	9,645,000	59,842,000,000	6,204.46
1937	10,591,000	65,724,000,000	6,205.65
1938	9,131,000	53,503,000,000	6,078.52
1939	9,967,000	61,340,000,000	6,154.31
1940	10,882,000	70,313,000,000	6,461.40
1941	13,137,000	98,069,000,000	7,465.10
1942	15,284,000	125,158,000,000	8,188.82
1943	17,402,000	153,843,000,000	8,840.54
1944	17,050,000	165,387,000,000	9,700.12
1945	15,186,000	154,481,000,000	10,172.59
1946	14,493,000	151,402,000,000	10,446.56
1947	15,215,000	191,010,000,000	12,554.06
1948	15,285,000	213,732,000,000	13,983.12
1949	14,187,000	199,993,000,000	14,096.92

THE ELECTRICAL MACHINERY INDUSTRY

1934	319,000	$ 770,000,000	$ 2,413.79
1935	338,000	930,000,000	2,751.48
1936	385,000	1,273,000,000	3,306.49
1937	461,000	1,566,000,000	3,396.96
1938	353,000	1,577,000,000	4,467.42
1939	398,000	1,861,000,000	4,675.88
1940	455,000	2,483,000,000	5,457.14
1941	607,000	3,769,000,000	6,209.23
1942	757,000	4,550,000,000	6,010.57
1943	960,000	5,734,000,000	5,972.92
1944	1,037,000	7,104,000,000	6,850.53
1945	925,000	6,302,000,000	6,812.97
1946	847,000	5,658,000,000	6,680.05
1947	929,000	8,299,000,000	8,933.26
1948	889,000	9,002,000,000	10,125.98
1949	778,000	8,523,000,000	10,955.01

SOURCES:
1. For The Lincoln Electric Company, for the years 1934-1941 from Petitioner's Exhibit 23, *The Lincoln Electric Company v. Commissioner of Internal Revenue*, United States Circuit Court of Appeals for the Sixth Circuit, No. 10,333, Transcript of Record, Vol. III, p. 729; for the years 1942-1949 compiled from the company's records and submitted by Ernst & Ernst, certified public accountants.
   For All Manufacturing Industries and for the Electrical Machinery Industry, for the years 1934-1941 from *National Income Supplement to the Survey of Current Business*, July 1947, Table 24, p. 36, United States Department of Commerce; for the years 1942-1949 from the *Survey of Current Business—National Income Number*, July 1950, p. 21.
2. For The Lincoln Electric Company, for the years 1934-1941 from Petitioner's Exhibit 20, *The Lincoln Electric Company v. Commissioner of Internal Revenue*, United States Circuit Court of Appeals for the Sixth Circuit, No. 10,333, Transcript of Record, Vol. III, p. 727; for the years 1942-1949 from data compiled by Ernst & Ernst and submitted per covering letter dated May 7, 1951 and signed by A. W. Geater, Resident Partner.
   For All Manufacturing Industries and for the Electrical Machinery Industry, for the years 1939-1949 from *Survey of Current Business*, U. S. Department of Commerce, October 1950, p. 18; for the years 1934-1938 from corporate sales data in Table 29, p. 41 of *National Income Supplement to Survey of Current Business*, July, 1947, adjusted to include unincorporated sales of All Manufacturing Industries by multiplying the corporate sales by 106.939% and those of the Electrical Machinery Industry by 100.787%—the average relationship obtaining in the years 1939-1941 for which both sets of data are available from the two sources listed above.
3. Derived by dividing the data in Column 2 by the data in Column 1.

CHART V

This chart shows the actual employment cost per dollar of sales. If this were based on units of product rather than dollars, the relative cost of The Lincoln Electric Company would be less than half of that shown, or approximately 12½%, rather than 25%, as shown.

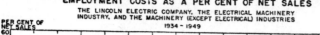

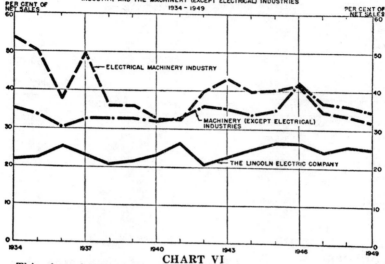

CHART VI

This chart is a continuation of Chart V, showing the comparison with three representative companies. The same comment should be made regarding the relative employment cost which is made in Chart V.

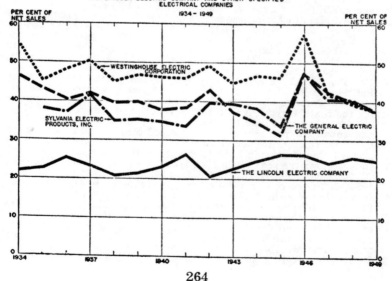

264

CHART VII

This chart is a continuation of Chart VI, showing the comparison with other manufacturers. The same comment as in Chart VI is proper.

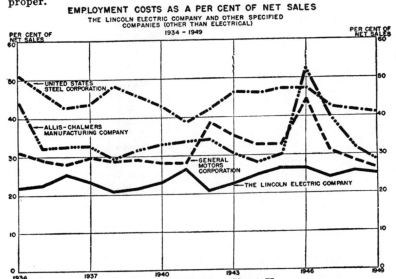

EMPLOYMENT COSTS AS A PER CENT OF NET SALES
THE LINCOLN ELECTRIC COMPANY AND OTHER SPECIFIED COMPANIES (OTHER THAN ELECTRICAL)
1934 - 1949

Supporting Data—Chart V

EMPLOYMENT COSTS* AS A PER CENT OF NET SALES, THE LINCOLN ELECTRIC COMPANY, THE ELECTRICAL MACHINERY INDUSTRY, AND THE MACHINERY (EXCEPT ELECTRICAL) INDUSTRIES, 1934-1949

		Employment Costs	
Year	Net Sales[1] (Col. 1)	Amount[2] (Col. 2)	Per Cent of Net Sales[3] (Col. 3)
THE LINCOLN ELECTRIC COMPANY			
1934	$ 4,064,821	$ 884,028	21.75
1935	5,262,474	1,183,965	22.50
1936	8,290,876	2,103,681	25.37
1937	10,709,085	2,488,634	23.24
1938	6,791,433	1,411,049	20.78
1939	9,257,613	1,988,660	21.48
1940	13,570,320	3,136,914	23.12
1941	24,024,095	6,315,790	26.29
1942	33,515,445	6,938,023	20.70
1943	32,987,734	7,443,883	22.57
1944	28,190,452	6,952,741	24.66
1945	24,306,430	6,427,868	26.45
1946	23,717,156	6,251,149	26.36
1947	31,297,319	7,561,752	24.16
1948	31,162,119	7,967,572	25.57
1949	25,662,744	6,372,832	24.83
ELECTRICAL MACHINERY INDUSTRY			
1934	$ 770,000,000	$ 412,000,000	53.51
1935	930,000,000	465,000,000	50.00
1936	1,273,000,000	480,000,000	37.71
1937	1,566,000,000	774,000,000	49.43
1938	1,577,000,000	566,000,000	35.89
1939	1,861,000,000	669,000,000	35.95
1940	2,483,000,000	804,000,000	32.38
1941	3,769,000,000	1,218,000,000	32.32
1942	4,550,000,000	1,797,000,000	39.49
1943	5,734,000,000	2,466,000,000	43.01
1944	7,104,000,000	2,814,000,000	39.61
1945	6,302,000,000	2,525,000,000	40.07
1946	5,658,000,000	2,353,000,000	41.59
1947	8,299,000,000	2,863,000,000	34.50
1948	9,002,000,000	2,999,000,000	33.31
1949	8,523,000,000	2,715,000,000	31.85

CHART V (Continued)
MACHINERY (EXCEPT ELECTRICAL) INDUSTRIES

1934	$ 1,950,000,000	$ 685,000,000	35.13
1935	2,486,000,000	831,000,000	33.43
1936	3,451,000,000	1,048,000,000	30.37
1937	4,258,000,000	1,389,000,000	32.62
1938	3,089,000,000	1,007,000,000	32.60
1939	3,571,000,000	1,165,000,000	32.62
1940	4,697,000,000	1,502,000,000	31.98
1941	7,390,000,000	2,430,000,000	32.88
1942	10,370,000,000	3,705,000,000	35.73
1943	12,286,000,000	4,310,000,000	35.08
1944	12,907,000,000	4,344,000,000	33.66
1945	11,640,000,000	4,056,000,000	34.85
1946	9,824,000,000	4,144,000,000	42.18
1947	13,697,000,000	5,043,000,000	36.82
1948	15,540,000,000	5,598,000,000	36.02
1949	14,027,000,000	4,872,000,000	34.73

*For The Lincoln Electric Company, employment costs include salaries, wages, commissions, bonuses, annuity premiums and profit sharing trust. For the Electrical Machinery Industry and the Machinery (Except Electrical) industries they include (according to the definitions on page 8 of the *National Income Supplement to the Survey of Current Business*) WAGES AND SALARIES which "consist of the monetary remuneration of employees commonly regarded as wages and salaries, inclusive of executives' compensation, commissions, tips, and bonuses, and of payments in kind which represent income to the recipients" and SUPPLEMENTS TO WAGES AND SALARIES which consist of "the monetary compensation of employees not commonly regarded as as wages and salaries. It consists of employer contributions for social insurance, employer contributions to private pension and welfare funds, compensation for injuries, directors' fees, pay of the military reserve, and a few other minor items of labor income."

SOURCES:

1. For The Lincoln Electric Company for the years 1934-1941 from Petitioner's Exhibit 20, *The Lincoln Electric Company v. Commissioner of Internal Revenue,* United States Circuit Court of Appeals for the Sixth Circuit, No. 10,333, Transcript of Record, Vol. III, p. 727; for the years 1942-1949 from data compiled by Ernst & Ernst and submitted per covering letter dated May 7, 1951 and signed A. W. Geater, Resident Partner. For the "Electrical Machinery" Industry and for the "Machinery Except Electrical" industries for the years 1939-1949 from *Survey of Current Business,* U. S. Department of Commerce, October 1950, p. 18; for the years 1934-1938 from corporate sales data in Table 29, p. 41 of *National Income Supplement to Survey of Current Business,* July, 1947, adjusted to include sales of unincorporated businesses by multiplying the corporate sales of the "Electrical Machinery" industry by 100.787% and those of the "Machinery, Except Electrical" industries by 102.326%—the average relationships obtaining in the years 1939-1941 for which both sets of data are available from the two sources listed above.

2. For the Lincoln Electric Company for the years 1934-1941 from data in Petitioner's Exhibit 52. *The Lincoln Electric Company v. Commissioner of Internal Revenue,* United States Circuit Court of Appeals for the Sixth Circuit, No. 10,333, Transcript of Record, Vol. III, p. 769; for the years 1942-1949 from data compiled by Ernst & Ernst and submitted per covering letter dated May 7, 1951 and signed A. W. Geater, Resident Partner. For the "Electrical Machinery" industry and for the "Machinery Except Electrical" industries,

APPENDIX

for the years 1934-1942 from *"National Income Supplement to Survey of Current Business,"* July 1947, Table 14, p. 27 for Wages and Salaries and Table 15, p. 28, for Supplements to Wages and Salaries; for the years 1943-1949 from *Survey of Current Business* National Income Number, July 1950, tables with corresponding numbers, pages 15-16.

3. Derived by dividing the data in Column 2 by the data in Column 1.

SUPPORTING DATA—CHARTS VI AND VII

EMPLOYMENT COSTS AS A PER CENT OF NET SALES, THE LINCOLN ELECTRIC COMPANY AND OTHER SPECIFIED COMPANIES, 1934-1949

Year	Net Sales* (Col. 1)	Salaries and Wages** (Col. 2)	Supplements to Salaries and Wages*** (Col. 3)	Amount (Col. 4)	Per Cent of Net Sales (Col. 5)
			EMPLOYMENT COSTS****		

THE LINCOLN ELECTRIC COMPANY[1]

Year	Net Sales*	Salaries and Wages**	Supplements to Salaries and Wages***	Amount	Per Cent
1934	$ 4,064,821	$ 884,028	a	$ 884,028	21.75
1935	5,262,474	1,183,965	a	1,183,965	22.50
1936	8,290,876	2,103,681	a	2,103,681	25.37
1937	10,709,085	2,488,634	a	2,488,634	23.24
1938	6,791,433	1,411,049	a	1,411,049	20.78
1939	9,257,613	1,988,660	a	1,988,660	21.48
1940	13,570,320	3,136,914	a	3,136,914	23.12
1941	24,024,095	6,315,790	a	6,315,790	26.29
1942	33,515,445	6,938,023	a	6,938,023	20.70
1943	32,987,734	7,443,883	a	7,443,883	22.57
1944	28,190,452	6,952,741	a	6,952,741	24.66
1945	24,306,430	6,427,868	a	6,427,868	26.45
1946	23,717,156	6,251,149	a	6,251,149	26.36
1947	31,297,319	7,561,752	a	7,561,752	24.16
1948	31,162,119	7,967,572	a	7,967,572	25.57
1949	25,662,744	6,372,832	a	6,372,832	24.83

THE GENERAL ELECTRIC COMPANY[2]

Year	Net Sales*	Salaries and Wages**	Supplements to Salaries and Wages***	Amount	Per Cent
1934	$ 164,797,317	$ 75,227,000	$ 925,292b	$ 76,152,292	46.21
1935	208,733,433	88,746,000	1,091,576b	89,837,576	43.04
1936	268,544,587	106,784,000	1,313,443b	108,097,443	40.25
1937	349,739,514	145,385,000	1,788,236b	147,173,236	42.08
1938	259,484,341	101,511,000	1,248,585b	102,759,585	39.60
1939	304,680,270	120,130,000	1,477,599b	121,607,599	39.91
1940	411,938,259	153,497,000	1,888,013b	155,385,013	37.72
1941	679,333,760	257,364,000	3,165,577b	260,529,577	38.35
1942	901,738,503c	382,039,000	4,699,080b	386,738,080	42.89
1943	1,288,431,590c	471,650,000	5,801,295b	477,451,295	37.06
1944	1,358,012,132	463,564,192	5,701,840b	469,266,032	34.56
1945	1,298,221,886	399,521,045	4,914,109b	404,435,154	31.15
1946	768,863,313d	359,300,000	4,419,390b	363,719,300	47.31
1947	1,330,776,375d	559,756,000	6,884,999b	566,640,999	42.58
1948	1,632,707,606d	662,665,000	•	662,665,000	40.59
1949	1,613,563,611d	606,685,000	•	606,685,000	37.60

WESTINGHOUSE ELECTRIC CORPORATION[3]

Year	Net Sales*	Salaries and Wages**	Supplements to Salaries and Wages***	Amount	Per Cent
1934	$ 92,158,893	$ 50,175,038	——	$ 50,175,038	54.44
1935	122,588,556	55,074,684	$ 258,000f	55,332,684	45.14
1936	154,469,031	73,198,987	1,000,000	74,198,987	48.03
1937	206,348,307	102,957,277	1,330,000	104,287,277	50.54
1938	157,953,216	70,459,766	604,597	71,064,363	44.99
1939	175,071,364	80,916,341	906,932	81,823,273	46.74
1940	239,431,448	109,743,043	1,230,852	110,973,895	46.35
1941	369,094,125	168,722,772	1,402,504	170,125,276	46.09
1942	487,274,551g	239,734,071	1,215,678	240,849,749	49.43
1943	709,342,717g	316,858,542	1,250,266	318,108,808	44.85
1944	830,480,435g	388,092,970	1,227,428	389,320,398	46.88
1945	685,132,854g	317,082,522	1,261,142	318,343,664	46.46
1946	377,965,646h	217,726,856e	——	217,726,856	57.60
1947	821,253,749h	342,530,755e	1,626,586	344,157,341	41.91
1948	970,673,847	381,998,267	1,616,100	383,614,367	39.52
1949	945,699,382	353,361,656	1,826,597	355,188,253	37.56

267

Chart VI and VII (Continued)

SYLVANIA ELECTRIC PRODUCTS, INC.[3]

Year					
1934	$ 7,949,648	$ n.a.	$ ——	$ n.a.	n.a.
1935	7,913,989	3,000,000	——	3,000,000	37.91
1936	10,234,322	3,788,000	——	3,788,000	37.01
1937	9,417,035	3,925,000	——	3,925,000	41.68
1938	7,957,066	2,776,816	——	2,776,816	34.90
1939	11,022,424	3,886,677	——	3,886,677	35.26
1940	14,358,808	5,013,375	——	5,013,375	34.91
1941	20,561,246	6,892,078		6,892,078	33.52
1942	32,338,870	12,745,749	40,676	12,786,425	39.54
1943	60,473,821	23,247,803	519,196	23,766,999	39.30
1944	100,398,043	37,650,402	573,377	38,223,779	38.07
1945	125,750,512	41,361,457	717,459	42,078,916	33.46
1946	69,313,127	32,246,337	645,766	32,892,103	47.45
1947	95,715,638	37,980,906	627,579	38,608,485	40.34
1948	99,347,751	39,275,890	961,109	40,236,999	40.50
1949	102,539,866	n.a.	n.a.	n.a.	n.a.

ALLIS-CHALMERS MANUFACTURING COMPANY[2]

Year					
1934	$ 20,332,142	$ 9,000,000	[1]	$ 9,000,000	44.26
1935	38,764,764	12,500,000	[1]	12,500,000	32.25
1936	58,948,888	18,000,000	[1]	18,000,000	30.53
1937	87,310,981	28,500,000	[1]	28,500,000	32.64
1938	77,512,764	22,720,054	[1]	22,720,054	29.31
1939	74,304,258	23,450,005	[1]	23,450,005	31.56
1940	87,053,207	28,670,004	[1]	28,670,004	32.93
1941	121,939,798	41,044,674	[1]	41,044,674	33.66
1942	196,040,342	66,802,605	[1]	66,802,605	34.08
1943	295,996,435	90,006,843	[1]	90,006,843	30.41
1944	379,485,631	106,185,084	[1]	106,185,084	27.98
1945	290,375,325	87,217,834	[1]	87,217,834	30.04
1946	93,840,030[j]	49,357,069[j]	[1]	49,357,069[j]	52.60[j]
1947	211,949,890	84,591,922	[1]	84,591,922	39.91
1948	328,101,328	105,925,073	[1]	105,925,073	32.28
1949	351,097,878	99,888,251	[1]	99,888,251	28.45

GENERAL MOTORS CORPORATION[4]

Year					
1934	$ 862,672,670	$ 263,204,225	$ 3,975,455	$ 267,179,680	30.97
1935	1,155,641,511	323,030,599	11,721,786	334,752,385	28.97
1936	1,439,289,940	384,153,022	18,694,460	402,847,482	27.99
1937	1,606,789,841	460,451,744	13,907,757	474,359,501	29.52
1938	1,066,973,000	300,825,930	3,572,681	304,398,611	28.53
1939	1,376,828,337	386,292,203	11,551,514	397,843,717	28.90
1940	1,794,936,642	492,246,017	11,387,010	503,633,027	28.06
1941	2,436,800,977	669,744,870	12,386,479	682,131,349	27.99
1942	2,250,548,859	859,314,062	5,273,650	864,587,712	38.42
1943	3,796,115,800	1,321,999,829	7,250,587	1,329,250,416	35.02
1944	4,262,249,472	1,380,032,467	9,088,254	1,389,120,721	32.59
1945	3,127,934,888	1,007,563,689	10,775,900	1,018,339,589	32.56
1946	1,962,502,289	870,215,992	——	870,215,992	44.34
1947	3,815,159,163	1,155,388,163	29,112,475	1,184,500,638	31.05
1948	4,701,770,340	1,283,865,090	48,927,690	1,332,792,780	28.35
1949	5,700,835,141	1,440,690,450	60,000,000	1,500,690,450	26.32

UNITED STATES STEEL CORPORATION[5]

Year			
1934	$ 420,900,000[k]	$ 214,800,000[l]	51.03
1935	539,400,000	253,900,000	47.07
1936	790,500,000	339,000,000	42.88
1937	1,028,400,000	447,100,000	43.48
1938	611,100,000	294,400,000	48.18
1939	846,000,000	386,500,000	45.69
1940	1,079,100,000	464,300,000	43.03
1941	1,622,300,000	628,300,000	38.73
1942	1,863,000,000	782,700,000	42.01
1943	1,972,300,000	912,900,000	46.29
1944	2,082,200,000	957,200,000	45.97
1945	1,747,300,000	825,500,000	47.24
1946	1,496,100,000	704,500,000	47.09
1947	2,122,800,000	903,600,000	42.57
1948	2,481,500,000	1,035,700,000	41.74
1949	2,301,700,000	945,900,000	41.10

* Data on sales are generally labeled "Net sales" or "Net sales billed," except for the United States Steel Corporation where they are labeled "Products & Services Sold."

** Data shown in this column are labeled "total wages," "payrolls," "amount of payrolls," or by some similar designation, but in all cases they include salaries and all other forms of compensation commonly treated under the heading of "salaries and wages."

*** In some cases supplements to salaries and wages are shown separately in this column, but in all others except for Allis-Chalmers they are included in the total employment costs. The approximate nature of these payments is indicated in connection with the appropriate company.

**** Under this heading are included the totals of data in columns 2 and 3. In the case of the United States Steel Corporation, the data shown in this column are headed "Employment Costs" in the company's annual reports to stockholders.

n.a. Not readily available.

ᵃ Included in salaries and wages column.

ᵇ During the years 1933-1947 a general profit sharing plan was in effect for employees generally. It was discontinued as of December 31, 1947. Distributions were based on length of service and during the life of the plan "earnings thereunder aggregated about $45,982,000, or an average of approximately $3,537,000 per year." (*Standard Corporation Records*, Feb.-Mar. 1950, p. 6594, Standard & Poor's Corporation, Publishers, 345 Hudson St., New York). These distributions figured on the average at about 1.23% of total wages and salaries for employees and the amounts in this column have been computed on that basis. Since 1934 there was also provided extra compensation, based on the company's profits, for a selected group of key employees for work performance. Furthermore, a plan was inaugurated on October 1, 1948 for a bonus paid with the company's stock on the basis of employees' savings through the purchase of U. S. Savings Bonds. However, no data are available on the distributions under these two plans; consequently the employment costs are understated by such amounts, thereby making the percentage of such costs in terms of net sales lower than they actually were.

ᶜ Revised to give effect to renegotiation settlement.

ᵈ Through 1945 for parent company only; since 1946 including subsidiaries consolidated.

ᵉ See footnote ᵇ, above.

ᶠ Payments to participants under management bonus plan approved April 10, 1935 for additional compensation for the management group. In addition, in 1948 a supervisory incentive plan was adopted but no amounts involved are available, hence the total employment costs for the years 1948 and 1949 are understated by such amounts.

ᵍ Revised to give effect to renegotiation settlement in 1942-44 and to contract termination settlement in 1945.

ʰ Revised to include additional subsidiaries into consolidation.

ⁱ It is not known whether the company operated during the period covered under any plan calling for additional compensation under some bonus or profit sharing system not covered by the data on total wages and salaries paid during the year as shown here. Furthermore, for the years 1934-1937 the data are approximated from a chart on p. 7 of the company's Annual Report to stockholders for 1942.

ʲ Not comparable, due to prolonged strikes during the year.

ᵏ Amounts of sales and employment costs are given in millions of dollars with one decimal place, but have been spelled out in this table.

[1] Employment costs, in addition to payrolls, include pension costs, social security taxes, insurance costs, and payments to industry welfare and retirement funds for other employee benefits.

SOURCES:

[1] Net sales for the years 1934-1941 from Petitioner's Exhibit 20, *The Lincoln Electric Company v. Commissioner of Internal Revenue,* United States Circuit Court of Appeals for the Sixth Circuit, No. 10,333, p. 727. Employment costs for the years 1934-1941 from Petitioner's Exhibit 52, op. cit., p. 769. Data for the years 1942-1949 compiled from company's records by Ernst & Ernst and submitted per covering letter dated May 7, 1951 and signed A. W. Geater, resident Partner.

[2] Sales (billed) for the years 1934-1941 from Petitioner's Exhibit 87, *The Lincoln Electric Company v. Commissioner of Internal Revenue,* United States Circuit Court of Appeals for the Sixth Circuit, No. 10,333 Transcript of Record, Vol. III, p. 823; for the years 1942-1949 the basic data were compiled from the annual issues of "Moody's Manual of Investments—Industrials," Moody's Investors Service, 65 Broadway, New York, and from *Standard Corporation* Records, Feb.-Mar. 1950, Standard & Poor's Corporation, Publishers, 345 Hudson St., New York.

[3] Data on net sales were obtained from the company's Annual Report to stockholders for the year 1948, p. 14 for the years 1934-1948 and for the year 1949 from "Moody's Manual on Investments—Industrials."

Data on Payroll for the years 1934-1949 were not readily available. For the year 1935 they were approximated from a chart on page 17 of the company's Annual Report for 1945; for the years 1936-1946 from the Annual Report for 1946, p. 8 and for the years 1947 and 1948 from the Annual Reports for the years 1947 and 1948, pages 13 and 15, respectively.

Data on Supplements to Salaries and Wages were obtained from the several Annual Reports to stockholders. Slightly less than half of the amounts for employee benefits for the years 1942-1948 shown have been contributed by the employees (see p. 9 of Annual Report for 1947). For 1942 the employee benefits covered only sickness, eyeglasses, hospital and death. Beginning with 1943 payments were being made into a savings and retirement fund. The amounts contributed by the company for the years 1942-1945 were estimated at half the total payments and for the years 1946-1948 the exact amounts paid by the company are given as shown in the respective Annual Reports (pages 8 of the 1946 report, 13 of the 1947 report, and 15 of the 1948 report).

[4] Data on sales for all the years, on provision for payments under the employees bonus for all the years, and on payrolls for the years 1936-1949 from the company's Annual Report for 1949, pp. 41-42; payrolls for the years 1934-1935 from the annual issues of "Moody's Manual of Investments—Industrials," Moody's Investment Service, 65 Broadway, New York.

[5] Basic data from United States Steel Corporation Annual Report for 1950, p. 29.

APPENDIX

CHART VIII

In spite of the low selling price and high wages shown in the previous charts, the dividend rates that have been paid by the Company over the seventeen years' experience with incentive management show that the stockholder is well rewarded, and continuously rewarded.

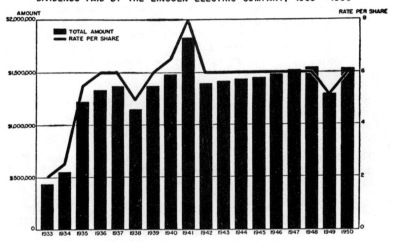

DIVIDENDS PAID BY THE LINCOLN ELECTRIC COMPANY, 1933 – 1950

DIVIDENDS PAID BY THE LINCOLN ELECTRIC COMPANY
1933-1950

Year	Dividends Paid	
	Total Amount	Rate Per Share
1933	$ 435,868.50	$2.00
1934	549,175.00	2.50
1935	1,219,756.00	5.50
1936	1,347,869.00	6.00
1937	1,373,776.00	6.00
1938	1,152,072.00	5.00
1939	1,375,502.00	6.00
1940	1,483,680.00	6.50
1941	1,835,094.00	8.00
1942	1,397,333.00	6.00
1943	1,417,281.00	6.00
1944	1,434,789.00	6.00
1945	1,459,969.00	6.00
1946	1,488,182.00	6.00
1947	1,522,400.75	6.00
1948	1,545,054.50	6.00
1949	1,294,338.75	5.00
1950	1,532,295.50	6.00

271

CHART VIII (Continued)

Source: Data for the years 1933-1941 from Petitioner's Exhibit 20,
*The Lincoln Electric Company v. Commissioner of Internal
Revenue*, United States Circuit Court of Appeals for the
Sixth Circuit, No. 10,333, Transcript of Record, Volume III,
p. 727; for the years 1942-1950 from the company's annual
statements by Ernst & Ernst and submitted per covering
letter dated May 23, 195 and signed A. W. Geater, Resident
Partner.

CHART IX

This chart shows the obvious result of incentive management. Work
stoppage with incentive management is an impossibility.

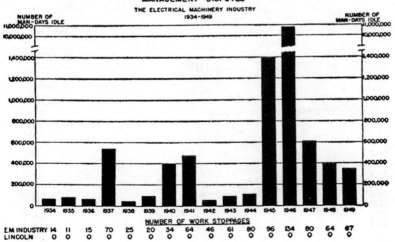

MAN-DAYS IDLE RESULTING FROM WORK STOPPAGES CAUSED BY LABOR-MANAGEMENT DISPUTES

THE ELECTRICAL MACHINERY INDUSTRY
1934-1949

	1934	1935	1936	1937	1938	1939	1940	1941	1942	1943	1944	1945	1946	1947	1948	1949
EM INDUSTRY	14	11	15	70	25	20	34	64	46	61	80	96	134	80	64	67
LINCOLN	0	0	0	0	0	0	0	0	0	0	0	0	0	0	0	0

NUMBER OF WORK STOPPAGES

APPENDIX

SUPPORTING DATA—CHART IX

WORK STOPPAGES CAUSED BY LABOR MANAGEMENT DISPUTES, ALL INDUSTRIES, THE ELECTRICAL MACHINERY INDUSTRY, AND THE MACHINERY (EXCEPT ELECTRICAL) INDUSTRIES, 1934-1949

Year	Work Stoppages	Workers Involved	Man-days Idle (all stoppages)	
			Number	Per Worker Involved*
ALL INDUSTRIES[1]				
1934	1,856	1,470,000	19,600,000	13.4
1935	2,014	1,120,000	15,500,000	13.8
1936	2,172	789,000	13,900,000	17.6
1937	4,740	1,860,000	28,400,000	15.3
1938	2,772	688,000	9,150,000	13.3
1939	2,613	1,170,000	17,800,000	15.2
1940	2,508	577,000	6,700,000	11.6
1941	4,288	2,360,000	23,000,000	9.8
1942	2,968	840,000	4,180,000	5.0
1943	3,752	1,980,000	13,500,000	66.8
1944	4,956	2,120,000	8,720,000	4.1
1945	4,750	3,470,000	38,000,000	11.0
1946	4,985	4,600,000	116,000,000	25.2
1947	3,693	2,170,000	34,600,000	15.9
1948	3,420	3,276,000	34,104,000	10.4
1949	3,600	3,059,000	53,500,000	17.5
THE ELECTRICAL MACHINERY INDUSTRY[2]				
1934	14	5,043	66,937	13.3
1935	11	3,782	82,978	21.9
1936	15	2,286	66,671	29.2
1937	70	29,901	538,266	18.0
1938	25	4,352	45,696	10.5
1939	20	4,613	96,195	20.9
1940	34	8,906	393,572	44.2
1941	64	19,954	475,060	23.8
1942	46	20,202	53,041	2.6
1943	61	33,235	95,008	2.9
1944	80	35,278	111,944	3.2
1945	96	121,200	1,390,000	11.5
1946	134	232,000	10,800,000	46.6
1947	80	36,100	611,000	16.9
1948	64	31,000	402,000	13.0
1949	67	27,100	352,000	13.0
THE MACHINERY (EXCEPT ELECTRICAL) INDUSTRIES[3]				
1934	43	23,521	511,442	21.7
1935	39	12,377	292,766	23.7
1936	58	26,961	878,049	32.6
1937	191	61,724	805,992	13.1
1938	60	16,806	534,594	31.8
1939	65	20,414	335,093	16.4
1940	96	26,711	416,665	15.6
1941	222	108,453	1,738,851	16.0
1942	130	46,811	103,878	2.2
1943	210	62,125	138,544	2.2
1944	311	141,078	507,917	3.6
1945	335	228,200	2,965,000	13.0
1946	324	244,000	13,700,000	56.1
1947	252	114,000	2,910,000	25.5
1948	189	152,000	2,090,000	13.8
1949	176	116,000	2,720,000	23.4

CHART IX (Continued)

*For all industries data were taken from "Handbook of Labor Statistics," 1947 Edition; for the other specified industries they were computed by dividing the number of workers involved into the number of man-days idle.

SOURCES:

1. "Handbook of Labor Statistics," 1947 Edition, Table E-3, p. 136, Bureau of Labor Statistics, United States Department of Labor for the years 1934-1947; for 1948 and 1949 they were computed from monthly data in the *Survey of Current Business*, U. S. Department of Commerce.

   *For all industries data were taken from "Handbook of Labor Sta-Bulletin No. 651, August 1937, Bureau of Labor Statistics, United States Department of Labor, Table 37. To obtain the data for Machinery (except electrical) the data for electrical machinery were deducted from those for "Machinery, not including transportation equipment" shown on pages 128-129.
   For the years 1937-1940, May issues of "Monthly Labor Review."
   For 1941, "Strikes in 1941 and Strikes Affecting Defense Production," Bulletin No. 711, Bureau of Labor Statistics, United States Department of Labor, Table 22, p. 37. Data for Machinery (except electrical) were obtained by deducting the data for electrical machinery from those given for "Machinery, not including transportation equipment."

   For 1942, "Strikes in 1942," Bulletin No. 741, Bureau of Labor Statistics, United States Department of Labor, Table 18, p. 22.

   For 1943, "Strikes in 1943," Bulletin No. 782, Bureau of Labor Statistics, Table 3, p. 5

   For 1944, "Strikes and Lockouts in 1944," Bulletin No. 833, Bureau of Labor Statistics, Table 3, p. 5.

   For 1945, "Work Stoppages in 1945," *Monthly Labor Review*, May 1945, Table 4, p. 726.

   For 1946, "Work Stoppages in 1946," *Monthly Labor Review*, May 1947, Table 3, p. 792.

   For 1947, "Work Stoppages in 1947," *Monthly Labor Review*, May 1948, Table 2, p. 484.

   For 1948, "Work Stoppages in 1948," *Monthly Labor Review*, May 1949, Table 3, p. 511.

   For 1949, "Work Stoppages in 1949," *Monthly Labor Review*, May 1950, Table 4, p. 504.

APPENDIX

CHART X

Low labor turnover is an obvious result of incentive management. Much of the labor turnover shown is the result of the war, during which people took temporary jobs which they relinquished when the war was over.

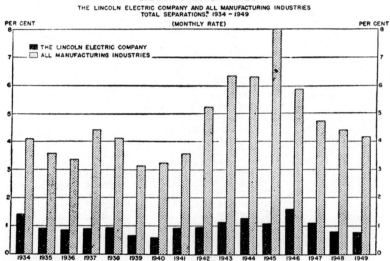

LABOR TURNOVER RATES
THE LINCOLN ELECTRIC COMPANY AND ALL MANUFACTURING INDUSTRIES
TOTAL SEPARATIONS, 1934 – 1949
(MONTHLY RATE)

*Excluding separations for military service.

LABOR TURNOVER RATES (TOTAL SEPARATIONS* THE LINCOLN ELECTRIC COMPANY AND ALL MANUFACTURING INDUSTRIES, 1934-1949

	Average Rate of Turnover Per Month	
Year	Lincoln[1]	All Manufacturing Industries[2]
1934	1.411%	4.108%
1935	0.928	3.567
1936	0.860	3.367
1937	0.901	4.433
1938	0.938	4.108
1939	0.667	3.142
1940	0.574	3.242
1941	0.928	3.567
1942	0.948	5.242
1943	1.144	6.367
1944	1.277	6.325
1945	1.073	8.000
1946	1.607	5.900
1947	1.102	4.742
1948	0.811	4.425
1949	0.796	4.158

*Excludes separations for military service and, for manufacturing industries, it also excludes some small but unknown amount of miscellaneous separations.

275

CHART X (Continued)

Sources: 1. For the years 1939-1941 from Petitioner's Exhibit 24, *The Lincoln Electric Company v. Commissioner of Internal Revenue*, United States Circuit Court of Appeals, for the Sixth Circuit, No. 10,333, Transcript of Record, Vol. III, p. 731; for the years 1934-1938 from data on separations submitted per covering letter dated March 9, 1950 and signed G. F. Clipsham, Assistant to the President, and from the average number of employees compiled by Ernst & Ernst and submitted per covering letter signed A. W. Geater, Resident Partner; for the years 1942-1949 from data compiled by Ernst & Ernst and submitted per covering letter dated May 23, 1951 and signed A. W. Geater, Resident Partner. For the latter years persons employed by the company for less than sixty days have been excluded from the number of persons leaving employment of the company.

2. For the years 1934-1947 from "Handbook of Labor Statistics," 1947 Edition, United States Department of Labor, p. 42; for the years 1948-1949 from current issues of the *Survey of Current Business*, Bureau of Foreign and Domestic Commerce, United States Department of Commerce. For each of the years the average monthly labor turnover was obtained by averaging the monthly rates (per 100 employees) as published by the Bureau of Labor Statistics. For the years 1940-1949 miscellaneous separations including military were deducted from total separations.

CHART XI

INDEXES OF PRODUCTIVITY, AS MEASURED BY INDUSTRIAL PRODUCTION, PER PRODUCTION WORKER, *ALL MANUFACTURING INDUSTRIES AND THE MACHINERY (INCLUDING ELECTRICAL) INDUSTRY, UNITED STATES, 1934-50

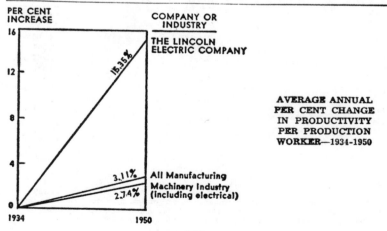

APPENDIX
CHART XI (Continued)

This chart shows that the increase in the productivity per production worker under incentive management was about five times as great as for all manufacturing, and for the machinery industries was 5.6 times as great. For Lincoln production workers, the productivity increase, or the annual improvement factor, averaged 15.35 per cent for a seventeen year period.

PRODUCTIVITY, IN CONSTANT NET SALES DOLLARS, * PER FACTORY EMPLOYEE THE LINCOLN ELECTRIC COMPANY, 1934-1950

Year	Number of Factory Workers (Average) (Col. 1)	Net Sales* Total Amount (Col. 2)	Net Sales* Per Factory Employee (Col. 3)	Index of Productivity (1934-100) (Col. 4)	Per Cent Change in Productivity from Preceding Year (Col. 5)
1934	279	$ 4,104,198.16	$14,710.39	100.00	......
1935	345	5,609,134.65	16,258.36	110.52	+10.52
1936	364	10,096,910.51	27,738.77	188.57	+70.62
1937	457	13,556,555.82	29,664.24	201.66	+ 6.94
1938	444	8,867,068.08	19,970.87	135.76	−32.68
1939	428	13,078,258.85	30,556.68	207.72	+53.01
1940	515	19,815,359.70	38,476.43	261.56	+25.92
1941	734	36,667,077.58	49,955.15	339.59	+29.83
1942	978	57,143,218.56	58,428.65	397.19	+16.96
1943	991	63,097,604.00	63,670.64	432.83	+ 8.97
1944	866	54,874,721.00	63,365.73	430.75	− 0.48
1945	855	46,930,554.00	54,889.54	373.13	−13.38
1946	891	40,889,243.00	45,891.41	311.97	−16.39
1947	888	50,832,719.00	57,244.05	389.14	+12.47
1948	807	47,585,792.00	58,966.29	400.85	+ 3.01
1949	724	37,156,143.00	51,320.64	348.87	−12.97
1950	695a	43,589,852.00	62,719.21	426.36	+22.21

Average increase in productivity per year...+15.35

*In terms of 1934 selling prices.

a. Adjusted to exclude the equivalent in number of factory workers as determined by the time spent (number of man-hours) in the fabrication of equipment items for the new factory and other work in connection with the new factory to which moving of welder operations and all offices was completed in September of 1951. For the year 1951 the data represent the average number of factory employees for the first six months after the above-mentioned adjustment. The actual data before the adjustment consisted of 701 for 1950 and 720 for 1951.

CHART XI (Continued)

Year	Production Workers (Average Number, Thousands) (Col. 1)	Industrial Production		Index of Productivity (1934=100) (Col. 4)	Per Cent Change in Productivity from Preceding Period (Col. 5)
		F.R.B. Index of Industrial Production (1935-1939=100) (Col. 2)	Index Numbers per 1,000 Production Workers (Col. 3)		

MACHINERY (INCLUDING ELECTRICAL)

Year	(Col. 1)	(Col. 2)	(Col. 3)	(Col. 4)	(Col. 5)
1934	597	69	.11558	100.00	......
1935	671	83	.12370	107.03	+ 7.03
1936	776	105	.13531	117.07	+ 9.38
1937	932	126	.13519	116.97	− 0.09
1938	704	82	.11648	100.78	−13.84
1939	788	104	.13198	114.19	+13.31
1940	935	136	.14545	125.84	+10.20
1941	1,315	221	.16806	145.41	+15.55
1942	1,656	340	.20531	177.63	+22.16
1943	2,034	443	.21779	188.43	+ 6.08
1944	2,011	439	.21830	195.64	+ 3.83
1945	1,747	343	.19634	169.87	−13.17
1946	1,570	240	.15287	132.26	−22.14
1947	1,795	276	.15376	133.03	+ 0.58
1948	1,771	277	.15641	135.33	+ 1.73
1949	1,553	234	.15068	130.37	− 3.67
1950	1,677	270	.16100	139.30	+ 6.85

Average increase in productivity per year.................................2.74%

ALL MANUFACTURING INDUSTRIES

Year	(Col. 1)	(Col. 2)	(Col. 3)	(Col. 4)	(Col. 5)
1934	6,811	74	.01086	100.00	......
1935	7,269	87	.01197	110.22	+10.22
1936	7,900	104	.01316	121.18	+ 9.94
1937	8,666	113	.01304	120.07	− 0.92
1938	7,372	87	.01180	108.66	− 9.50
1939	8,192	109	.01331	122.56	+12.79
1940	8,811	126	.01430	131.68	+ 7.44
1941	10,825	168	.01552	142.91	+ 8.53
1942	12,617	212	.01680	154.70	+ 8.25
1943	14,560	258	.01772	163.17	+ 5.48
1944	14,126	252	.01784	164.27	+ 0.67
1945	12,437	214	.01721	158.47	− 3.33
1946	11,745	177	.01507	138.77	−12.43
1947	12,890	194	.01505	138.58	− 0.14
1948	13,102	198	.01511	139.13	+ 0.40
1949	11,597	183	.01578	145.30	+ 4.43
1950	12,264	209	.01704	156.91	+ 7.99

Average increase in productivity per year.................................3.11%

*In the "Handbook of Labor Statistics," 1947 Edition, p. 14, the term, "production worker," is defined as follows: "Production workers include working foremen and all nonsupervisory workers engaged in fabricating, processing, assembling, inspection, receiving, storage, handling, packing, warehousing, shipping, maintenance, repair, janitorial, watchman services, product development, auxiliary production for plant's own use (e.g., power plant), and record-keeping and other services closely associated with the above production operations. Excluded are supervisory employees (above the working foreman level) and their clerical staffs, routemen, salesmen, and certain other groups of employees. Prior to 1945, production workers were identified as wage earners."

278

CONCLUSION

The conclusion that must be drawn from these facts is obvious although it is considered radical because of present custom. That conclusion is this: The American economy must adopt incentive management. We cannot afford to let the outmoded plan of labor-management civil war continue. America cannot allow the benighted leadership of government and labor unions to throttle progress.

We cannot allow selfish politicians to build up labor union power that has for its only purpose the condemning of all Americans to be "common men," without hope, without pride and without opportunity to be self-respecting individuals.

We see what developed man can be and what the economy can become when made by such developed men. We must not stop short of this goal.

There is another phase of this problem that needs attention, particularly at this time. We are seeing the exploitation of the minority by the majority by rigged income taxes that rob the successful minority by the less successful majority. We also have seen the exploitation by clever legislation of the majority by an active minority. We have seen this exploitation of the public by tariffs, by unearned wages that the consumer must pay, by farm parity, by so-called social security and by the philosophy that all must be winners in the game of life. It is obvious that the present "do-gooder" program cannot continue with our present representative government. Only a dictatorship can make it continue.

279

The government we now have is already far from that formed by our Founding Fathers. They made it the way they did in order to guard against the very things that the unthinking are now insisting that government do.

Our present representative government can continue only if all people will understand and accept the responsibility of a government of a free people. Unfortunately, the average voter now is not interested. He will not be bothered. He feels that it is easier to follow demagogues and their programs than to spend the necessary thought and study to find and support the truth. Such government, controlled by such people, must disappear as has been demonstrated by all past history.

The responsibilities and rewards that are inherent in incentive management and the consequent growth of those involved are a complete and unfailing answer to this threat. No man developed under incentive management will allow his freedom to be infringed upon by anyone, be that infringer a self-seeking politician, union leader, employer or a thoughtless voter.

It is only the undeveloped "common man," depended on by self seekers to keep themselves in power, who make our problem and threaten our freedom.

Addendum to Appendix

This addendum is added to the appendix to carry forward some of the statistical data in the foregoing charts. A selection of data has been made and presented in new charts to indicate that incentive management at The Lincoln Electric Company has continued in the same directions as were indicated by the information published in this appendix in 1951.

CHART XII

WELDER SELLING PRICE IN RELATION TO COSTS

Since 1934, the year that the Incentive Program was started, Lincoln worker's compensation has increased five-fold, the cost of copper almost four-fold, and steel sheets and bars slightly more than three-fold. These are the major cost elements in a motor-generator welder. Yet in spite of these increases, the selling price is approximately 20 per cent less than it was in 1934. The machine is essentially the same, with of course improvements and refinements. The profit per dollar of sales has remained approximately constant during the period shown.

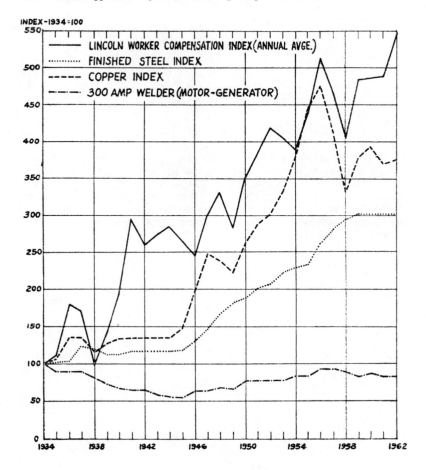

CHART XIII

ELECTRODE SELLING PRICE IN RELATION TO COST OF WIRE PURCHASED

The Lincoln Electric Company in 1959 paid almost four times as much as it did in 1934 for the steel rod from which it manufactures electrodes. The selling price of 5/32 inch Fleetweld 5 electrode was still less than it was in 1934. This electrode, one of the largest selling types, is made from essentially the same materials it was in 1934. An electrode is a piece of steel wire drawn to a relatively small diameter and covered with a complex chemical coating.

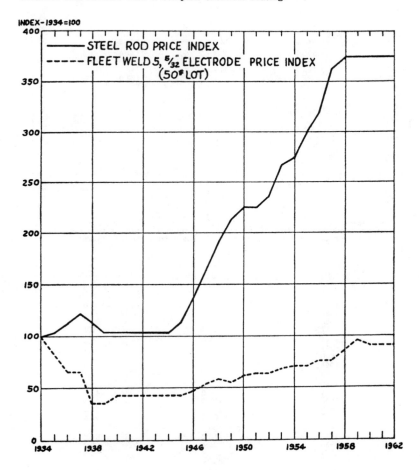

INDEX-1934=100

STEEL ROD PRICE INDEX

FLEET WELD 5, $\frac{5}{32}''$ ELECTRODE PRICE INDEX (50# LOT)

283

CHART XII

PRICE INDICES OF LINCOLN COMPENSATION[a], FINISHED STEEL, COPPER, AND 300 AMP WELDERS, 1934-1962. (1934 = 100)

	Lincoln Compensation	Finished Steel	Copper	300 Amp Welder
1934	100.0	100.0	100.0	100.0
1935	111.6	100.8	106.3	88.4
1936	179.7	103.3	134.8	88.4
1937	170.7	123.6	134.8	88.4
1938	99.2	119.9	116.0	80.6
1939	142.7	112.7	126.8	71.3
1940	193.7	112.2	133.7	67.4
1941	294.8	116.8	134.8	64.3
1942	259.5	116.8	134.8	64.3
1943	273.3	116.8	134.8	58.9
1944	285.0	116.8	134.8	55.8
1945	264.7	119.4	148.0	55.8
1946	244.8	131.0	198.4	62.8
1947	298.7	146.9	248.0	62.8
1948	331.4	167.4	237.9	67.4
1949	283.9	181.0	222.0	65.9
1950	352.0	188.3	261.7	76.7
1951	383.8	201.4	277.7	76.7
1952	419.6	206.6	301.4	76.7
1953	404.8	220.3	333.1	76.7
1954	388.6	229.9	380.7	78.4
1955	439.4	242.7	444.1	78.4
1956	512.3	261.2	475.9	92.2
1957	464.5	282.8	411.4	92.2
1958	404.4	295.5	331.4	88.4
1959	478.4	302.1	377.1	83.7
1960	485.8	302.1	393.3	86.8
1961	489.0	302.1	371.4	82.9
1962	547.4	302.1	377.3	82.9

[a]Computed from Company prices and employee compensation records, steel from **Iron Age** price series and copper from **American Metal Market.**

CHART XIII

PRICE INDICES OF WIRE AND FW 5 ELECTRODES[a]. (1934 = 100)

	Wire Price	FW 5 Electrodes
1934	100.0	100.0
1935	104.9	82.5
1936	112.2	65.0
1937	121.9	65.0
1938	112.2	37.5
1939	104.9	37.5
1940	104.9	42.5
1941	104.9	42.5
1942	104.9	42.5
1943	104.9	42.5
1944	104.9	42.5
1945	112.2	42.5
1946	148.8	47.5
1947	161.0	52.5
1948	190.2	57.5
1949	212.2	55.0
1950	224.4	60.0
1951	224.4	62.5
1952	235.4	62.5
1953	265.8	67.5
1954	273.2	70.0
1955	300.0	70.0
1956	320.7	77.5
1957	361.0	77.5
1958	373.2	85.0
1959	373.2	95.0
1960	373.2	90.0
1961	373.2	90.0
1962	373.2	90.0

[a]Computed from Company records of prices and wire costs.

284

CHART XIV

SALES VALUE OF PRODUCTS PER EMPLOYEE

The productivity of the Lincoln organization as measured by sales value of product per employee is more than double that of the average of All Manufacturing Industries in the United States as classified and determined by U. S. Department of Commerce Statistics. The sales value of products per employee is determined by dividing the total number of employees, including all branch sales and warehouse personnel, into the total dollar volume for the year.

This comparison is made in dollars rather than units. In evaluating the comparison, the significance of Charts XII and XIII must be considered. Had Lincoln selling prices increased in proportion to material and labor costs, the sales value of products per employee would now be more than double what it is.

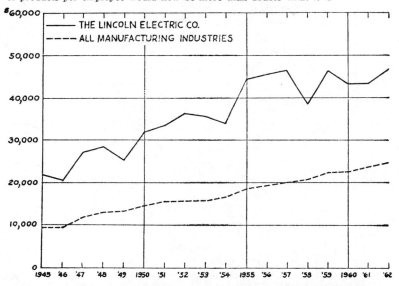

PRODUCTIVITY PER WORKER, MEASURED BY SALES DOLLAR, FOR LINCOLN ELECTRIC, AND ALL MANUFACTURERS, 1945-1962

	Lincoln Electric[a]	All Mfg.[b]
1945	$21,897	$ 9,135
1946	20,323	9,446
1947	27,050	11,684
1948	28,354	12,896[y]
1949	25,012	13,007
1950	31,736	14,484
1951	33,116	15,583
1952	35,677	15,640
1953	35,113	15,832
1954	33,892	16,572
1955	44,142	18,280
1956	45,738	19,098
1957	46,495	20,002
1958	38,169	20,348[z]
1959	46,152	22,075[z]
1960	43,068	22,296[z]
1961	43,074	23,220[z]
1962	46,936	24,420[z]

[a]Computed from Company records.

[b]Computed from **National Income**, various years, Supplement to **Survey of Current Business**, U.S. Dept. of Commerce.

[y]Change in base from 1948 on introduces a slight degree of noncomparability with earlier years.

[z]Series originally used now discontinued; these values estimated from other series.

CHART XV

TOTAL COMPENSATION PER EMPLOYEE

As compensation for outstanding productivity, the average annual earnings of Lincoln employees are approximately double those of employees in the All Manufacturing Industries classification. This average is determined by dividing the total compensation for personal services by the average number of full-time employees. The total compensation includes all earnings including year-end incentive bonus, retirement annuities purchased by the Company, and other benefits.

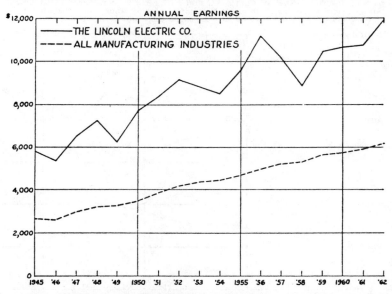

ANNUAL EARNINGS OF EMPLOYEES OF LINCOLN ELECTRIC, AND ALL MANUFACTURERS, INCLUDING ALL SUPPLEMENTS TO WAGES AND SALARIES, 1945-1962

	Lincoln Electric[a]	All Mfg.[b]
1945	$5,791	$2,646
1946	5,357	2,634
1947	6,536	2,927
1948	7,250	3,180[y]
1949	6,211	3,252
1950	7,701	3,509
1951	8,397	3,870
1952	9,180	4,115
1953	8,857	4,356
1954	8,502	4,428
1955	9,615	4,696
1956	11,209	4,952
1957	10,164	5,199
1958	8,848	5,269[z]
1959	10,467	5,648[z]
1960	10,630	5,764[z]
1961	10,700	5,944[z]
1962	11,978	6,175[z]

[a]Computed from Company records.

[b]Computed from **National Income,** various years, Supplement to **Survey of Current Business,** U.S. Dept. of Commerce.

[y]Change in base from 1948 on introduces a slight degree of noncomparability with earlier years.

[z]Series originally used now discontinued, these values estimated from other series of earnings.

CHART XVI

MONTHLY LABOR TURNOVER RATES

The separation rate of employees per month per one hundred employees includes all terminations. The low Lincoln rate, in comparison with All Manufacturing Industries, indicates employee satisfaction and results in many efficiencies and cost reductions through the retention of skills and attitudes and the elimination of training costs.

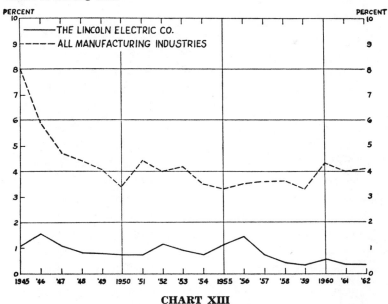

CHART XIII

STABILITY OF WORK FORCE AS MEASURED BY MONTHLY LABOR SEPARATION RATE FOR LINCOLN ELECTRIC AND U.S. INDUSTRY, 1945-1962.

	Lincoln Electric[a]	All Industry[b]
1945	1.07	8.0
1946	1.60	5.9
1947	1.10	4.7
1948	.81	4.4
1949	.79	4.1
1950	.73	3.4
1951	.75	4.4
1952	1.17	4.0
1953	.90	4.2
1954	.73	3.5[x]
1955	1.11	3.3[x]
1956	1.44	3.5[x]
1957	.72	3.6
1958	.43	3.6
1959	.33	3.3[x]
1960	.51	4.3[z]
1961	.32	4.0[z]
1962	.36	4.1[z]

[a]Computed from Company records.

[b]From **Monthly Labor Review,** various dates, Bureau of Labor Statistics data.

[x]Computed from monthly rates averaged.

[z]Bureau of Labor Statistics revised entire index in 1960 to include Food Processing Industries and the printing, publishing, and related industries. These figures are from the revised index.